The New UCI LISP Manual

Edited by
James R. Meehan
University of California, Irvine

With contributions by
Lynn H. Quam
Whitfield Diffie
Robert J. Bobrow
Richard R. Burton
Jeffrey M. Jacobs
Daryle Lewis
Rick LeFaivre

LAWRENCE ERLBAUM ASSOCIATES, PUBLISHERS
1979 Hillsdale, New Jersey

Lawrence Erlbaum Associates, Inc., Publishers
365 Broadway
Hillsdale, New Jersey 07642

ABSTRACT: This manual describes the PDP-10 LISP 1.6 system developed at Stanford University, the University of California at Irvine, and Rutgers University. It is intended to unify the Stanford LISP Manual (SAILON 28.7), the UCI LISP Manual (Tech Report 21, October 1973), and the Rutgers/UCI LISP Manual (April 1978).

ISBN 0-89859-012-4

Printed in the United States of America

The New UCI LISP Manual

edited by
James R. Meehan
Dept. of Information and Computer Science
University of California, Irvine
Irvine, California 92717

June 1979

Including contributions by:

Lynn H. Quam
Whitfield Diffie
Robert J. Bobrow
Richard R. Burton
Jeffrey M. Jacobs
Daryle Lewis
Rick LeFaivre

ABSTRACT: This manual describes the PDP-10 LISP 1.6 system developed at Stanford University, the University of California at Irvine, and Rutgers University. It is intended to unify the Stanford LISP Manual (SAILON 28.7), the UCI LISP Manual (Tech Report 21, October 1973), and the Rutgers/UCI LISP Manual (April 1978).

CONTENTS

INTRODUCTION

This is a new reference manual on LISP, combining the Stanford LISP manual, the UCI LISP manual, and the recent additions from Rutgers.

The first UCI LISP manual was published in 1973 as a 175-page "addendum" to the 75-page Stanford manual. The new versions of LISP from Rutgers were accompanied by 50-page documents describing changes. The task of finding an accurate reference was made nearly impossible since the various manuals often disagreed. Those just learning LISP were hopelessly lost.

The present work, then, is not merely a concatenation of old documents, but rather a unification, resolving discrepancies. Much of the text has been rewritten. Some new sections, such as the description of the scanner, reflect extensions to the system. Other sections, such as the chapter on compiled LISP, describe previously undocumented information. The chapter on the LISP structure editor has been greatly reorganized and includes more material for the new user. There are many new examples, and many more LISP definitions of system functions than in previous manuals. The Table of Contents in the front and the extensive Index in the back provide a quick way to locate almost any item. There are summaries of the commands for the Break Package and the Editor.

Documentation Conventions

The single-quote mark (') is the preferred symbol for quoting S-expressions and is used throughout this book.

(FN A B C) denotes a function FN with 3 parameters, A, B, and C, that are evaluated before the function is called.

(FN "A" "B" "C") denotes a function FN whose arguments are not evaluated.

(FN A {B}) denotes a function with an optional second parameter. Missing parameters default to NIL, but we use this notation to indicate a function that is commonly called without the full set of parameters. Such functions often use a different default for their missing (NIL) parameters. For example, (SPRINT X) is evaluated as (SPRINT X NIL), but the SPRINT function itself tests to see whether its second parameter is NIL; if so, it uses the number 1 instead.

(FN "A" . "B") denotes a function with parameters that are not evaluated. The first parameter is referred to as A. The rest are collectively called B.

Function descriptions are underlined for ease of reading. If two underlined functions appear on adjacent lines, then either they are completely synonymous (e.g., PRIN and PRIN1) or they are closely related (e.g., APPEND and *APPEND).

Acknowledgements

LISP and its documentation are the work of many people. In this section are excerpts from the acknowledgements for the various versions, in chronological order.

Stanford LISP 1.6

[The Stanford LISP 1.6 Manual (SAILON 28.7) was written by Lynn H. Quam and Whitfield Diffie.]

The Stanford A.I. Lisp 1.6 System was originally an adaptation of one developed by the Artificial Intelligence Project at M.I.T. Since 1966, that system has been largely rewritten by John Allen and Lynn Quam.

John R. Allen implemented the storage reallocation system which makes it possible for the user to change the sizes of the various memory spaces. He also ... wrote the first loader interface, and generally maintained and debugged the system. ...

UCI LISP (1973)

[The UCI LISP Manual was published in October 1973 as Technical Report 21 of the Department of Information and Computer Science, University of California, Irvine. The authors of the manual were Robert J. Bobrow, Richard R. Burton, Jeffrey M. Jacobs, and Daryle Lewis.]

Introduction

UCI LISP is a compatible extension of the Stanford LISP 1.6 programming system for the DEC PDP-10. The extensions make UCI LISP a powerful and convenient interactive programming environment for research and teaching in artificial intelligence and advanced list processing applications. All Stanford LISP programs (except those using the BIGNUM package) can be run directly in UCI LISP. In addition, the extended features of UCI LISP make it much easier to transfer interpreted LISP programs from BBN LISP and MIT AI LISP. ...

... UCI LISP represents a substantial extension to Stanford LISP, and from our own experience presents a major improvement in the habitability of the system for both naive and experienced users. (A majority of the extensions were suggested by the features of BBN LISP, ... now called INTERLISP.)

The major extensions to Stanford LISP can be briefly described as follows:

1) Improvements in storage utilization:
   a) UCI LISP is reentrant and compiled code may be placed in the sharable high segment.
   b) The allocator allows reallocation of all spaces (including Binary Program Space) at any time, and new versions of GETSYM and PUTSYM are now available to permit relocation of MACRO-10 and FORTRAN coded routines.
   c) A new data type, the BLOCK, ... allows users freer access to Binary Program Space and permits the construction of data items such as the system OBLIST, which is both a list and a contiguous block of storage (to provide efficient use as a sequential hash table).

2) Powerful interactive debugging facilities, including:
   a) sophisticated conditional breakpoint and function tracing facilities
   b) a powerful list structure editor for editing function definitions and data

c) facilities for examining, correcting, and continuing to run in the context of a program which has been interrupted by an error or by a user initiated temporary interrupt.

3) Extensions to the I/O facilities available in the basic system, including:
   a) convenient I/O to disk files, including use of project/programmer designations and ways to save and restore functions and data
   b) Read Macros (patterned after MIT AI LISP) for extending the LISP READ routine
   c) a routine for printing circular or deeply nested expressions
   d) routines to modify the control table of the LISP READ routine
   e) the ability to change the OBLIST used by INTERN (and, hence, READ) at any time by changing the value of the atom OBLIST to a properly structured BLOCK list ...
   f) the ability to RENAME and DELETE files from within LISP
   g) the ability to read file directories for any accessible project-programmer number, to see if a file exists in a directory
   h) several useful functions for carriage positioning, teletype echo, and prompt character control, reading input a line at a time, reading list structures without interning their atoms, etc.

4) Functions for examining and modifying the special pushdown stack which holds the context of ongoing computations.

5) Error protection facilities:
   a) NIL, T and other atoms cannot be easily damaged by RPLACA, RPLACD, SETQ and SET.
   b) The system will no longer go into an infinite loop when searching for the function definition of the CAR of a form.
   c) Changes [were made] to the disk output routine DSKOUT so that it uses the RENAME facility to provide a backup for user files (minimizing the risk of unintentionally clobbering files).

6) Extended basic functions including:
   a) new predicates for data types, and most predicates now return useful non-NIL values, rather than T
   b) new list construction and modification functions

c) multiple sequential form evaluation in LAMBDA expressions
d) an efficient n-way switch
e) availability of the FORTRAN mathematical functions
f) mapping functions with several arguments, and ones which build new lists using NCONC to join segments

As mentioned, we have made UCI LISP a reentrant system which may be used by several users simultaneously. Thus, while the new features of UCI LISP require a larger system than the original Stanford LISP, this impact is minimized in any environment with more than one LISP user. In addition, since the basic LISP system contains many features previously available only in the various extension files ... or which had to be written by the user, it is possible to write and debug meaningful jobs in the basic system, without getting extra core. ...

The ability to put compiled code in the sharable segment and to reallocate Binary Program Space makes it possible to build systems in which much of the systems code is compiled LISP expressions. All of the advantages of higher level coding are obtained, and the LISP compiler (borrowed from Stanford with some small modifications) produces better results than most assembly language coders. Such partially compiled systems can now be used without closing off the possibility of the user extending Binary Program Space to store his own compiled code. In general, it is now possible to compile a system incrementally. The user can save the low segment which contains the partially compiled system, then test out new material in interpreted form before extending the Binary Program Space in the segment to load the new compiled material.

The debugging facilities form the bulk of the extensions to Stanford LISP, and are identical with the equivalent facilities available in BBN LISP in the summer of 1971. (BBN LISP has been extended in the intervening period.) They make it possible for the user to track down bugs in complicated recursive programs by making it easier for him to investigate the context in which the bug occurred (e.g. to see at what point erroneous data was passed as an argument, or at what point the flow of control went awry, etc.) The user does not have to plan in advance or set breakpoints to get access to the context of the error. The system holds the context of any error automatically, allowing the user to perform whatever investigations he wishes, and make any corrections which may be useful. This also makes it possible to patch up a small error, like an unbound atom or simple undefined function, in the middle of a large computation and to continue the computation without having to start from scratch. Similarly, the user can try out ideas for correcting the error, without leaving the context of the error, and go on only when he has pinned down the error and its possible solution. If the information available at the time the LISP system discovers the error is insufficient to pin down the cause of the error, the user can have the system repeat the computation, with a special trace feature that prints out whatever the user wishes to know at various points in the computation. (The user can specify both what data is to be printed and under what conditions he wishes it printed.) The user can also force the system to establish a breakpoint anywhere in his computation, so he can investigate the context before the error has covered its tracks.

The UCI LISP editor (borrowed with some modifications from the BBN LISP system) is actually a language for incremental modification of list structures. It can be used by a user at a terminal to modify function definitions (even during the middle of a break while the function is still on the context stack) or to change complicated data structures. It can also be used as a subroutine by other functions, making it convenient for one function to modify another function. This is actually done by the BREAK package, to implement the function BREAKIN which inserts a breakpoint at any arbitrary point in a user function. ...

The design and overall direction of the implementation of this system are the responsibility of Robert Bobrow, who also made the first modifications to Stanford LISP, including the original error package, accessible context stack and storage reallocator. In large part the existence of the final system and its extensive documentation is due to the Herculean efforts of Daryle Lewis, who did the bulk of the modifications to the assembly language code (including making Stanford LISP reentrant) and corrected the compiler and LAP systems. He singlehandedly transferred the entire BBN LISP editor and its documentation to our system, and in general performed vital and arduous design, programming and documentation tasks, too numerous to mention. Richard Burton did yeoman's labor by transferring (and extending) the BBN LISP ERROR and BREAK packages, and providing their documentation. Jeff Jacobs maintained the system for many months, correcting may old Stanford compiler and garbage collector bugs; he also implemented many extensions, such as ... the disk file directory functions, the user-switchable OBLIST, and the BLOCK data type. Bill Earl has also provided great service in maintaining the system and its documentation. Whitfield Diffie of Stanford has helped us out of several sticky problems with the LISP system and its compiler. The original implementation of the editor and several I/O functions is due to Rodger Knaus, as well as many helpful suggestions. Finally, but of vital importance, is Alan Bell, whose great knowledge of the

PDP-10 operating system helped us through many rough times, and who has done much of the transferring of BBN LISP and MIT AI LISP programs.

We are triply indebted to the designers, implementers and documenters of BBN LISP, particularly Daniel Bobrow and Warren Teitelman. Most of the debugging and interactive facilities as well as the general design philosophy of UCI LISP were inspired by the BBN LISP system. Secondly, we were able to use much of their code directly, since it was written in LISP, making it possible to obtain a large, well-written and debugged system in a fraction of the time and effort it would have taken to write it from scratch. Finally, we have made extensive use of the BBN LISP TENEX REFERENCE MANUAL as a source of raw material for our documentation. In particular, much of the material in the chapters on the BREAK and ERROR packages and the editor is a revised version of the material in the BBN LISP MANUAL. We take full responsibility for the errors and deficiencies produced by such an arrangement, while gratefully acknowledging BBN's aid in providing much of the basic documentation. We are also in debt to several people at BBN for their aid in obtaining and explaining this material, particularly Jim Goodwin, Alice Hartley and the director of the Artificial Intelligence Group, Jaime Carbonell.

This manual is the work of many people as well as the listed authors - in particular Warren Teitelman, formerly of BBN and now at Xerox Palo Alto Research Center, who produced the original BBN LISP documentation and the lion's share of the original code. ...

Rutgers LISP

The Rutgers/UCI LISP Manual was written by Rick LeFaivre. The second version was released in April 1978 with a revised system containing LISP, LISPC (the compiler), and three AI systems: PLANNER, CONNIVER, and FUZZY.

Many features were added to 1973 UCI LISP. For example:

1. Control-C's are trapped, permitting breaks in running code.

2. Missing arguments to EXPR's default to NIL.

3. The CAR and CDR of NIL are defined to be NIL.

4. Macros are expanded once and saved for later use.

5. Strings are handled as a separate class of atoms. Like numbers, they evaluate to themselves and cannot take properties. They are processed more efficiently than in Stanford LISP.

6. Loop-functions (DO, DO WHILE, etc.) have been added.

7. Arithmetic functions have synonyms, + for PLUS, etc.

8. MAKNAM and READLIST accept integer arguments for ASCII codes.

9. File protection can be specified. Subfile directories (SFD's) have been implemented. Random access to bytes within a file is possible. This code was written by Mabry Tyson and Rich Cohen at the University of Texas.

10. There are new, efficient ways of commenting LISP code.

11. New printing and pretty-printing functions are available.

12. The compiler and Break Package have been improved.

13. The SORT, MERGE, and INSERT functions from Carnegie-Mellon's LISPX package have been included.

LeFaivre is responsible for having corrected many old bugs and cleaning up a great deal of code. The new version of the compiler produces excellent code.

UCI LISP (1978,1979)

The current version of LISP at UCI has new functions to allow easier access to the scanner tables, to manipulate lists, and to generate new symbols (the NEWSYM package, by Chris Riesbeck at the Yale AI Project). The file-accessing functions have been changed to give correct error messages, to use the Break Package, and to allow default file extensions on input. Prettyprint command lists can be built automatically during DSKIN. Control-P was added to the interrupt package as a measure of last resort (it HALTs).

TYOLIST and TYILIST provide "logical" I/O channels. Perhaps the most useful addition is DSKLOG, which makes a file copy of terminal input and output.

The Packaging of UCI LISP

In this book, we describe LISP as a single system. In fact, it is a collection of subsystems, many of which are independent of each other, or nearly so. You may choose your own configuration of subsystems. In many installations, where core limitations, pricing policies, or scheduling algorithms mitigate against large jobs, this is especially important. While it is possible to include all the subsystems (the INTERLISP syndrome), it is by no means necessary.

At UCI, for example, we maintain several separate LISP systems (configurations). Our basic system includes the LISP interpreter, LAP assembler, LISP system functions, prettyprinter, editor, and break package. We also support MLISP (an ALGOL-like dialect of LISP); that system includes the MLISP-to-LISP translator, the LISP-to-MLISP prettyprinter, and some runtime support functions. Our LISPC system has the code for the compiler but not the editor, since LISPC is rarely used interactively. We also have two experimental systems, one for LISP and one for MLISP, that use a screen-oriented editor instead of the structure editor described in chapter 22.

The details of assembling a LISP system are given in section 25.2, but the point being emphasized here is that UCI LISP is flexible in size, depending on what "custom options" you choose to include.

The system itself is available from the ICS Department at UCI, at no charge; just send a tape.

Editor's Note

Throughout the book, I have included definitions taken from the actual implementation as well as equivalent definitions. It was a feature of the original Stanford manual -- not followed in the later manuals -- that I felt to be effective as a teaching tool and essential for a complete understanding of LISP.

I have tried to avoid (or remove) two types of description in the text, "new" and "powerful" (although instances remain in the quoted Acknowledgements). In the first case, there is scarcely a single function that has not been revised since 1973. Bugs in such basic functions as APPLY and READLIST were fixed recently; NIL isn't even the same. The term "new" has no well-defined expiration date, and what is new to one reader may be old hat to another.

Likewise, the term "powerful" may be good advertising but is neither accurate not objective. "Often-used" is a far more significant characteristic.

In choices between giving a few details or giving many, I have usually opted for giving many. I find little point in hiding the implementation details from readers who wish to know them, and I have some sympathy for those who are confronted by some great, undocumented mystery and are forced either to disappear into source listings and DDT, or to abandon all hope of understanding the system.

On the other hand, one of my goals in producing the book was to make it easier to learn LISP by organizing the material better. There's a new chapter on the basics of LISP, for example, a response to complaints that CAR and CDR shouldn't have to wait until Chapter 10. By making a larger number of chapters, each of which covers a smaller range of issues, it should be easier to find the answers to specific questions and references for forgoteen details. And finally, it's my hope that the present format will make it easier to learn more about LISP: the fine details are separated from the basic information, and while the beginner will see that the formidable Chapter 23 on compiled code is eminently ignorable, the um, dedicated user may find it more inviting.

Inevitably, installations will change details of the system, and no single document can cover all the variations of UCI LISP. But it is my hope that the advantages of a comprehensive text will outweigh the disadvantages of minor differences.

This document was formatted by a version of DEC's RUNOFF extended by Steve Reiss (formerly at Yale, now at Brown). It includes such features as macros, hyphenation, and an automatic table of contents. I would not have written the manual without it.

The ICS Department at UCI supplied the computer time for me to produce the first version of this book in the fall of 1978 and the current revision as well, for which I am very grateful. Thanks also to the UCI Computing Facililty for keeping the 10 in such fine shape, and to the many students and other users who commented on previous versions of this book.

Jim Meehan, July 1979

CHAPTER 1

RUNNING LISP

1.1 Starting

To use the UCI LISP system, log in and type the following command at the monitor level:

```
.R LISP
```

You are then at what is called the top level of LISP, which can be described simply by saying that LISP types a prompt character (*), reads a LISP expression from your terminal, evaluates it (executes it), prints the result, and starts over again. This is called the READ-EVAL-PRINT loop -- there are actual LISP functions called READ, EVAL, and PRINT that do this.

LISP has several areas of dynamic storage; their sizes are fixed unless you ask LISP to allocate more, which you can do by typing

```
.R LISP 40
```

for example. Alternatively, you can ask for more core once you have already started, by using the function REALLOC.

1.2 Errors

LISP is very tolerant of errors, and there is a group of functions known as the Break Package that helps you fix an error and continue computing. It is called automatically when an error occurs. This section presents several useful features of the LISP Break Package. Chapter 21 has the complete documentation.

When the Break Package is called, computation is suspended, an error message is printed, and a break prompt (e.g., "1:") appears instead of the asterisk. Being in the Break Package is much like being at top level: you are free to examine any aspect of the program environment using normal LISP functions. Example:

```
*(FOO)                        <-- you call the function FOO

UNDEFINED FUNCTION - FOO      <-- an error message appears

(FOO BROKEN)                  <-- the break-point is FOO

1:                            <-- Break prompt for level 1
```

If you cause an error while at level 1 in the Break Package, you will enter level 2 of the Break Package, and so on.

Here are four useful operations in the Break Package.

1. ^ (up-arrow)
   This command cancels the current break and takes you one level back in the Break Package. If you are already at level 1 (as in the example shown above), the up-arrow returns you to the top level of LISP, and you get the "*" prompt again.

2. ^^ (two up-arrows)
   This command returns you to the top level of LISP from any level of the Break Package.

3. BKF
   This command prints the names of the functions that are still pending (in the process of being executed).

4. BKFV
   This command prints both the names and the parameters of the functions pending.

1.3 Interrupting computation

LISP includes an interrupt-handling routine, which may be called at any time by typing one or two Control-C's (one if LISP was waiting for TTY input, two otherwise). LISP responds:

INTERRUPT (?=HELP):

and waits for you to type something. Typing "?" will

produce the following list of choices:

```
CR = Continue (Ignore ^C)
^D = Return to top level
^X = Exit to Monitor via (EXIT NIL)
^H = Break next function call
^B = Back up and break last function call
^G = (ERR 'ERRORX)
^E = (ERR NIL)
^R = Restore System OBLIST
^A = (LISPSCAN) and return to top level
^P = HALT (escape PFH trap)
```

CR (carriage return) causes LISP to resume what it was doing.

^D (Control-D) causes an immediate return to the top level of LISP.

^X (Control-X) causes an exit to the monitor. The proper way to leave LISP is to type ^C^X or to call (EXIT). Once at the monitor level, a ".CONTINUE" command will cause LISP to continue where it left off, while ".START" and ".REENTER" cause it to restart at the top level (like ^D).

^H (Control-H) causes the computation to continue, but a break will occur the next time a LISP function is called. A message of the form (<name> BROKEN) is typed and you are in the Break Package.

^B (Control-B) causes the system to back up to the most recently evaluated LISP expression. Then it puts you in the Break Package.

^G (Control-G) calls (ERR 'ERRORX) which returns to the last function that called (ERRSET ... ERRORX). This enables you to Control-C out of the Break package or the Editor, reenter and return to the appropriate command level. If you were several levels deep in the Editor, for example, Control-G would return you to the correct command level of the Editor.

^E (Control-E) calls (ERR NIL), which returns NIL to the last ERRSET. (See Chapter 18.)

^R (Control-R) restores the standard system OBLIST (symbol table). Another control character must be typed after this character is typed. This will often recover after a GARBAGED OBLIST message.

^A (Control-A) calls (LISPSCAN) which restores the standard LISP READ scanner. (This is needed only in systems running with MLISP.)

^P (Control-P) executes a HALT instruction and is intended to be a guaranteed way to get out of LISP. If the interrupt system gets stuck in a loop, for example, this drastic measure may be used. (On some virtual memory systems, the Page Fault Handler (PFH) may cause this to happen.)

All other characters are ignored by the interrupt routine. The system is protected against interrupts at the wrong time. ^C during garbage collection will be ignored until garbage collection is complete. (If several interrupts occur withing a single garbage collection, however, it will be aborted.) If the loader is running when an interrupt occurs, LOAD will abort and return to its caller.

1.4 Other interrupts from the terminal

There are three special control characters for terminal input.

<u>(ERRCH CHAR)</u>

Typing ^G calls (ERR 'ERRORX). That character may be changed with this function. CHAR should be an ASCII value of the new interrupt character. ERRCH returns the ASCII value of the old interrupt character.

<u>(REREADCH CHAR)</u>

If you make a typing error on the current line of input, you may use the standard line-editing characters: RUBOUT and ^H delete a character, ^U deletes the entire line, and ^R retypes the line. But if you're typing a multi-line expression and you make a mistake <u>past</u> the first line, you may type the "re-read character," ^Z, which causes READ to start over.

The function REREADCH changes the re-read character and returns the old one.

<u>(EDITCH CHAR)</u>

Occasionally you may not discover a typing error until a good deal of typing has taken place. Rather than starting over, you can type the "edit character," ^F (for "fix"), which calls the LISP Editor when the expression is completed. (The ^F may appear anywhere in the expression.) You may then edit the expression and return the corrected version by typing OK to the Editor.

The function EDITCH changes the edit character and returns the old one.

1.5 Quoted expressions

The standard quote character is ' (single-quote), but @ (at-sign) is also recognized as an input quote character. The single-quote is used on output.

1.6 Top-level printing

The print function used at the top level is specified by the value of the global variable %PRINFNTOP, which is initialized to 'PRIN.

CHAPTER 2

BASICS

LISP's data structures are called *S-expressions*. There are two kinds of S-expressions: *atoms* and *CONS-cells*.

```
                    S-expressions
                   /             \
                  /               \
              atoms               CONS-cells
             /  |  \
            /   |   \
           /    |    \
  identifiers   |     strings
                |
             numbers
             /     \
            /       \
       integers    reals
        /      \
       /        \
    small      large
```

A CONS-cell is represented as a word in Free Storage. The left half (18 bits) is called the CAR, and the right half (18 bits) is called the CDR. The CAR and CDR are either addresses of other S-expressions or small integers (called INUM's).

```
 ______________________
|          |           |
|   CAR    |    CDR    |
|__________|___________|
```

An *atom* is represented as the address of a word in Free Storage with -1 (777777Q) in its left half (to distinguish it from CONS-cells) and the address of the atom's property list in the right half. The exception is the INUM (small integer), which is represented by using an address outside the legal range to indicate the value of the number itself.

A *list* is a CONS-cell whose CDR is either the atom NIL or another list. The atom NIL is the identifier that represents the empty list and the Boolean concept "false." Its value is pre-defined to be NIL and cannot be changed.

In keeping with its character as both an atom and the empty list, the CAR and CDR of NIL are defined to be NIL. Like other atoms, NIL has a property list, although it is not stored on the CDR. GET, PUT, etc., are all aware of its actual location.

The atom T represents the Boolean concept "true." Its value is pre-defined to be T and cannot be changed.

Graph notation

Throughout the book, we use a graph notation for list structures. A CONS-cell is denoted by a period (.), CARs descend, and CDRs go off to the right. If the CDR is NIL, it is not labeled. The CAR of an atom header is indicated by "-1". Elements in Full-Word Space are enclosed in quotes.

```
.----CDR      .----.-----CDDR      .-----------CDR      etc.
|             |    |               |
CAR           CAR  CADR            .-----CDAR
                                   |
                                   CAAR
```

2.1 Syntax

```
<atom> ::= <identifier>
       ::= <string>
       ::= <number>

<S-expression> ::= <atom>
               ::= ( )
               ::= ( <S-expression list> )
               ::= ( <S-expression list> . <S-expression> )

<S-expression list>  ::= <S-expression>
                     ::= <S-expression> <S-expression list>
```

2.2 Representation

```
Notation                Representation

(A . (B . C))           .--.--C
                        |  |
                        A  B
```

(A) is equivalent notation for (A . NIL).
(A B) is equivalent notation for (A . (B . NIL))
(A B . C) is equivalent notation for (A . (B . C))

```
((A . B) (C . D) E)       .-----.-----.--
                          |     |     |
                          .--B  .--D  E
                          |     |
                          A     C
```

<u>(CAR X)</u>

CAR returns the S-expression pointed to by the left half of the CONS-cell X. The CAR of the atom NIL is defined to be NIL, but the CAR of any other atom contains a -1, which will cause an illegal memory reference if used as an address.

<u>(CDR X)</u>

CDR returns the S-expression pointed to by the right half of the CONS-cell X. The CDR of NIL is defined to be NIL. (The CDR's of other atoms are described in the chapters on identifiers, numbers, and strings.)

Examples:

```
(CAR '(A B C)) = A
(CAR 'A)       is illegal
(CDR '(A B C)) = (B C)
(CDR 'A)       = the property list of A
(CDR '(A))     = NIL
```

(CAAR X)
(CADR X)
...
(CDDDDR X)

All of the composite CAR-CDR functions with up to four A's and D's are available.

Examples:
(CADR X) = (CAR (CDR X))
(CAADDR X) = (CAR (CAR (CDR (CDR X))))

(CONS X Y)

CONS creates a new cell whose left half (CAR) points to X and whose right half (CDR) points to Y. X and Y may be any S-expressions.

Example: (CONS 'A 'B) = (A . B)

(CONS 'D NIL) = (D)

LISP uses call by address, although it normally appears to use call by value. There are only two functions in LISP that take advantage of call by address, RPLACA and RPLACD. They differ from all others in that they actually modify existing list structure rather than constructing new list structure. Any function that uses RPLACA or RPLACD can also modify existing list structure.

NOTE

These functions should be used with caution since it is easy to create structures which will confuse or destroy the interpreter.

(RPLACA X Y)

RPLACA replaces the CAR of X with Y. The value of RPLACA is the modified S-expression X.

Example:
(RPLACA '(A B C) '(D E)) = ((D E) B C)

```
                 X -> .--.--.--        Y -> .--.--
BEFORE                |  |  |               |  |
                      A  B  C               D  E
```

```
                 X -> .-------.--.--
AFTER                 |       |  |
                 Y -> .--.--  B  C
                      |  |
                      D  E
```

(RPLACD X Y)

RPLACD replaces the CDR of X by Y. The value of RPLACD is the modified S-expression X.

(LIST X1 ... XN)

= (CONS X1 (CONS X2 ...(CONS Xn NIL)...))

LIST evaluates all of its arguments and returns a list of their values.

Examples:

```
(LIST) = NIL
(LIST 'A) = (A)
(LIST 'A 'B) = (A B)
(LIST 'A (LIST 'B 'C) 'D) = (A (B C) D)
```

(ATOM X)

The value of ATOM is T if X is an identifier, a number, or a string; it is NIL otherwise.

Examples:

```
(ATOM T)          = T
(ATOM 1.23)       = T
(ATOM '(X Y Z))   = NIL
(ATOM (CDR '(X))) = T
(ATOM NIL)        = T
```

<u>(CONSP X)</u>

The value of CONSP is X if X is not an atom.

Examples:

```
(CONSP T)            = NIL
(CONSP 1.23)         = NIL
(CONSP '(X Y Z))     = (X Y Z)
(CONSP (CDR '(X)))   = NIL
(CONSP NIL)          = NIL
```

<u>(LITATOM X)</u>

The value of LITATOM is T if X is an identifier, NIL otherwise.

<u>(NUMBERP X)</u>

The value of NUMBERP is X if X is a number of any type, NIL otherwise.

<u>(INUMP X)</u>

The value of INUMP is X if X is an INUM ("small" integer), NIL otherwise.

<u>(STRINGP X)</u>

The value of STRINGP is X if X is a string, NIL otherwise.

<u>(SETQ "X" Y)</u>

SETQ is LISP's "assignment statement." It changes the value of X to Y and returns Y. X is not evaluated; Y is. Note that values in LISP are actually pointers (addresses).

<u>(EQ X Y)</u>

The value of EQ is T if X and Y are the same pointer, i.e., the same internal address. Identifiers on the OBLIST have unique addresses and therefore EQ will be T if X and Y are the same identifier. EQ will also return T for equivalent INUMs, since they are represented as addresses. However, EQ will not compare equivalent numbers of any other kind. For non-atomic S-expressions, EQ is

T if X and Y are the same pointer.

Examples:

```
(EQ T T)          = T
(EQ T NIL)        = NIL
(EQ 'A 'B)        = NIL

(EQ 1 1.0)        = NIL
(EQ 1 1)          = T
(EQ 1.0 1.0)      = NIL
(SETQ Z 1.0)      = 1.0
(SETQ Y Z)        = 1.0
(EQ Y Z)          = T
     because Y and Z are the same pointer

(EQ '(A) '(A))    = NIL
(SETQ Z '(A))     = (A)
(SETQ Y Z)        = (A)
(EQ Y Z)          = T
```

(NEQ X Y)

NEQ is the opposite of EQ, i.e., (NOT (EQ X Y)).

(EQUAL X Y)

The value of EQUAL is T if X and Y are identical S-expressions. EQUAL can also test for equality of numbers of mixed types. EQUAL is equivalent to:

```
(DE EQUAL (X Y)
  (COND [(EQ X Y) T]
        [(AND [NUMBERP X] [NUMBERP Y]) (ZEROP (*DIF X Y))]
        [(OR [ATOM X] [ATOM Y]) NIL]
        [(EQUAL (CAR X) (CAR Y)) (EQUAL (CDR X) (CDR Y))]))
```

Examples:

```
(EQUAL T T)       = T
(EQUAL 1 1)       = T
(EQUAL 1 1.0)     = T
(EQUAL '(A B) '(A B))      = T
(EQUAL '(T) T)            = NIL
```

(NEQUAL X Y)

NEQUAL is the opposite of EQUAL, i.e., (NOT (EQUAL X Y)).

(EVAL X)

EVAL is described in detail in Chapter 8. In brief, if X is an identifier, EVAL returns the value of the atom, which is stored on the property list under the name VALUE. If there is no VALUE property, an error occurs (UNBOUND ATOM). If X is a number or a string, EVAL simply returns X. If X is a list, then the CAR (first element) of the list is assumed to be the name of a function and the remaining elements of the list, if any, are assumed to be the parameters (arguments) to that function. Depending on what kind of function it is, the arguments may be evaluated before the function is called.

Examples:

```
(SETQ A 3)     = 3
(SETQ B 'A)    = A
(EVAL B)       = 3
```

(QUOTE "X")

QUOTE returns X without evaluating it. The notation 'A and @A are both shorthand for (QUOTE A).

(LENGTH L)

LENGTH returns the number of top-level elements of the list L. LENGTH is equivalent to:

```
(DE LENGTH (L)
    (COND [(ATOM L) 0]
          [T (ADD1 (LENGTH (CDR L)))]))
```

2.3 Conditional expressions

COND is LISP's "if-then-else" statement. It has the following form:

```
(COND (e[1,1] e[1,2] ... e[1,n1])

      (e[2,1] e[2,2] ... e[2,n2])

      ...
```

```
(e[m,1] e[m,2] ... e[m,nm]))
```

where the e[i,j]s are any S-expressions.

The e[i,1]'s are considered to be predicates: they evaluate to NIL (false) or not-NIL (true). The e[i,1]'s are evaluated starting with e[1,1], e[2,1], etc., until the first e[k,1] is found whose value is not NIL. Then the corresponding e[k,2], e[k,3], ..., e[k,nk] are evaluated respectively and the value of e[k,nk] is returned as the value of COND. It is permissible for nk to equal 1, in which case the value of e[k,1] is the value of COND. If all e[i,1] evaluate to NIL, then the value of COND is NIL.

For ease of reading and writing, it is recommended that each "clause" be enclosed in brackets instead of parentheses. The prettyprinter already does this, as shown in the examples below.

```
Examples:
(DE NOT (X) (COND [X NIL] [T]))
(DE IMPLIES (X Y) (COND [X (COND [Y T])] [T]))

(DE TEST (X)
    (COND [(EQ X 1) 'A]
          [(EQUAL X 1.0) "KK"]
          [(NUMBERP X)]
          [T 'NONE/ OF/ THESE]))


(TEST 1)        = A
(TEST 1.0)      = "KK"
(TEST 2)        = 2
(TEST NIL)      = NONE/ OF/ THESE
(TEST (TEST 2)) = 2
(TEST (TEST 1)) = NONE/ OF/ THESE
```

2.4 Boolean Predicates

The Boolean predicates perform logical operations on the truth values NIL and T. A non-NIL value is considered equal to T.

<u>(NOT X)</u>
<u>(NULL X)</u>

= T if X is NIL
= NIL otherwise

<u>(AND X1 X2 ... XN)</u>

= Xn if all Xi are non-NIL
= NIL otherwise

AND evaluates its arguments from left to right until either NIL is found, in which case the remaining arguments are not evaluated, or until the last argument is evaluated.

(AND) = T.

<u>(OR X1 X2 ... XN)</u>

= the first Xi that is not NIL
= NIL otherwise

OR evaluates its arguments from left to right until either non-NIL is found, in which case the remaining arguments are not evaluated, or until the last argument is evaluated.

(OR) = NIL.

Examples:

```
(DE FLONUMP (X)
    (AND (NUMBERP X) (EQ (CADR X) 'FLONUM)))

(DE TEST (X) (OR (NUMBERP X) 12))
(TEST NIL)  =  12
(TEST 147)  =  147
```

2.5 Programs

<u>(PROG "VARLIST" . "BODY")</u>

PROG is roughly equivalent to a BEGIN-END block in ALGOL. VARLIST is a list of variables that are local to the PROG. They are initialized to NIL when the PROG is entered. BODY is a list of statements and statement labels. A statement is a non-atomic S-expression. A label is an identifier or an INUM.

PROG evaluates its statements in sequence until either RETURN or GO is evaluated, or until the list of statements is exhausted, in which case the value of PROG is NIL.

<u>(RETURN X)</u>

RETURN causes the PROG containing it to be exited with the value X.

<u>(GO "ID")</u>

GO causes the sequence of control within a PROG to be transferred to the statement that follows the label ID. In interpreted PROGs, if ID is non-atomic, it will be repeatedly evaluated until an atomic value is found. However, in compiled PROGs, ID is evaluated only once.

GO cannot transfer into or out of a PROG.

Example:
The function LENGTH may be defined as follows:

```
(DE LENGTH (X)
    (PROG (N)
          (SETQ N 0)
     LOOP (COND [(ATOM L) (RETURN N)])
          (SETQ N (ADD1 N))
          (SETQ L (CDR L))
          (GO LOOP)))
```

2.6 Defining functions

<u>(DE "ID" "ARGS" "FORM1" "FORM2" ...)</u>

DE is used for defining a function. ID is the name of the function. ARGS is the list of formal parameters; it may be NIL. FORM1, FORM2, etc., are the body of the procedure. Functions defined with DE are called EXPRs; EXPRs evaluate their arguments before entering the procedure body.

2.7 Sorting

(LEXORDER X Y)

The value of LEXORDER is T iff X is lexically (alphabetically) less than or equal to Y. Numbers are always less than identifiers. If X is not an atom, LEXORDER keeps taking the CAR of X until an atom is reached; likewise for Y. Thus, for example, LEXORDER may be used to sort either a list of atoms or a list of lists, sorted by the first atom in each list.

CHAPTER 3

IDENTIFIERS

3.1 Spelling rules

Identifiers are strings of characters which taken together represent a single atomic quantity. Identifiers are normally strings of characters beginning with a letter and followed by letters and digits. There are four classes of characters that can be used in identifiers.

LETTER This includes ABCDEFGHIJKLMNOPQRSTUVWXYZ
and abcdefghijklmnopqrstuvwxyz
and ! # % & * : ; < > _
and = ? \ ^ ¦ } + - $ ‾
and control-characters in the ranges 1Q-10Q, 16Q-30Q, and 34Q-37Q (Q means octal)

IGNORE This includes blank, comma, tab, line feed, vertical tab (13Q), form feed, and carriage return.

DIGIT This includes 0123456789

DELIM This includes ( ) . / [ ]

Any LETTER may be the first character of an identifier. IGNOREs, DELIMs, DIGITs and any of the four following characters

" { ' @

may be used as the first character only if they are "slashified," i.e., preceded with a slash (/).

<u>After</u> the first character, you may use a LETTER or a DIGIT or any one of the following three characters

{ ' @

in the identifier. IGNOREs, DELIMs, and the double-quote mark (") may be used only if they are slashified.

On input, you may slashify characters that don't need it. Thus AB, /AB, A/B, and /A/B are all the same identifier.

On output, PRIN (used by PRINT) will slashify only those characters that need it. PRINC does *not* print the slashes at all.

Examples:

```
A               /(
a               ?
FOObaz          /13245
TIME-OF-DAY     /,
A1B2            LPT:
<=>             *JOHN*
$restaurant     +WEIRD
-OO--OO-        A'B'C
A@B@C           BLANKS/ IN/ MIDDLE
```

3.2 Lower-Case Characters

READ normally converts lower-case letters to their upper-case counterparts. Thus, for example, nil and NIL represent the same atomic symbol. When the global variable *RAISE is NIL, however, READ will *not* convert lower-case letters to upper case. (*RAISE is *initially* T.) This applies only to non-string atomic symbols read via READ and LINEREAD; lower-case letters in strings, those which are slashified, and those read via READCH or TYI, will not be converted to upper case. *RAISE does not affect how the characters are echoed when you type, only how they are treated inside LISP. A separate flag, *RAISEDSK, is used by DSKIN for file input.

3.3 Representation

An identifier is internally represented as a CONS-cell, called an *atom header*. (A reference to the identifier is the address *of this cell*.)

```
identifier -> .-----(property list)
              |
             "-1"
```

The CDR of an identifier gives the property list of the identifier (see Chapter 13). The CAR of an identifier gives the pointer -1 (777777 octal), which will cause the error ILLEGAL MEMORY REFERENCE if used as an address, as in

(CAR (CAR 'A)). The CAR of an identifier is interpreted by PRINT as if it were the number 65536 decimal (200000 octal). If you see this number in your output, chances are excellent that you've taken the CAR of an atom.

<u>EXCEPTION</u>

The CAR and CDR of NIL are defined to be NIL.

3.4 The OBLIST

The OBLIST (object list) is LISP's symbol table.

In order that occurrences of identifiers with the same print names have the same internal address (and hence the same value), a special list is used to store all identifiers seen by READ, READLIST, LINEREAD, and IASCII. This list is the value of a global variable called OBLIST. The OBLIST is structured as a list of lists. The top-level lists are called hash buckets. To put an identifier into the OBLIST, LISP uses hash coding on the print name of the identifier, producing a number which is the index of one of the hash buckets. Each bucket is a list of all distinct identifiers with the same hash code. Thus, (CAR OBLIST) is the first bucket, and (CAAR OBLIST) is the first identifier of the first bucket.

The function BLKLST (see 6.2) can be used to create new symbol tables.

INTERNed identifiers (those on the OBLIST) are protected from garbage collection. Un-INTERNed identifiers are not.

3.4.1 OBLIST Functions

<u>(INTERN I)</u>

INTERN puts the identifier I in the appropriate bucket of OBLIST. If the identifier is already in the OBLIST, then INTERN returns a pointer to the identifier already there. Otherwise, INTERN returns I.

NOTE

INTERN is necessary only when an identifier which was created by GENSYM, MAKNAM, or ASCII needs to be stored uniquely. READ, READLIST, LINEREAD, and IASCII automatically INTERN symbols.

(REMOB "X1" "X2 ... "XN")

REMOB removes all of the identifiers X1, X2, ..., Xn from the OBLIST and returns NIL. None of the Xi's are evaluated.

Example: (REMOB FOO BAZ)

3.5 Creating new identifiers

(GENSYM)

GENSYM increments the generated symbol counter and returns a new identifier specified by the counter. The GENSYM counter is initialized to the identifier G0000. Successive executions of (GENSYM) will return G0001, G0002, G0003, ...

(CSYM "I")

CSYM initializes the GENSYM counter to the identifier I, and returns I. CSYM does not evaluate its argument.

Example:

```
(CSYM ARY00)      = ARY00
(GENSYM)          = ARY01
(GENSYM)          = ARY02
```

(NEWSYM "L")

NEWSYM is a more general version of GENSYM. NEWSYM returns an INTERNed identifier formed by concatenating the name L to the symbol counter for L. The symbol counter is stored on the property list of L under the name SCNTR. If there is no counter, a counter of 0 will be used and added to the property list. There are no leading zeroes, and there is no restriction on the length of the name (as there is with GENSYM).

```
Example:  (NEWSYM JAZZ) = JAZZ0
          (NEWSYM JAZZ) = JAZZ1
          (NEWSYM JAZZ) = JAZZ2
                ...
```

<u>(INITSYM "L")</u>

INITSYM is used for initializing symbol counters. L should be a list of identifiers, whose symbol counters will be initialized to zero, or lists (A B) where B is the initial symbol counter (an integer) for the identifier A. INITSYM returns a list of identifiers using the new symbol counters.

```
Example:  (INITSYM ROCK (ROLL 3) (BLUES 8))
               = (ROCK0 ROLL3 BLUES8)
          (NEWSYM ROCK) = ROCK1
          (NEWSYM ROLL) = ROLL4
          (NEWSYM BLUES) = BLUES9
```

<u>(OLDSYM "L")</u>

OLDSYM returns the identifier using the current symbol counter for L, rather than creating a new identifier.

```
Example:  (INITSYM (ROKK 3)) = (ROKK3)
          (OLDSYM ROKK) = ROKK3
```

<u>(SYMSTAT "L")</u>

For each identifier in the list L, SYMSTAT returns a list of the identifier and its current symbol counter.

```
Example:   (following the examples above)
           (SYMSTAT ROCK ROLL ROKK)
              = ((ROCK 1) (ROLL 4) (ROKK 3))
```

<u>(ALLSYM "L")</u>

If L is an identifier, ALLSYM returns a list of all the created identifiers between zero and the current symbol counter for L. Otherwise, L should be a list of the form (A B), in which case, ALLSYM returns a list of all the identifers between B and the current symbol counter for A.

```
Example:   (ALLSYM ROLL) = (ROLL0 ROLL1 ROLL2 ROLL3
                            ROLL4)
```

(ALLSYM (ROLL 2)) = (ROLL2 ROLL3 ROLL4)

(REMSYM "L")

For each item I in L, REMSYM REMOB's all the created identifiers between zero and the current symbol counter for I, or between A and the current symbol counter for B if I is of the form (A B), and returns the identifier with the current symbol counter.

Example: (REMSYM ROCK (ROLL 2)) = (ROCK1 ROLL4)

(ASCII N)

ASCII creates a single character identifier whose ASCII print name equals N. The identifier is not INTERNed.

Example:
(ASCII 101Q) is an identifier with print name A.

(IASCII N)

IASCII is equivalent to (INTERN (ASCII N)), but more efficient.

3.6 Transforming lists of characters

(MAKNAM L)

MAKNAM transforms a list of single-character identifiers (it actually takes the first character of each identifier) and ASCII values into an S-expression identical to that which would be produced by READing those characters. The numbers 0 through 9 are equivalent to the digits /0 through /9. All other numbers are treated as ASCII codes. Only the right-most 7 bits are used; 200Q through 211Q are used to represent ASCII 0 through 11Q.

MAKNAM does not INTERN any of the identifiers in the S-expression it produces.

Examples:

```
(MAKNAM '(A P P L E))        = APPLE
(MAKNAM '(// /)))            = /)
(MAKNAM '(101Q 102Q))        = AB
(MAKNAM '(P 11Q))            = P9
(MAKNAM '(P 211Q))           = P<tab>
(MAKNAM '(/( A /, B /))      = (A B)
```

(READLIST L)

READLIST is identical to MAKNAM except that READLIST does INTERN all the identifiers in the S-expression it produces. READLIST has a logical inverse, EXPLODE; i.e.,

```
(READLIST (EXPLODE L)) = L
(EXPLODE (READLIST L)) = L
```

(EXPLODE L)

EXPLODE transforms an S-expression into a list of single-character identifiers identical to the sequence of characters which would be produced by PRIN.

Examples:

```
(EXPLODE 'APPLE) = (A P P L E)
(EXPLODE 'AA/ BB) = (A A // /  B B)
(EXPLODE '(1 2)) = (/( 1 /  2 /))
(EXPLODE '(/1A /2A))
   = (/( // 1 A /  // 2 A /))
```

(EXPLODEC L)

EXPLODEC is the same as EXPLODE, except that PRINC is used for unpacking instead of PRIN.

Examples:

```
(EXPLODEC 'APPLE) = (A P P L E)
(EXPLODEC 'AA/ BB) = (A A /  B B)
(EXPLODEC '(1 2)) = (/( 1 /  2 /))
(EXPLODEC '(/1A /2A))
   = (/( 1 A /  2 A /))
```

(AEXPLODE X)
(AEXPLODEC X)

These are like EXPLODE and EXPLODEC, except that they return a list of ASCII values (integers), and they're more efficient since they don't have to create and interm single-character atoms. If the print name of X contains a character in the range ASCII 0 to ASCII 11Q, that character will be translated to a number in the range 200Q to 211Q to maintain compatibility with MAKNAM and READLIST.

```
(AEXPLODE X) = (TYOLIST (PRIN X))
(AEXPLODEC X) = (TYOLIST (PRINC X))
```

(FLATSIZE L)

= (LENGTH (EXPLODE L))

(FLATSIZEC L)

= (LENGTH (EXPLODEC L))

(NTHCHAR X N)

```
= (CAR (NTH (EXPLODEC L) N)) if N > 0
= (CAR (NTH (REVERSE (EXPLODEC L)) N)) if N < 0
= NIL if N = 0 or |N| > (FLATSIZEC L)
```

(ANTHCHAR X N)

ANTHCHAR is like NTHCHAR, but it returns an ASCII value instead of a character atom.

(CHRVAL X)

= (ANTHCHAR X 1)
CHRVAL returns the ASCII representation of the first character of the print name of X.

(AT X)

AT "atomizes" any S-expression, including lists and strings.

```
(DE AT (X)
    (READLIST (MAPCAN 'EXPLODE (EXPLODEC X))))
```

(ATCAT X1 X2 ... XN)

ATCAT concatenates X1, X2, ..., Xn, and then "atomizes" the result.

```
Example:   (ATCAT "FOO" 3 PERIOD BLANK 'BAZ)
               = FOO3/./ BAZ
```

3.7 Predefined character atoms

The following global variables have been predefined.

```
(SETQ QT '/')              ~ single quote
(SETQ LPAR '/()            ~ left parenthesis
(SETQ RPAR '/))            ~ right parenthesis
(SETQ LABR '<)             ~ left angle-bracket
(SETQ RABR '>)             ~ right angle-bracket
(SETQ LSBR '/[)            ~ left square-bracket
(SETQ RSBR '/])            ~ right square-bracket
(SETQ DASH '-)             ~ minus-sign
(SETQ STAR '*)             ~ asterisk
(SETQ PLUSS '+)            ~ plus-sign
(SETQ SLASH '//)
(SETQ BLANK '/ )
(SETQ COLON ':)
(SETQ COMMA '/,)
(SETQ PERIOD '/.)
(SETQ DOLLAR '$)
(SETQ EQSIGN '=)
(SETQ LARROW '_)                    ~ left-arrow
(SETQ DBQUOTE '/")                  ~ double quote
(SETQ PERCENT '%)                   ~ percent-sign
(SETQ CIRCLEX (IASCII 26Q))         ~ control-V
(SETQ UNDERBAR (IASCII 30Q))        ~ control-X
(SETQ SEMICOLON ';)
(SETQ BELL (IASCII 7Q))
(SETQ TABCHR (IASCII 11Q))
(SETQ LF (IASCII 12Q))              ~ line feed
(SETQ VT (IASCII 13Q))              ~ vertical tab
(SETQ FF (IASCII 14Q))              ~ form feed
(SETQ CR (IASCII 15Q))              ~ carriage return
(SETQ ALTMODE (IASCII 33Q))
(SETQ NULLCH (IASCII 0))            ~ null character
```

CHAPTER 4

NUMBERS

LISP has two types of numbers: integers and real numbers.

4.1 Integers

<integer> ::= {<sign>} <digits> {. ¦ Q}

<digits> ::= <digit> {<digits>}

<sign> ::= + ¦ -

4.1.1 Input

Integers followed by "." are always read in base 10; integers followed by "Q" are always read in base 8. Otherwise, integers are read according to the value of the global variable IBASE (input radix). IBASE is initially 10.

4.1.2 Output

Integers are printed according to BASE and *NOPOINT. BASE is the output radix, initially 10. *NOPOINT is initially NIL and specifies whether to print a decimal point (.) or an "octal point" (Q): a decimal point will be printed if BASE = 10 and *NOPOINT is NIL; an octal point will be printed if BASE = 8 and *NOPOINT is NIL.

NOTE

> It is highly recommended that *NOPOINT be left NIL. Otherwise, a file written while BASE=8, for example, and read while IBASE=10 will probably cause trouble. Also note that some LISP systems use 8 as the initial value for BASE and IBASE.

In order to allow the user to disable the printing of octal or decimal points when interacting from the terminal but still have points printed when writing on a file (so that it can later be read in correctly), DSKOUT uses the global variable *NOPOINTDSK, also initialized to NIL, instead of *NOPOINT.

4.1.3 36-Bit Integers

Integers may be input and output as either signed 35-bit or unsigned 36-bit numbers. On input, the last 36 bits are retained (there is no overflow). For example, -1Q and 777777777777Q input as the same quantity. On output, the decision to print as 36 bits or sign plus 35 bits is under the control of the global variable BASE. If BASE is positive, negative integers will be printed with a sign. If BASE is negative, negative numbers will be printed as a 36-bit number.

There are no built-in precautions against setting BASE and IBASE to bizarre values (e.g., 0, NIL, 16). With BASE = 16, for example, the number 222 prints as =>. If you make BASE or IBASE a local variable inside a PROG, they'll be initialized to NIL as all PROG variables are; be sure to give them reasonable values before you call READ or PRINT.

Examples with IBASE = 8, BASE = -8, and *NOPOINT = NIL

input		meaning		prints as
-13	=	-11.	= -11 base 10	777777777765Q
1000	=	512.	= +512 base 10	1000Q
19	=	17. (!)	= +17 base 10	21Q
19.	=	19.	= +19 base 10	23Q
1000Q	=	512.	= +512 base 10	1000Q

4.1.4 Representation of integers

By convention, addresses in UCI LISP range from 0 to 377777Q. The remaining PDP-10 addresses up to 777776Q are used to represent "small" integers, called INUMS. 577777Q, the midpoint of that range, is defined as the representation for the integer zero (called INUM0). Integers outside that range are called FIXNUMS. Their ranges are as follows:

INUM $|n| < K$ $K = 200000Q = 65536.$

FIXNUM $K \leq |n| < 2^{35}$

4.1.5 Representation of INUMs

INUMs are represented directly as addresses equal to the INUM plus a constant offset of 577777Q.

Examples	INUM	Representation
	+65535.	777776Q
	+2	600001Q
	+1	600000Q
	0	577777Q
	-1	577776Q
	-2	577775Q
	-65535.	400000Q

4.1.6 Representation of FIXNUMs

FIXNUMs are represented by list structure of the following form:

```
atom header -> .-----.-------(value)
               |     |
              "-1"  FIXNUM
```

where value is the 2's-complement representation of the fixed-point number, stored in Full-Word Space.

Examples:

```
+100000000Q  -> .-----.-------"000100000000"
                |     |
               "-1"  FIXNUM
```

```
-14000000032Q -> .-----.-------"776377777746"
                 |     |
                "-1"  FIXNUM
```

4.2 Reals

4.2.1 Syntax

```
<real>     ::= {<sign>} <digits> {.} <exponent>
           ::= {<sign>} {<digits>} . <digits> {<exponent>}
<exponent> ::= E {<sign>} <digits>
```

Examples:

number	meaning
3.14159	+3.14159
+1E-3	+0.001
-196.37E4	-1963700.0
0.3	+0.3
-0.3E+1	-3.0

4.2.2 Restrictions

The radix for real numbers is always decimal. A real number x must be in the (approximate) range:

$$10^{-38} < |X| < 10^{+38} \quad \text{or} \quad x = 0$$

A real number has approximately eight significant digits of accuracy.

4.2.3 Representation of Reals

```
atom header -> .-----.-------(value)
               |     |
              "-1"  FLONUM
```

where value is in PDP-10 2's-complement floating-point representation, and is stored in Full-Word Space.

4.3 Functions on numbers

There are two types of functions which operate on numbers to create new numbers: arithmetic functions and bit operations. Some of the numerical predicates also return numbers; others return T or NIL.

4.3.1 Arithmetic functions

Unless otherwise noted, the following functions are defined for integer, real, and mixed combinations of arguments, and they evaluate all their arguments. The result is real if any argument is real, and integer if all arguments are integer. Most arithmetic functions may cause overflow, which produces an error message.

<u>(MINUS X)</u>

= -X

<u>(*PLUS X Y)</u>
<u>(+ X Y)</u>

= X + Y

<u>(PLUS X1 X2 ... XN)</u>

= X1 + X2 + ... + Xn

<u>(*DIF X Y)</u>
<u>(- X Y)</u>

= X - Y

<u>(DIFFERENCE X1 X2 ... XN)</u>

= X1 - X2 - ... - Xn

<u>(*TIMES X Y)</u>
<u>(* X Y)</u>

= X * Y

(TIMES X1 X2 ... XN)

= X1 * X2 * ... * Xn

(*QUO X Y)
(// X Y)

= X / Y

(QUOTIENT X1 X2 ... XN)

= X1 / X2 / ... / Xn

For integer arguments, *QUO and QUOTIENT give the integer part of the real quotient of the arguments.

Examples:
(*QUO 5 2) = 2
(*QUO -5 2) = -2

(REMAINDER X Y)

= X - (X / Y) * Y

NOTE

REMAINDER, DIVIDE, and GCD are not defined for real arguments.

(DIVIDE X Y)

= (CONS (QUOTIENT X Y) (REMAINDER X Y))

(GCD X Y)

GCD returns the greatest common divisor of the integers X and Y.

<u>(ADD1 X)</u>
<u>(+I X)</u>

= X + 1

<u>(INCR X)</u>

This is a MACRO that expands to (SETQ X (ADD1 X)).

<u>(SUB1 X)</u>
<u>(-I X)</u>

= X - 1

<u>(DECR X)</u>

This is a MACRO that expands to (SETQ X (SUB1 X)).

<u>(ABS X)</u>

= ¦X¦

<u>(FIX X)</u>

Returns the largest integer not greater than X.

Examples:
(FIX 1) = 1
(FIX 1.1) = 1
(FIX -1.1) = -2 not -1

<u>(*MIN X Y)</u>

= Minimum of X and Y

<u>(MIN X1 X2 ... XN)</u>

= Minimum of X1, X2, ..., Xn

(*MAX X Y)

= Maximum of X and Y

(MAX X1 X2 ... XN)

= Maximum of X1, X2, ... , Xn

4.3.2 Other functions

Other arithmetic functions can be defined as follows:

```
(DE FLOAT (X) (*PLUS X 0.0))
(DE RECIP (X) (*QUO 1 X))
(DE SIGN (X) (COND [(ZEROP X) 0]
                   [(MINUSP X) -1]
                   [T 1]))
(DE ROUND (X) (TIMES (SIGN X) (FIX (PLUS (ABS X) 0.5)))
```

4.3.3 Examples

```
(MINUS 1)              = -1
(MINUS -1.2)           = 1.2
(PLUS 1 2 3.1)         = 6.1
(PLUS 6 ·3 -2)         = 7
(DIFFERENCE 6 3 1)     = 2
(TIMES -2 2.0)         = -4.0
(QUOTIENT 5 2)         = 2
(QUOTIENT 5.0 2)       = 2.5
(QUOTIENT -5 2)        = -2
(REMAINDER 5 2)        = 1
(REMAINDER -5 2)       = -1
(REMAINDER 5.0 2)      = error
(ABS -32.5)            = 32.5
(FIX 32.5)             = 32.
(FIX -32.5)            = -33.
(ROUND .5)             = 1
(ROUND .49)            = 0
(ROUND -.49)           = 0
(ROUND -35.1)          = -35
```

4.3.4 Predicates

(NUMBERP X)

= X if X is a number of any type
= NIL otherwise

(DE NUMBERP (X) (COND [(NUMTYPE X) X]))

(INUMP X)

= X if X is an INUM
= NIL otherwise

(NUMTYPE X)

= INUM if X is an INUM
= FIXNUM if X is a FIXNUM
= FLONUM if X is a real number
= NIL otherwise

(ZEROP X)

= X if X is zero of any numerical type
= error if X is a non-numerical quantity
= NIL otherwise

(=0 X)

= (EQ X 0)

(MINUSP X)

= X if X is a negative number of any type
= error if X is a non-numerical quantity
= NIL otherwise

(*GREAT X Y)
(GT X Y)
(> X Y)

= T if X and Y are numbers of any type and X > Y.
= error if either X or Y is not a number
= NIL otherwise

(LE X Y)

= (NOT (*GREAT X Y))

(*LESS X Y)
(LT X Y)
(< X Y)

= (*GREAT Y X)

(GE X Y)

= (NOT (*LESS X Y))

(GREATERP X1 X2 ... XN)

= T if X1 > X2 > ... > Xn
= error if any Xi is a non-numerical quantity
= NIL otherwise

(LESSP X1 X2 ... XN)

= T if X1 < X2 < ... < Xn
= error if any Xi is a non-numerical quantity
= NIL otherwise

4.3.5 Other predicates

Other numerical predicates may be defined as follows:

```
(DE FLOATP (X) (COND [(EQ X (PLUS X 0)) NIL]
                     [(EQ (CADR X) 'FLONUM) T]))
(DE FIXP (X) (NOT (FLOATP X)))
(DE ONEP (X) (ZEROP (DIFFERENCE X 1)))
(DE EVENP (X) (ZEROP (REMAINDER X 2)))
```

4.3.6 Bit Functions

The following functions are intended to operate on integers. Their results are not defined for real numbers.

(BOOLE V X1 X2 ... XN)

> BOOLE causes a 36-bit Boolean operation to be performed on its arguments. The value of V specifies which of 16 Boolean operations to perform. In this description, the terms AND, OR, NOT, EQ, and NEQ refer to bit-operations, not LISP functions.

For n = 2, each bit[i] in (BOOLE V A B) is defined:

V	result	V	result
0	0	10Q	NOT (A[i]) AND NOT (B[i])
1	A[i] AND B[i]	11Q	A[i] EQ B[i]
2	NOT (A[i]) AND B[i]	12Q	NOT (A[i])
3	B[i]	13Q	NOT (A[i]) OR B[i]
4	A[i] AND NOT (B[i])	14Q	NOT (B[i])
5	A[i]	15Q	A[i] OR NOT (B[i])
6	A[i] NEQ B[i]	16Q	NOT (A[i]) OR B[i]
7	A[i] OR B[i]	17Q	1

For n > 2, BOOLE is defined:

(BOOLE V ... (BOOLE V (BOOLE V X1 X2) X3) ... Xn)

(LSH X N)

LSH performs a logical left shift of N places on X. If N is negative, X will be shifted right. In both cases, vacated bits are filled with zeros.

4.3.7 Examples

```
(BOOLE 1Q 76Q 133Q)        = 32Q
(BOOLE 1Q 76Q 133Q 70Q)    = 30Q
(BOOLE 12Q 13Q 0Q)         = 777777777764Q
(BOOLE 7Q 7Q 12Q)          = 17Q
(LSH 15Q 2Q)               = 64Q
(LSH 15Q -2Q)              = 3Q
(LSH -1Q -2Q)              = 177777777777Q
```

CHAPTER 5

STRINGS

5.1 Syntax

string ::= " <any characters except double-quote> "

A string is an arbitrary sequence of characters enclosed in double quotes and not containing double quotes.

Examples:

```
          "A STRING     with blanks !"
          "1,3-X.5"
```

5.2 Representation of strings

Strings are represented by a list structure of the following form:

```
atom header -> .-----.-------.--------.--------.--------
               |     |       |        |        |
               "-1"  STRING  "abcde"  "fghij"  "klmno"
```

Strings may not take properties. Strings evaluate to themselves, like numbers, and cannot be assigned values. The atom STRING is a reserved property name, like FIXNUM, FLONUM, and PNAME.

Characters are stored in Full-Word Space, five ASCII characters per word. The enclosing double-quotes are not stored. Words are filled in with null (zero) bytes. Strings that are an exact multiple of 5 characters long are not followed by a null word (as in ASCIZ).

5.3 INTERNing strings

Strings are not automatically INTERNed on the OBLIST, so that they will be garbage-collected when no longer referenced. However, READ will INTERN all strings if the global variable INTERNSTR has the value T; it is initially NIL. Strings appearing in compiled code will always be referenced, however, so LAP has been modified to INTERN them (by setting INTERNSTR to T). This has the advantage that functions which are compiled may reference the same string a number of times without penalty - only one copy will be stored.

5.4 Functions on strings

<u>(EQSTR A B)</u>

EQSTR compares the PNAMEs of atoms A and B, returning T if they are identical and NIL if they differ. Useful for use with any un-INTERNed atomic symbols (including, of course, strings).

<u>(SUBSTRING STR M N)</u>

SUBSTRING returns a new string consisting of characters M through N of STR. M and N may be positive integers (count from left) or negative integers (count from right). If M is non-numeric, a value of 1 (first character) is assumed, and if N is non-numeric, -1 (last character) is assumed. Although STR will typically be a string, SUBSTRING will actually work with <u>any</u> argument; the indicated characters are simply extracted from the print name of STR and formed into a string.

<u>(CONCAT STR1 STR2 ...)</u>

CONCAT returns a new string which is the concatenation of STR1, STR2, ... As in SUBSTRING, the arguments needn't be strings - CONCAT will return a string consisting of the concatenation of the characters in the PRINC character strings.

Functions on strings

(STR X)

= (CONCAT X "")
STR simply converts X into a string.

(STRLEN X)

= (LENGTH (EXPLODEC X))
STRLEN returns the length of the string X.

(PRINTSTR X)

= (TERPRI (PRINC X))
Strings are usually printed with PRINC so that the quotes don't appear in the output.

CHAPTER 6

ARRAYS AND BLOCKS

6.1 Arrays

(ARRAY "ID" TYPE B[1] B[2] ... B[N])

ARRAY is a function which declares an array with name ID, and places an array-referencing function on the property list of ID. TYPE determines the type of an array as follows:

TYPE	INITIAL VALUE	ARRAY ELEMENT
T	NIL	LISP S-expressions stored as pointers (2 per word)
NIL	0.0	Real numbers stored one per word in PDP-10 floating-point representation
36.	0	36-bit 2's-complement integers stored 1 per word
$0 < m < 36.$	0	m-bit positive integers (bytes) packed 36/m (rounded down) per word

B[1], B[2], ..., B[n] ($n \leq 5$) determine the subscript bounds. If B[i] is an integer K, then the the lower bound for that subscript is 0, and the upper bound is K-1 (not K). Otherwise, B[i] should be a dotted pair (L . U), where L is the lower bound and U is the upper bound. The elements of an array are referenced by:

```
(ID i[1] i[2] ... i[n])
```

The subscripts must be integers and must be within the bounds. Array elements are stored in Binary Program Space.

Examples:

1. To declare a 1-dimensional array CHARS of 7-bit bytes, with subscripts from 1 to 50:

   ```
   (ARRAY CHARS 7 '(1 . 50))
   ```

   The first element of CHARS is (CHARS 1).

2. To declare a 2-dimensional array A of real numbers, with subscripts 0 to N and 0 to M:

   ```
   (ARRAY A NIL N M)
   ```

3. To declare a 1-dimensional array FOO of S-expressions, with subscripts from -P to P:

   ```
   (ARRAY FOO T (CONS (MINUS P) P))
   ```

<u>(EXARRAY "ID" TYPE B[1] B[2] ... B[N])</u>

EXARRAY is identical to ARRAY except that array elements are stored in the body of a subroutine loaded by the LOADER (see Chapter 24), and exarray elements are not initialized. The array-referencing subroutine is stored in Binary Program Space as with ARRAY. EXARRAY searches the symbol table for ID (see GETSYM in Chapter 24).

NOTE

Both ARRAY and EXARRAY consume Binary Program Space. If there is insufficient room there (see Chapter 20), the error message "BINARY PROGRAM SPACE EXCEEDED" will result.

(STORE ("ID" I[1] I[2] ... I[N]) X)

STORE changes the value of the specified array element to X, and returns X. STORE evaluates its second argument first.

Examples: (same arrays as above)

```
(STORE (FOO 0) '(A B))
(STORE (FOO (BAZ L)) 1)
(STORE (A I J) (A J I))
(STORE (CHARS 1) 17)
```

6.2 Contiguous blocks of storage

A BLOCK consists of contiguous storage locations in Binary Program Space. BLOCKs are similar to arrays in that they may contain pointers that are protected from garbage collection, or their contents may be ignored by the garbage collector. They differ, however, in the means of access. BLOCKs are accessed by a pointer into Binary Program Space and all of the functions which will act on a CONS-cell will work equally well on an element of a block. BLOCKs can be used for setting up lists that are also tables, as in setting up multiple OBLISTs.

NOTE

The value returned by the BLOCK functions is a true address, not a LISP number.

(GTBLK N GC)

GTBLK is a SUBR that returns a zeroed BLOCK of N words. If GC is NIL, then the contents of the BLOCK are ignored by the garbage collector. If GC is non-NIL, then the contents are treated as pointers and the cells pointed to will not be collected.

(BLKLST L N)

BLKLST is a SUBR that returns a pointer-type BLOCK of N words. It chains the words in the BLOCK such that the CDR of each word is the succeeding word. The top level of L is then mapped into the CAR's of the block. If N is NIL (or missing), then the length of the list is used. If (LENGTH L) is less than N, then the CARs of the remainder of the BLOCK are set to NIL. If (LENGTH L) is greater than N, the list is truncated.

To create a new, empty symbol table to be used later as the OBLIST, use:

```
(SETQ SYMTABLE (BLKLST NIL (LENGTH OBLIST)))
```

Alternatively, you might want to use everything in the current symbol table:

```
(SETQ SYMTABLE (BLKLST OBLIST))
```

Atoms INTERNed after this table is installed will appear only in the new table.

To install a new symbol table to be used by INTERN, READ, etc., use:

```
(SETQ OBLIST SYMTABLE)
```

(It's probably a good idea to save the value of OBLIST somewhere before you do that.) To clear a symbol table, you can use:

```
(MAP 'RPLACA SYMTABLE)
```

This is merely a compact way of saying (MAP (FUNCTION (LAMBDA (I) (RPLACA I NIL))) SYMTABLE).

If you get into trouble switching OBLISTs, ^C^R will restore the original OBLIST.

CHAPTER 7

LAMBDA EXPRESSIONS

LAMBDA expressions are procedure bodies; they compute a result when values are assigned to their formal parameters. A LAMBDA expression can be assigned to an identifier; you can then treat that identifier as a function name. There are several types of function definitions which determine how arguments are bound to the LAMBDA expression. The following is a LAMBDA expression:

(LAMBDA "LAMBDA-VARS" "FORM1" "FORM2" ... "FORMN")

LAMBDA defines a function by specifying a list of identifiers called the LAMBDA variables (formal parameters), and one or more FORMs, each of which is an S-expression. When such a LAMBDA expression is applied to a list of arguments (actual parameters), the arguments are bound to the LAMBDA variables, and each FORM is evaluated in sequence. The value of the LAMBDA expression is the value of the last FORM.

LAMBDA expressions may have no more than five arguments if they are to be compiled.

Examples:
(LAMBDA NIL 1)
This LAMBDA expression of no arguments always evaluates to 1.

(LAMBDA (X) (PRINT X) (TIMES X X))
This LAMBDA expression prints its argument and then computes the square. (If X is not a number, an error will result.)

Examples where LAMBDA expressions are applied to actual parameters:

```
((LAMBDA (X) (PLUS 1 (CAR X)) '(6)) = 7

((LAMBDA (X Y) (CONS X Y)) NIL T) = (NIL . T)
```

<u>(LABEL "ID" "LAMBDA-EXPR")</u>

LABEL creates a temporary name ID for its LAMBDA expression. This makes it possible to construct recursive functions with temporary names.

Example:

```
(DE REVERSE (L)
  ((LABEL REVERSE1
          (LAMBDA (L M)
           (COND [(ATOM L) M]
                 [T (REVERSE1 (CDR L)
                              (CONS (CAR L) M))])))
   L
   NIL))
```

LABEL is rarely used.

7.1 EXPRs and SUBRs

EXPRs are the most common type of function. An EXPR is an identifier which has a LAMBDA expression on its property list under the property name EXPR. EXPRs are evaluated by binding the values of the actual parameters to their corresponding formal parameters. DE (see Chapter 2) is useful for defining EXPRs. The compiled form of an EXPR is called a SUBR.

An EXPR may have any number of parameters; a SUBR may have no more than five.

If there are fewer actual parameters than formal parameters, the missing parameters are defined to be NIL. (See Chapter 24 for information concerning compiling calls to EXPRs with missing parameters.)

Examples:

```
(DE SQUARE (X) (TIMES X X))
(DE *MAX (X Y) (COND [(GREATERP X Y) X] [T Y]))
(GET '*MAX 'EXPR) =
        (LAMBDA (X Y) (COND [(GREATERP X Y) X] [T Y]))
(DE ID-E (X) X)
(ID-E (PLUS 1 2)) = 3
```

```
(ID-E) = NIL    (missing args default to NIL)
```

7.2 FEXPRs and FSUBRs

A FEXPR is an identifier which has a LAMBDA expression on its property list under the property name FEXPR. The LAMBDA expression has one formal parameter. FEXPRs are evaluated by binding the list of actual parameters to the single formal parameter; the actual parameters are not evaluated. Many input/output functions, particularly those whose parameters are file names, are FEXPRs.

DF (see Chapter 14) is useful for defining FEXPRs. The compiled form of an FEXPR is called an FSUBR.

Examples:

```
(DF QUOTE (X) (CAR X))

(DF OLDSYM (ID)
  (SETQ ID (CAR ID))
  (READLIST (NCONC (EXPLODE ID) (EXPLODE (GET ID 'SCNTR)))))

(DF ID-F (L) L)
(ID-F (PLUS 1 2)) = ((PLUS 1 2))
(ID-F) = NIL
```

7.3 LEXPRs and LSUBRs

A LEXPR is an EXPR that takes an arbitrary number of parameters. Its LAMBDA expression has an atomic argument "list" of the form:

```
(LAMBDA "ID" "FORM1" "FORM2" ... "FORMn")
```

The actual parameters are evaluated. ID is bound to the number of actual parameters. They are referred to by the special functions ARG and SETARG. The compiled form of an LEXPR is called an LSUBR.

(ARG N)

ARG returns the value of the Nth argument to a LEXPR.

Examples:

```
(DE MAX N
   (PROG (M)
         (SETQ M (ARG N))
       L (SETQ N (SUB1 N))
         (COND [(ZEROP N) (RETURN M)]
               [(GREATERP (ARG N) M) (SETQ M (ARG N))])
         (GO L)))
(MAX 1 1.2 4 3 -50) = 4
```

```
(DE LIST N
   (PROG (X)
    LOOP (COND [(EQ N 0) (RETURN X)])
         (SETQ X (CONS (ARG N) X))
         (SETQ N (SUB1 N))
         (GO LOOP)))
```

```
(DE ID-L N N)
(ID-L (PLUS 1 2)) = 1
(ID-L) = 0
```

<u>(SETARG N V)</u>

SETARG sets the value of the Nth argument to V and returns V.

7.4 MACROs

A MACRO is an identifier which has a LAMBDA expression on its property list under the property name MACRO. The LAMBDA expression has one formal parameter. MACROs are evaluated by binding the <u>entire list</u> containing the macro name and the actual parameters (unevaluated) to the formal parameter. The body in the LAMBDA expression is evaluated and should result in another "expanded" form. In the interpreter, that expanded form is evaluated; in the compiler, it is compiled. DM (see Chapter 14) is useful for defining MACROs.

```
(DM ID-M (X) X)
(ID-M (PLUS 1 2)) = (ID-M (PLUS 1 2))
(ID-M) = (ID-M)
```

(MCONS L)

The CONS of an arbitrary number of arguments can be defined:

```
(DM MCONS (L)
    (COND [(NULL (CDDR L)) (CADR L)]
          [T (LIST 'CONS
                   (CADR L)
                   (CONS 'MCONS (CDDR L)))]))
```

(MCONS A B C) calls MCONS with L = (MCONS A B C). MCONS then forms the list (CONS A (MCONS B C)). Evaluating this will again call MCONS with L = (MCONS B C). When that is evaluated, MCONS will be called with L = (MCONS C). MCONS will finally return C. The effect of (MCONS A B C) is then (CONS A (CONS B C)).

Example:

```
*(MCONS 1 2 3)
Enter MCONS:
!     L = (MCONS 1 2 3)
MCONS = (CONS 1 (MCONS 2 3))
Enter MCONS:
!     L = (MCONS 2 3)
MCONS = (CONS 2 (MCONS 3))
Enter MCONS:
!     L = (MCONS 3)
MCONS = 3
(1 2 . 3)
```

(*EXPAND2 L FN)

*EXPAND2 is generally useful for MACRO expansion:

```
(DE *EXPAND2 (L FN)
 (COND [(NULL (CDR L)) (CAR L)]
       [T (LIST FN (CAR L) (*EXPAND2 (CDR L) FN))]))
```

The actual definition of MCONS is:

```
(DM MCONS (L) (*EXPAND2 (CDR L) 'CONS))
```

MACROs are more general than FEXPRs and LEXPRs. In fact, the previous definition of MAX can be replaced by the following MACRO:

```
(DM MAX (L) (*EXPAND2 (CDR L) '*MAX))
```

(MAX A B C D) would then expand to:

```
(*MAX A (*MAX B (*MAX C D)))
```

<u>(*EXPAND L FN)</u>
<u>(*EXPAND1 L FN)</u>

*EXPAND and *EXPAND1 are MACRO-expanding functions used by PLUS, TIMES, etc. They are equivalent to:

```
(DE *EXPAND (L FN) (*EXPAND1 (REVERSE (CDR L)) FN))
```

```
(DE *EXPAND1 (L FN)
 (COND [(NULL (CDR L)) (CAR L)]
       [T (LIST FN (*EXPAND1 (CDR L) FN) (CAR L))]))
```

Examples:

```
(DM PLUS (L) (*EXPAND L '*PLUS))
```

(PLUS A B C D) now expands to:

```
(*PLUS (*PLUS (*PLUS A B) C) D)
```

The difference between *EXPAND and *EXPAND2 is the order in which the arguments are passed to the function, left-to-right versus right-to-left. The arguments are <u>evaluated</u> left-to-right with either macro.

7.5 The MACROEXPANSION Feature

<u>(UNMACEXPAND X)</u>

If the global variable MACROEXPANSION is set to T (its default setting), all macro expansions will be automatically saved so the expansion is done only once. The original macro call is restored when the function is prettyprinted, edited, or broken. If necessary, the function

(UNMACEXPAND X)

may be used to restore all macro calls in X to their original states. (There is normally no reason to call UNMACEXPAND directly.) The macro-saving feature may be disabled by setting MACROEXPANSION to NIL.

Example:

```
*(DE ADD (X Y) (PLUS X Y))  ~ PLUS is a macro
ADD


*(GET 'ADD 'EXPR) ~ Look at the definition.
(LAMBDA (X Y) (PLUS X Y))


*(ADD 3 4)        ~ Now use it. MACRO is expanded.
7


*(GET 'ADD 'EXPR) ~ Now look at the definition.
(LAMBDA (X Y)
        (MACROEXPANSION (*PLUS X Y) (PLUS X Y)))


*(PP ADD)               ~ Prettyprint it.

(DEFPROP ADD (LAMBDA (X Y) (PLUS X Y)) EXPR)


*(GET 'ADD 'EXPR) ~ PP called UNMACEXPAND.
(LAMBDA (X Y) (PLUS X Y))
```

The call to PLUS was replaced with a call to an FSUBR named MACROEXPANSION, which simply evaluates its first argument:

```
(DF MACROEXPANSION (L) (EVAL (CAR L)))
```

<u>(EXPANDMACRO S)</u>

This function returns its parameter with all its macros (if any) expanded. It is defined as:

```
(DE EXPANDMACRO (SEXP)
  (COND [(OR [ATOM SEXP]
             [EQ (CAR SEXP) 'QUOTE]
             [AND [CDR SEXP] [ATOM (CDR SEXP)]])
         SEXP]
        [(EQ (CAR SEXP) 'MACROEXPANSION)
         (EXPANDMACRO (CADR SEXP))]
        [(AND [LITATOM (CAR SEXP)]
              [GET (CAR SEXP) 'MACRO])
         (EXPANDMACRO ((LAMBDA (MAC S) (MAC S))
                       (GET (CAR SEXP) 'MACRO)
                       SEXP))]
        [T (MAPCAR (FUNCTION EXPANDMACRO) SEXP)]))
```

CHAPTER 8

EVALUATION OF S-EXPRESSIONS

This chapter describes the heart of the LISP interpreter, the mechanism for evaluating S-expressions.

<u>(EVAL E)</u>
<u>(*EVAL E)</u>

EVAL and *EVAL evaluate the value of the S-expression E. EVAL may take an optional second argument (see 8.2).

Example:
(EVAL (LIST 'ADD1 3)) = 4

The top level of LISP is:

```
(PROG NIL
 L    (%PRINFNTOP (EVAL (READ)))
      (TERPRI)
      (GO L))
```

%PRINFNTOP is initially PRIN.

<u>(APPLY FN ARGS)</u>
<u>(*APPLY FN ARGS)</u>

APPLY and *APPLY bind each S-expression in the value of ARGS to the corresponding argument of the function FN, and return the value of FN. APPLY may take an optional third argument (see 8.2). FN must be an EXPR, SUBR, LSUBR, or a LAMBDA-expression.

Example:
```
(APPLY (FUNCTION APPEND) '((A B) (C D)))
      = (A B C D)
```

(APPLY# FN ARGS)

APPLY# is similar to APPLY except that FN may be a function of any type, including MACRO.

When either APPLY or APPLY# is given an EXPR as its first argument, the second argument is evaluated by APPLY# or APPLY, but the elements of the resulting list are directly bound to the LAMBDA variables of the EXPR, and are not evaluated again even though it is an EXPR.

Examples:
```
(APPLY# 'PLUS '(3 2 2)) = 7
(APPLY# 'CONS (LIST 'A 'B)) = (A . B)
```

(QUOTE "E")

QUOTE returns the S-expression E without evaluating it.

```
(DF QUOTE (E) (CAR E))
```

NOTE

The single-quote (') and the at-sign (@) are both abbreviations for QUOTE. 'FOO = @FOO = (QUOTE FOO)

(FUNCTION "FN")

FUNCTION is the same as QUOTE in the interpreter. In the compiler, FUNCTION causes the S-expression FN to be compiled if FN is a LAMBDA expression, but QUOTE generates an S-expression constant. See *FUNCTION in 8.2 for the special FUNARG feature.

<u>(F:L L)</u>

This is a MACRO that saves some typing.

```
(F:L (I) (PRINT I) (ADD1 I))
```

expands into:

```
(FUNCTION (LAMBDA (I) (PRINT I) (ADD1 I)))
```

F:L is defined:

```
(DM F:L (L) (LIST 'FUNCTION (CONS 'LAMBDA (CDR L))))
```

Definitions of EVAL and APPLY

The following function definitions lack some details but explain the essence of EVAL and APPLY. The A-LIST feature of these functions is not shown, but will be explained in 8.2.

```
(DE EVAL (X)
  (PROG (Y)
        (RETURN
         (COND
          [(OR [NUMBERP X] [STRINGP X]) X]
          [(ATOM X)
           (COND [(SETQ Y (GET X 'VALUE)) (CDR Y)]
                 [T (ERROR '(UNBOUND VARIABLE))])]
          [(ATOM (CAR X))
           (COND [(SETQ Y
                        (GETL (CAR X) '(EXPR MACRO FEXPR)))
                  (COND [(EQ (CAR Y) 'EXPR)
                         (APPLY (CADR Y)
                                (MAPCAR 'EVAL (CDR X)))]
                        [(EQ (CAR Y) 'MACRO)
                         (EVAL (APPLY (CADR Y) (LIST X)))]
                        [T (APPLY (CADR Y) (LIST (CDR X)))])
                  ]
                 [(SETQ Y (GET (CAR X) 'VALUE))
                  (EVAL (CONS (CDR Y) (CDR X)))]
                 [T (ERROR '(UNDEFINED FUNCTION))])]
          [T (APPLY (CAR X) (MAPCAR 'EVAL (CDR X)))]))))


(DE APPLY (FN ARGS)
  (COND [(ATOM FN)
         (COND [(GET FN 'EXPR) (APPLY (GET FN 'EXPR) ARGS)]
               [T (APPLY (EVAL FN) ARGS)])]
        [(EQ (CAR FN) 'LAMBDA)
         (PROG2 (BIND (CADR FN) ARGS)
                (EVAL (CADDR FN))
                (UNBIND (CADR FN)))]
        [T (APPLY (EVAL FN) ARGS)]))
```

The functions BIND and UNBIND implement variable bindings as described in the next section.

8.1 Variable Bindings

Briefly, LISP uses dynamic scoping (shallow binding) of variables as APL does, for example, rather than static scoping (deep binding) as ALGOL does.

8.1.1 Bound and Free Occurrences

A variable has a "bound occurence" when it appears in the formal parameter list of the innermost LAMBDA or PROG; otherwise it has a "free occurence."

Examples:

```
(LAMBDA (X) (TIMES X Y))
       X has a bound occurrence.
       Y has a free occurrence.

(LAMBDA (Y Z) (MAPCAR (FUNCTION (LAMBDA (X) (CONS X Y))) Z))
       X and Z have only bound occurrences.
       Y is bound by the outer LAMBDA and free in the inner.
```

Functions defined with DE, DF, and DM implicitly use LAMBDA. E.g., (DE FOO (L) (CAR L)) is the same as (DEFPROP FOO (LAMBDA (L) (CAR L)) EXPR).

8.1.2 Scope of Bindings

Variables are automatically bound by LAMBDA and PROG. Unbound variables can be bound _globally_ with SETQ. The binding of a variable X is superseded by executing a LAMBDA or PROG that also binds X. The old binding is saved, and will be restored upon return from the LAMBDA or PROG, but is inaccessible in the meantime. For example,

```
(DE A (X) (C))            ~ A binds X and calls C.
(DE B (X) (A (PLUS X 1))) ~ B also binds X.
(DE C () (PRINT X))       ~ C doesn't bind at all.
```

The variable X has a free occurence in C; that is, C _uses_ X but does not bind it. If we call (A 3), then A will _bind_ X to 3 and call C. When C calls (PRINT X), X is still bound, so C prints 3. If we call (B 14), B will bind X to 14, so (PLUS X 1) evaluates to 15. Then A is called, and A binds X to 15, superseding the old binding. A calls C, C calls PRINT, and PRINT uses the most recent binding of X, namely 15. If we call (C) directly, we get the error message UNBOUND VARIABLE.

8.1.3 SPECIAL Variables and the compiler

Suppose we define a function F:

```
(DE F (X Y) (PLUS X Y 3))
```

When this function is executed, the values passed to F for X and Y are attached to the property lists of X and Y by the binding mechanism, and when X and Y are later evaluated by PLUS, that's where the values are retrieved from. If we compile this function, the values passed to F are placed on the Regular Pushdown List and retrieved from there when PLUS is called. The property lists of X and Y are unaffected. It doesn't matter, therefore, what the names of the parameters were, since we're not accessing their property lists.

But suppose we try to compile the function G:

```
(DE G (X Y) (PLUS X Y Z))
```

X and Y are no problem; they're on the Regular Pushdown List. But Z has a free occurrence in G, and the compiler has no way of knowing whether Z has already been put on the Regular Pushdown List, so it assumes that it has not. It compiles code that accesses Z's property list. It also prints out the message UNDECLARED FREE VARIABLE. The "declaration" it wants is (SPECIAL Z), which simply puts T on the property list of Z under the name SPECIAL, i.e., (DEFPROP Z T SPECIAL). In this example, the compiler could detect that Z should be SPECIAL.

But that may not be good enough. Consider the function H:

```
(DE H (Z) (PRINT Z) (PRINT (G 1 2))
```

If we compile H, then the value passed to H for Z will not go on Z's property list, but rather on the Regular Pushdown List, just as X and Y did in function F. Z will be unaffected. But when we get to the function G from H, G is expecting to find Z's value on its property list, not on the Regular Pushdown List. In this case, you *must* declare Z to be SPECIAL before compiling H, so that it *will* compile code to access Z's property list.

In compiled functions, then, any variable that is bound in a LAMBDA or PROG and has a free occurrence elsewhere must be declared SPECIAL, except inside MAP functions (they're compiled in-line).

Examples:
(LAMBDA (A B) (PLUS X A B))
The variable X has a free occurrence and must be declared SPECIAL if the LAMBDA expression is to be compiled.

```
(DE FOO (A L) (MAPC (FUNCTION (LAMBDA (I) (PLUS A I))) L))
```

The variable A has a free occurence, but it does not need to be declared SPECIAL since it occurs inside a MAP function.

8.1.4 Binding Mechanisms

8.1.4.1 Interpreted variables - All variables in interpreted functions, and SPECIAL variables in compiled functions, store their values in the following way. A CONS-cell, called the variable's SPECIAL cell, is placed on the variable's property list under the property name VALUE. The actual value is placed in the CDR of the SPECIAL cell, called the VALUE cell (see diagram in 13.2). These variables are bound at the entry to a LAMBDA or PROG by saving their previous values on the Special Pushdown List and storing their new values in the VALUE cells. All references to these variables are made directly to their SPECIAL cells. When the LAMBDA or PROG is exited, the old values are restored from the Special Pushdown List.

If the variable was not previously bound, then a new SPECIAL cell is put on the property list, and the un-INTERNed atom UNBOUND is saved on the Special Pushdown List whe the LAMBDA or PROG is entered, and placed in the VALUE cell on exit. This is more efficient than removing the VALUE property and adding a new one every time the variable is bound. To EVAL, then, an unbound variable is one that either lacks a VALUE property altogether or has the atom UNBOUND in its VALUE cell.

(UNBOUND)

UNBOUND returns the un-INTERNed atom UNBOUND which the system places in the CDR of an atom's special cell (i.e., in the value cell) to indicate that the atom currently has no assigned value even though it has a VALUE property on its property list.

(BOUNDP X)

BOUNDP is used to test whether X (which should evaluate to the name of an identifier) has a value. Definition:

```
(DE BOUNDP (X)
  (AND [LITATOM X]
       [SETQ X (GET X 'VALUE)]
       [NEQ (CDR X) (UNBOUND)]))
```

8.1.4.2 Compiled variables - In compiled functions, all variables not declared SPECIAL are stored on the Regular Pushdown List. Their SPECIAL cells (if they exist) are not referenced at all.

8.2 The A-LIST and FUNARG Features

The A-LIST which is used in some LISP systems to implement recursive variable bindings does not exist here, but its effects are simulated through a special A-LIST feature. The functions EVAL and APPLY allow an extra last argument to be passed which is either a list of paired identifiers and values (like an A-LIST) or a "binding context pointer" (BCP), which is a pointer into the Special Pushdown List.

In the case of an A-LIST argument, EVAL and APPLY will bind the special cells of the variables in the A-LIST to their specified values, saving their previous bindings on the Special Pushdown List. When EVAL and APPLY return, the variable bindings are restored to their previous values. Example:

```
*(DE F (X) (PLUS X Y))
F

*(SETQ Y 3)
3

*(EVAL '(F 5))
8

*(EVAL '(F 5) '((Y . 6)))
11

*Y
3
```

A BCP designates a level in recursive variable binding. When EVAL and APPLY receive a BCP as their second argument, all value cells are re-bound to the values they had at the time the BCP was generated. This causes EVAL and APPLY to reference these variables in the context which existed when the BCP was generated. This feature is primarily used to prevent variable-name conflicts when using EVAL, APPLY, and functional arguments. As with the A-LIST, when EVAL and APPLY exit, the previous bindings are restored.

There are three ways to generate a BCP:

If a FEXPR is defined with two arguments, then the second argument will point to the Special Pushdown List level at the time the FEXPR is called.

The second way to generate a BCP is with *FUNCTION.

(*FUNCTION "FN")

*FUNCTION returns a list of the following form:

(FUNARG FN . <BCP>)

where BCP points to the Special Pushdown List level at the time *FUNCTION is called. Whenever such a functional form is used in functional context, all SPECIAL bindings are restored to the values they had at the time *FUNCTION was evaluated. When the functional argument has been APPLYed, the previous bindings are restored as with the A-LIST.

The third and most direct way to generate a BCP is with the stack-pointer functions described in Chapter 19.

8.3 Order of precedence among properties

When EVAL is given the expression (F X), it looks through the property list of F for the first property name that is a member of the list (SUBR LSUBR EXPR FSUBR MACRO FEXPR). If it doesn't find one, then it will look for the VALUE of F. If there is a value, it repeats the process with the value; otherwise, it causes the error UNDEFINED FUNCTION.

It is particularly important to remember this when using parameters as functions. Example:

```
(DE G (X CAR) (CAR X))
(DE H (X FOO) (FOO X))
```

While the functions look similar, G will effectively ignore its second parameter and always call the system function CAR because, as indicated in the list above, EVAL looks for SUBR before VALUE. Unless there is a function named FOO, the function H will use its second parameter.

To avoid doubt, use APPLY#.

```
(DE H (X FOO) (APPLY# FOO (LIST X)))
```

Since APPLY# evaluates its arguments first, this will not conflict with a function named FOO. For examples, see the definitions of the MAP functions (12.5).

CHAPTER 9

COMMENTS

There are two kinds of comments, those that are invisible to READ (scanner comments), and those that are not (program comments).

9.1 Scanner Comments

Scanner comments begin with any one of the characters defined as comment-beginners. The current set includes tilde (~, ASCII 176Q), control-Y (ASCII 31Q), and control-Z (ASCII 32Q). Scanner comments end with any one of the characters defined as comment-enders. The current comment-ender is line-feed (ASCII 12Q).

You can redefine the comment-beginning and -ending characters. See Chapter 16.

When any of the input functions (e.g., READ, TYI, READCH) encounter a comment-beginner, they continue to scan the input until they reach a comment-ender, ignoring everything else. Scanner comments are thus useful for allowing descriptive text that will be completely ignored when read. They also make it possible to extend atoms (identifiers, strings, and numbers) across line boundaries without any of the characters in the comment becoming part of the atom. That is, when the printing functions run out of space on a line, they print a comment-beginner (the most recently defined one), a carriage-return, a line-feed, and a comment-ender (the most recently defined one). (If that's also a line-feed, they print only one.) Then they continue printing the atom. In this way, the output may be read later on.

9.1.1 Scanner Comments and the TTY

Since output to the TTY cannot be input later, this procedure is skipped when printing there. Note also that Control-Z is the initial reread character (see Chapter 1), which takes precedence over its being a scanner comment-beginner.

9.2 Program comments

Program comments are S-expressions that always evaluate to NIL. They may be placed in function definitions anywhere a NIL could be placed without harm, e.g., at the top level of LAMBDAs and PROGs. When the function is subsequently compiled, these expressions will disappear.

<u>(NILL "L")</u>

```
(DF NILL (L) NIL)
```

The list of parameters is not evaluated or used in any way. Note that the parameters must be syntactically well-formed, however. For example,

```
(NILL DOES X = Y?)
```

is a legal comment, but

```
(NILL YES X = Y.)
```

is <u>not</u> legal, since the dot after the Y will cause a DOT CONTEXT ERROR.

<u>(; "L")</u>
<u>(;; "L")</u>

A more useful commenting facililty is provided by the functions ; and ;;. These functions are also defined as printmacros (see Chapter 17) that cause the parameters to be printed in block form as a comment. ; comments are intended to be used for detailed descriptions of code: they are printed starting in column 40. ;; comments are intended to serve as top-level descriptions of functions or segments of code: they are printed at the current level of indentation.

In order to cause comments to be stored as compactly as possible, a new readmacro character ("{", left brace) is used for reading comments:

{; This is a comment.}

causes everything from the ";" up to the "}" to be read as a string, so this comment will be stored internally as

(; "This is a comment.")

In addition to being more compact, the use of {...} allows special characters such as periods and commas (and lower-case letters, if *RAISE=T) to appear in comments without having to "slashify" them. The comment-printer knows about such packed comments, and prints them correctly. The prettyprinter will print all comments in braces unless the variable COMMENTSTR is set to NIL. Packed comments may be converted to lists for easier editing via the UNPACK edit command (see section 22.14).

Comment atoms are defined by placing the function name PP-COMMENT on the property list of the atom under the PRINTMACRO property, and putting either T (print at current indentation level) or the desired starting print column on the property list under the property COMMENT. You can disable ; or ;; as comment atoms by removing these two properties, or change the starting column or add new comment atoms if desired.

Note that comments are intended primarily to comment symbolic files -- when printing to the terminal all comments appear simply as *COMMENT* unless the special variable COMMENTFLG is non-NIL. The functions PP; and PPL; and the edit commands P; and PP; may be used to print function definitions with comments on the terminal (i.e., they first set COMMENTFLG to T).

CHAPTER 10

OTHER PROGRAMMING CONSTRUCTS

10.1 SELECTQ

(SELECTQ X "Y1" "Y2" ... "YN" Z)

This function selects a sequence of instructions based on the value of its first argument X. Each of the Y's is a list of the form (S E[1] E[2] ...) where S is the "selection key." S is either an atom or a list; it is *not* evaluated, but treated as a constant.

If S is an atom, and X is EQ to S, then the expressions E[1], E[2], ... are evaluated, and SELECTQ returns the value of the last E-expression. If there are no E-expressions, SELECTQ returns NIL.

If S is a list, and X is EQ to some element of S, then E[1], E[2], ... are evaluated as described above.

If Y is not selected in one of the two ways described, then the remaining Y's are tested. If none is selected, the value of SELECTQ is the value of Z. Z must be present.

Example:

```
(SELECTQ (CAR W)
         [Q (PRINT FOO) (FIE W)]
         [(A E I O U) (VOWEL W)]
         (COND [W 'STOP]))
```

which has two cases, Q and (A E I O U), and a default condition, which is a COND.

SELECTQ compiles in-line, and is therefore very fast.

10.2 Variations on PROG

<u>(PROG1 X1 X2 ... XN)</u>

PROG1 evaluates all expressions X1, X2, ..., Xn (n $\leq$ 5), and returns X1 as its value.

<u>(PROG2 X1 X2 ... XN)</u>

PROG2 evaluates all expressions X1, X2, ..., Xn (n $\leq$ 5), and returns the value of X2.

<u>(PROGN X1 X2 ... XN)</u>

PROGN evaluates all expressions X1, X2, ..., Xn (any n), and returns Xn as its value.

10.3 Loop-constructs (FOR, WHILE, etc.)

<u>(DO "E1" "E2" ...)</u>

DO is a macro which provides a general evaluation capability for LISP. In its simplest form, DO is equivalent to PROGN: each E is evaluated in turn, with the value of the last E returned as the value of the DO.

The following forms of DO expand into PROGs. The E's may thus contain labels and GOs, and the loop may be exited prematurely via RETURN.

<u>(DO WHILE "P" "E1" "E2" ...)</u>

DO-WHILE evaluates P. If that is non-NIL, it evaluates the E's. This is repeated until P evaluates to NIL, at which time the most recent value of the last E is returned. (The atom WHILE occurs literally in the call.)

(DO UNTIL "P" "E1" "E2" ...)

DO-UNTIL is equivalent to (DO WHILE (NOT P) E1 E2 ...). Note that, unlike the UNTIL-loop many programming languages, this one performs the test before evaluating the E's. (The atom UNTIL occurs literally in the call.)

(DO FOR "VAR" IN L "E1" "E2" ...)

(Similar to MAPC). VAR is bound to each element of L in turn, and the E's are evaluated for each binding. When L is exhausted, the last value of the last E is returned. If L is initially NIL, no E's are evaluated and DO returns NIL. VAR is local to the generated PROG, so any previous value of VAR will be saved and restored. (The atoms FOR and IN occur literally in the call.)

```
Example:  (DO FOR I IN '(FOO 1 BAZ 13.2 NIL)
                        (PRINT (NUMBERP I))
```

will print NIL, 1, NIL, 13.2, and NIL.

(DO FOR "VAR" ON L "E1" "E2" ...)

(Similar to MAP). Like DO-FOR-X-IN, except VAR is bound to successive tails of L. (The atoms FOR and ON occur literally in the call.)

(DO FOR "VAR" RPT N "E1" "E2" ...)

This is similar to DO-FOR-X-IN, except VAR takes on integer values from 1 to N. If N is initially less than 1, none of the E's are evaluated and DO returns NIL. (The atom RPT occurs literally in the call.)

(RPTQ N "E1" "E2" ...)

This is equivalent to (DO FOR RPTN RPT N E1 E2 ...).

(REPEAT N "E1" "E2" ...)

The expressions E1, E2, etc., will be evaluated, in turn, N times (if N > 1), as in RPTQ, but the loop counting is done with registers for speed; no LISP variables are used. REPEAT always returns NIL.

10.4 Programming advice

There is no single "LISP style" of programming, let alone a "best style" of LISP programming, but there are stereotypical patterns. Some of these, such as the use of recursion, are related to the structure of S-expressions, and one hears such glowing adjectives as "pure" and "natural" applied to highly patterned programs. Such praise is often made faint, however, when the patterns introduce gross inefficiency. The purpose of this section is neither to advocate nor to proscribe certain styles or patterns, but merely to comment on a few of the programming considerations that are important in LISP. Put simply, if you have some idea about what's going on behind the scenes, you can write better programs than someone who follows patterns blindly.

10.4.1 Recursion versus iteration

Recursive definitions often have the pedagogical advantages of being short and easy to understand. Sometimes, the recursion is used only to effect a loop through successive elements of a list. If the last thing a function does is to call itself on the CDR of its parameter, the function uses what is called _tail recursion_. Example:

```
(DE LENGTH (L)
        (COND [(ATOM L) 0]
              [T (ADD1 (LENGTH (CDR L)))]))
```

It's hard to fault that definition for clarity, but the implementation uses six locations on the Special Pushdown List for each call to LENGTH: one for the parameter, one for the recursive call, one for the call to COND, and three for internal bookkeeping (to permit tracing, etc.). There was no real need to save L on the stack, since all we did to the returned value was add a constant and return the sum. That's a cue for eliminating the recursion and replacing it with iteration: if the parameters aren't going to be used again after we return from the recursive call, then it might be better to use iteration.

Iteration comes in several flavors, of course. The obvious PROG-loop is this:

```
(DE LENGTH (L)
  (PROG (C)
        (SETQ C 0)
   LOOP (COND [(ATOM L) (RETURN C)])
        (SETQ C (ADD1 (C))
        (SETQ L (CDR L))
        (GO LOOP)))
```

Writing explicit loops can be a nuisance, and there are several ways to avoid that chore. For example, we could use the loop-constructs in the previous section:

```
(DE LENGTH (L)
  (PROG (C)
        (SETQ C 0)
        (DO WHILE (CONSP L) (INCR C) (POP L))
        (RETURN C)))
```

The DO-WHILE itself expands into a PROG, of course, but we didn't have to write the explicit control.

Notice that LENGTH stops when it reaches an ATOM. That's more general than testing for NIL, but also more expensive. You need it if there's a chance that the CDR of the LAST of the list will be some non-NIL atom, but that's rarely the case. If you know that it's a "proper" list, i.e., ending with NIL, then you can use the MAP functions:

```
(DE LENGTH (L)
  (PROG (C)
        (SETQ C 0)
        (MAPC (FUNCTION (LAMBDA () (INCR C))) L)
        (RETURN C)))
```

The MAP functions, defined in chapter 12, are simply loop functions coded at the assembly level for speed. They all terminate on a null check, and they cause an error if they reach a non-NIL atom. The compiler compiles the MAP functions "in-line"; that is, it wouldn't generate calls to MAPC (in our example), but rather it would expand the code as a loop and compile that, which is much more efficient.

10.4.2 Keeping recursion

Some functions, of course, _must_ be coded recursively. Typically, these functions call themselves on the CAR of their parameter and then on the CDR. Since they needed the parameter after the first recursive call (to take the CDR), we know that they're not like the simple tail-recursive functions.

(Strictly speaking, you could eliminate the recursive calls by keeping an explicit stack yourself, but that's just a different way of implementing recursion.)

Perhaps the simplest case of double recursion is SUBST:

```
(DE SUBST (X Y Z)
  (COND [(EQUAL Y Z) X]
        [(ATOM Z) Z]
        [T (CONS (SUBST X Y (CAR Z)) (SUBST X Y (CDR Z)))]))
```

Since we need the parameters after returning from (SUBST X Y (CAR Z)), we can't avoid the recursion. We can eliminate half of it, however. If Z ends with NIL we can use this variation, SUBST1:

```
(DE SUBST1 (X Y Z)
  (COND [(EQUAL Y Z) X]
        [(ATOM Z) Z]
        [T (MAPCAR (FUNCTION (LAMBDA (L) (SUBST1 X Y L)))
                   Z)]))
```

That is, we explicitly recurse on the CARs, but we let MAPCAR loop through the CDRs. (This technique is used, for example, in FLATTEN.)

You may notice that the first two parameters to SUBST are always the same. In this case, we can take advantage of LISP's scoping conventions to save stack space.

```
(DECLARE (SPECIAL !X !Y))
(DE SUBST2 (!X !Y Z) (SUBST2A Z))
(DE SUBST2A (Z)
  (COND [(EQUAL !Y Z) !X]
        [(ATOM Z) Z]
        [T (CONS (SUBST2A (CAR Z)) (SUBST2A (CDR Z)))]))
```

Once the parameters !X and !Y are bound on entry to SUBST2, they're accessible under those names by any function, until SUBST2 exits. The SPECIAL declaration is needed if we're going to compile SUBST2 and SUBST2A (see Chapter 8), and it's often a good idea to give SPECIAL variables unusual spellings to avoid conflicts.

We can combine the two preceding functions:

```
(DECLARE (SPECIAL !X !Y))
(DE SUBST3 (!X !Y Z) (SUBST3A Z))
(DE SUBST3A (Z)
  (COND [(EQUAL !Y Z) !X]
        [(ATOM Z) Z]
        [T (MAPCAR (FUNCTION SUBST3A) Z)]))
```

ALGOL-60 programmers do the same thing with nested

procedures and static scoping.

10.4.3 PROG, GO, and RETURN

For all their stylistic faults, PROGs are indispensable, and the implementation is efficient, so there's no reason to avoid them. Upon entry, the PROG interpreter saves the current stack pointer and two pointers to the PROG body, the second of which changes as successive statements are executed. (GO X) causes a linear search for X in the PROG body, starting from the top, like MEMQ. While there are certainly faster search algorithms in general, most require some preprocessing. The MEMQ solution, moreover, does well since the number of top-level statements in a PROG is often quite small. The stack pointer is reset when GO and RETURN are executed, since they can be nested deeply somewhere within the PROG, allowing such concoctions as (SETQ A (PLUS B (GO X))), as well as more reasonable examples. (The compiler is less sanguine about such things.)

10.4.4 NCONC versus APPEND

The call-by-address functions, RPLACA and RPLACD, and functions that use them, such as NCONC, are the bane of beginners but a necessity of life. Changing structures in place requires little time and no storage. Making repeated copies, even top-level copies, can require a lot of time and even more storage.

The most obvious examples are those where you're building a list of results, and you want to add each new result to the end of the list. APPEND seems like the right choice:

```
(SETQ RLIST (APPEND RLIST (LIST NEWRESULT)))
```

That will work, of course, but APPEND makes a top-level copy of its first parameter every time it's called, and for this kind of application, about one-half N-squared cells will be allocated, all but N of which are also deallocated, to form a list of N results: prohibitively inefficient beyond tiny N.

One simple and clean solution is to build the list backwards, and REVERSE it when you're done.

```
(SETQ RLIST (CONS NEWRESULT RLIST))
```

Even better, DREVERSE it. DREVERSE uses RPLACD to reverse the list in place, thus requiring no new storage.

But sometimes you need to have the list in the right order during the collection process. In that case, you might use

```
(SETQ RLIST (NCONC RLIST (LIST NEWRESULT)))
```

That adds the new item onto the end of the list, but it does that by traveling down the list until it reaches the LAST sublist (the one whose CDR is NIL), and then it uses RPLACD to attach the (LIST NEWRESULT).

The same idea is used by the TCONC and LCONC pointers described in Chapter 12. They do the same RPLACD, but they're faster than NCONC because they keep track of where the end of the list is, instead of searching down the whole length of the list every time. The MAP functions that return lists (e.g., MAPCAR) do the same thing.

If you always produce your new results one at a time, the suggested methods will suffice. But what if you also produce <u>segments</u> of new results, such as a 3-element list that you would like to APPEND to the end of the result list? The APPEND solution will allow you to do this:

```
(SETQ RLIST (APPEND RLIST NEWSEGMENT))
```

but you face the same storage problems as before. You probably do <u>not</u> want to do this:

```
(SETQ RLIST (NCONC RLIST NEWSEGMENT))
```

because that's going to change the structure from which NEWSEGMENT was taken. For example, if you got NEWSEGMENT by doing

```
(SETQ NEWSEGMENT OTHERDATA)  ~ or any CDR of OTHERDATA
```

and you later do

```
(SETQ RLIST (NCONC RLIST NEXTNEWSEGMENT))
```

you will have changed OTHERDATA, too, because prior to this most recent NCONC, (LAST RLIST) was the exact same cell as (LAST OTHERDATA), and when this NCONC does its RPLACD on (LAST RLIST), it's also changing (LAST OTHERDATA).

To avoid this, you can use

```
(SETQ RLIST (NCONC RLIST (COPY NEWSEGMENT)))
```

since that will use all new cells. But all you really need to do is

```
(SETQ RLIST (NCONC RLIST (APPEND NEWSEGMENT NIL)))
```

That may seem odd at first, but what it's doing is creating a copy of the top level of the list NEWSEGMENT; it is the last element of that top level that NCONC is going to change.

CHAPTER 11

FUNCTIONS ON S-EXPRESSIONS

This chapter describes functions that operate on general S-expressions. Chapter 12 describes functions that operate specifically on lists.

<u>(XCONS X Y)</u>

```
= (CONS Y X)
```

<u>(NCONS X)</u>

```
= (CONS X NIL)
```

<u>(SUBST X Y S)</u>

SUBST substitutes S-expression X for all EQUAL occurrences of S-expression Y in S-expression S. SUBST is defined:

```
(DE SUBST (X Y S)
    (COND [(EQUAL Y S) X]
          [(ATOM S) S]
          [T (CONS (SUBST X Y (CAR S))
                   (SUBST X Y (CDR S)))]))
```

Example:

```
(SUBST 5 'FIVE '(FIVE PLUS FIVE IS TEN))
     = (5 PLUS 5 IS TEN)
```

(COPY X)

= (SUBST 0 0 X)

(DSUBST X Y Z)

DSUBST is similar to SUBST, but it uses EQ, it does not copy Z (it changes the list structure Z itself), and it substitutes with a copy of X. It is more efficient than SUBST.

(LSUBST X Y Z)

LSUBST is also like SUBST, except X is substituted as a segment. X must be a list or NIL. Note that if X is NIL, LSUBST returns a copy of Z with all Y's deleted. For example:

```
(LSUBST '(A B) 'Y '(X Y Z)) = (X A B Z)
```

This manner of transforming a list is known as splicing. SUBST does one-for-one replacement, so the output has the same shape as the input. LSUBST and other splicing functions (e.g., LCONC, MAPCON, MAPCAN) can produce output with a different shape, as in the example above.

(SUBLIS ALST EXP)

ALST is a list of pairs ((U1 . V1) (U2 . V2) ... (Un . Vn)) with each U[i] atomic. The value of SUBLIS is the result of substituting each V for the corresponding U in EXP.

Example:

```
(SUBLIS '((A . X) (C . Y)) '(A B C D))
   = (X B Y D)
```

A new structure is created only if needed; i.e., if there are no substitutions, the result is EQ to EXP.

(SUBPAIR OLD NEW EXP)

SUBPAIR is similar to SUBLIS except that elements of NEW are substituted for corresponding atoms of OLD in EXP.

Example:

```
(SUBPAIR '(A C) '(X Y) '(A B C D))
   = (X B Y D)
```

SUBPAIR is defined:

```
(DE SUBPAIR (OLD NEW EXP)
    (SUBLIS (MAPCAR 'CONS OLD NEW) EXP))
```

NOTE

SUBLIS and SUBPAIR do not substitute copies of the appropriate expression, but substitute the identical structure.

<u>(INP X Y)</u>

INP tests whether X is EQ to Y or anywhere "inside" Y.

```
(DE INP (X Y)
  (COND [(EQ X Y) T]
        [(ATOM Y) NIL]
        [(INP X (CAR Y)) T]
        [T (INP X (CDR Y))]))
```

<u>(FLATTEN X)</u>

FLATTEN produces a single list of all the elements in X, equivalent to a pre-order traversal of X.

Example: (FLATTEN '((1 2) 3 ((4) 5))) = (1 2 3 4 5)

```
(DE FLATTEN (L)
  (MAPCAN (FUNCTION (LAMBDA (I)
                      (COND [(ATOM I) (NCONS I)]
                            [T (FLATTEN I)])))
          L))
```

CHAPTER 12

FUNCTIONS ON LISTS

This chapter describes functions for building, fragmenting, modifying, transforming, mapping, and searching lists.

12.1 List-building functions

(*APPEND X1 X2)
(APPEND X1 X2 ... XN)

APPEND joins lists together. *APPEND takes exactly two parameters; APPEND takes any number.

```
(DE *APPEND (X Y)
     (COND [(NULL X) Y]
           [T (CONS (CAR X) (*APPEND (CDR X) Y))]))
```

```
(APPEND X1 X2 ... Xn)
  = (*APPEND X1 (*APPEND X2 ...(*APPEND Xn NIL)...))
```

Examples:
```
(APPEND) = NIL
(APPEND '(A B) '(C D) '(E)) = (A B C D E)
```

(*NCONC X1 X2)
(NCONC X1 X2 ... XN)

NCONC is similar in effect to APPEND, but NCONC does not copy list structures. NCONC modifies list structures by using RPLACD to replace the last element of X1 by a pointer to X2, the last element of X2 by a pointer to X3, etc. The value of NCONC is the modified list X1, which is the concatenation of X1, X2, ..., Xn.

*NCONC takes exactly two arguments; NCONC takes any number.

```
(DE *NCONC (X1 X2)
   (COND [(NULL X1) X2]
         [T (RPLACD (LAST X1) X2) X1]))
```

Examples:
(NCONC) = NIL
(NCONC '(A B) '(C D)) = (A B C D)

```
                X1 -> .--.--        X2 -> .--.--
   BEFORE               |  |                |  |
                        A  B                C  D


                              X2
                              |
                              V
                X1 -> .--.--.--.--
   AFTER                |  |  |  |
                        A  B  C  D
```

Note: (EQ X2 (CDDR X1)) = T

(NCONC1 L V)

= (NCONC L (LIST V))
NCONC1 adds V to the end of L.

(ATTACH X L)

ATTACH destructively attaches X to the beginning of list L. For example, after

(SETQ L '(A))

(SETQ M (ATTACH 'B L))

L has value (B A). If L is NIL, ATTACH is equivalent to CONS, and L remains NIL. Otherwise L will be EQ to M.

(TCONC PTR X)

TCONC is useful for building a list by adding elements one at a time at the end. This could be done with NCONC. However, unlike NCONC, TCONC does not have to search to the end of the list each time it is called. It does this by keeping a pointer to the end of the list being assembled, and updating this pointer after each call. The savings can be considerable for long lists. The cost is the extra word required for storing both the list being assembled, and the end of the list. PTR is that word: (CAR PTR) is the list being assembled, (CDR PTR) is (LAST (CAR PTR)). The value of TCONC is PTR, with the appropriate modifications to its CAR and CDR. Note that TCONC is a destructive operation, using RPLACA and RPLACD.

Example:

```
(MAPC (FUNCTION (LAMBDA (X)
                  (SETQ FOO (TCONC FOO X))))
      '(5 4 3 2 1))

FOO = ((5 4 3 2 1) 1)
```

TCONC can be initialized in two ways. If PTR is NIL, TCONC will make up a pointer. In this case, the program must set some variable to the value of the first call to TCONC. After that it is unnecessary to reset it, since TCONC physically changes PTR:

```
(SETQ FOO (TCONC NIL 5))

FOO = ((5) 5)

(MAPC (FUNCTION (LAMBDA (X) (TCONC FOO X)))

      '(4 3 2 1))

FOO = ((5 4 3 2 1) 1)
```

If PTR is initially (NCONS NIL), the value of TCONC is the same as for PTR=NIL, but TCONC changes PTR:

```
(SETQ FOO (NCONS NIL))

FOO = (NIL)

(MAPC (FUNCTION (LAMBDA (X) (TCONC FOO X)))

      '(5 4 3 2 1))
```

FOO = ((5 4 3 2 1) 1)

The latter method allows the program to initialize the pointer and then call TCONC without having to use SETQ on its value.

<u>(LCONC PTR X)</u>

LCONC is the splicing version of TCONC: where TCONC adds <u>elements</u> at the end of a list, LCONC adds <u>lists</u> at the end. For example:

(SETQ FOO (NCONS NIL))

FOO = (NIL)

(LCONC FOO (LIST 1 2))

FOO = ((1 2) 2)

(LCONC FOO (LIST 3 4 5))

FOO = ((1 2 3 4 5) 5)

(LCONC FOO NIL)

FOO = ((1 2 3 4 5) 5)

Note that LCONC uses the same pointer conventions as TCONC for eliminating searching to the end of the list, so that the same pointer can be given to TCONC and LCONC interchangeably.

(TCONC FOO NIL)

FOO = ((1 2 3 4 5 NIL) NIL)

(LCONC FOO (LIST 3 4 5))

FOO = ((1 2 3 4 5 NIL 3 4 5) 5)

To splice in a top-level copy of the list X instead of X itself, use:

(LCONC PTR (APPEND X NIL))

12.2 Accessing parts of lists

(MEMQ L1 L2)
(MEMB L1 L2)

The value of MEMQ is the tail of the list L2 starting with the first top-level element that is EQ to L1, NIL otherwise.

MEMQ is equivalent to:

```
(DE MEMQ (L1 L2)
    (COND [(NULL L2) NIL]
          [(EQ L1 (CAR L2)) L2]
          [T (MEMQ L1 (CDR L2))]))
```

Examples:
```
(MEMQ 1 '(2 3 4)) = NIL
(MEMQ '(C D) '((A B)(C D) E)) = NIL
(MEMQ 'A '(Q A B)) = (A B)
```

(MEMBER L1 L2)

The value of MEMBER is the tail of the list L2 starting with the first top-level element that is EQUAL to L1, NIL otherwise.

MEMBER is equivalent to:

```
(DE MEMBER (L1 L2)
    (COND [(NULL L2) NIL]
          [(EQUAL L1 (CAR L2)) L2]
          [T (MEMBER L1 (CDR L2))]))
```

Examples:
```
(MEMBER '(C D) '((A B)(C D) E))    = ((C D) E)
(MEMBER 'C '(D))  = NIL
```

(TAILP X Y)

The value of TAILP is X iff X is a list and a tail of Y, i.e., X is EQ to some number of CDRs (possibly 0) of Y.

(LAST L)

LAST returns the last part of a list according to the following definition:

```
(DE LAST (L)
    (COND [(ATOM (CDR L)) L]
          [T (LAST (CDR L))]))
```

Examples:
(LAST '(A B C)) = (C) = (C . NIL)
(LAST '(A B . C)) = (B . C)

(NTH X N)

The value of NTH is the tail of X beginning with the Nth element. E.g., if N = 2, the value is (CDR X); if N=3, (CDDR X); etc. If N = 1, the value is X. If N < 1, the value is (CONS NIL X)..

(PRELIST L N)

PRELIST returns a copy of the first N elements of the list L. If there are fewer than N elements in it, PRELIST returns a copy of the entire list.

(SUFLIST L N)

SUFLIST returns the list formed by taking N CDR's of its first argument. If it exhausts its first argument before it runs out of CDR's, it stops at NIL (i.e., it will return NIL).

SUFLIST is the "compliment" of PRELIST in the sense that:

(APPEND (PRELIST L N) (SUFLIST L N)) = L

SUFLIST is defined:

```
(DE SUFLIST (L N)
    (COND [(CONSP L) (NTH L (ADD1 N))]))
```

<u>(LDIFF X Y)</u>

Y must be a tail of X, i.e., EQ to the result of applying some number of CDRs to X. LDIFF gives a list of all elements in X but not in Y, i.e., the list difference of X and Y. Thus (LDIFF X (MEMQ FOO X)) gives all elements in X up to the first FOO.

Note that the value of LDIFF is always new list structure unless Y=NIL, in which case (LDIFF X NIL) is X itself.

If Y is not a tail of X, LDIFF generates an error. LDIFF terminates on a null check, not an atom check.

12.3 Using lists as stacks

(PUSH "VAR" VAL)

This is a MACRO which expands into (SETQ VAR (CONS VAL VAR)).

(POP "VAR")

This is a MACRO which expands into (PROG1 (CAR VAR) (SETQ VAR (CDR VAR))).

12.4 Transforming lists

(REVERSE L)

REVERSE reverses the top level of list L. REVERSE is equivalent to:

```
(DE REVERSE (L) (REVERSE1 L NIL))
(DE REVERSE1 (L M)
        (COND [(NULL L) M]
              [T (REVERSE1 (CDR L)
                           (CONS (CAR L) M))]))
```

(DREVERSE L)

The value of (DREVERSE L) is EQUAL to (REVERSE L), but DREVERSE destroys the original list L and thus does not use any additional storage. It is more efficient than REVERSE. Definition:

```
(DE DREVERSE (L)
  (PROG (Y Z)
   LOOP (COND [(ATOM (SETQ Y L)) (RETURN Z)])
        (SETQ L (CDR L))
        (SETQ Z (RPLACD Y Z))
        (GO LOOP)))
```

(REMOVE X L)

Returns a COPY of L with all top-level elements EQUAL to X removed. Definition:

```
(DE REMOVE (X LIST)
  (COND [(ATOM LIST) LIST]
        [(EQUAL (CAR LIST) X) (REMOVE X (CDR LIST))]
        [T (CONS (CAR LIST) (REMOVE X (CDR LIST)))]))
```

(DREMOVE X L)

DREMOVE is like REMOVE, but it uses EQ instead of EQUAL, and it actually modifies the list L when removing X, and thus does not use any additional storage. It is more efficient than REMOVE.

NOTE

If X = (L ... L) (i.e., if every element of X is EQ to L) then the value returned by (DREMOVE X L) is NIL, but even after the destructive changes to X there is still one CONS cell left in the modified list which cannot be deleted. Thus if X is a variable and it is possible that the result of (DREMOVE X L) might be NIL, the user must set the value of the variable given to DREMOVE to the value returned by the function; e.g., (SETQ L (DREMOVE X L)).

(UNION L1 L2 ... LN)

UNION returns a list which is the union of the lists L1, L2, ..., Ln. Membership tests are made by whatever function the global variable MEMBFN is set to. Initially, MEMBFN = MEMBER.

(INTERSECTION L1 L2 ... LN)

INTERSECTION returns a list which is the intersection of L1, L2, ..., Ln. INTERSECTION also uses MEMBFN.

(ENTER V L)

ENTER returns L if V is already a member of L. Otherwise it returns L with V CONSed onto the front. As with UNION and INTERSECTION, MEMBFN is used to indicate whether MEMQ or MEMBER checks should be performed. Definition:

```
(DE ENTER (V L)
   (COND [(MEMBFN V L) L]
         [T (CONS V L)]))
```

(NODUPLES L)

NODUPLES returns the list L with all duplicate elements removed. NODUPLES is defined as (UNION L).

12.5 Mapping Functions

The MAP functions apply either to lists and their successive CDR's (MAP, MAPL, MAPCON) or to each CAR of the list (MAPC, MAPCL, MAPCAN).

12.5.1 Basic functions

<u>(MAP FN L1 L2 ... LN)</u>

MAP applies the function FN (which should be a function of n arguments, $n \leq 5$) to the lists L1 - Ln, then to successive CDRs of the lists, stopping when it reaches the end of the shortest list. The value of MAP is NIL. For a single list of arguments, MAP is equivalent to:

```
(DE MAP (FN L)
    (PROG (M)
     LOOP (COND [(NULL L) (RETURN NIL)])
          (SETQ M (CDR L))
          (APPLY# FN (LIST L))
          (SETQ L M)
          (GO LOOP)))
```

For two lists of arguments, MAP is equivalent to:

```
(DE MAP (FN L1 L2)
    (PROG (M1 M2)
     LOOP (COND [(OR [NULL L1] [NULL L2]
                 (RETURN NIL))])
          (SETQ M1 (CDR L1))
          (SETQ M2 (CDR L2))
          (APPLY# FN (LIST L1 L2))
          (SETQ L1 M1)
          (SETQ L2 M2)
          (GO LOOP)))
```

Example: (MAP (FUNCTION PRINT) '(X Y Z))

```
        PRINT:          (X Y Z)
        PRINT:          (Y Z)
        PRINT:          (Z)
        returns:        NIL
```

NOTE

In some LISP systems, the CDR of each list is evaluated _after_ the function is applied. This makes a difference only if the function changes the list in place (e.g., via RPLACD). In UCI LISP, doing so will not affect subsequent calls to the function.

(MAPC FN L1 L2 ... LN)

MAPC is like MAP except that MAPC applies the function FN to the CARs of the remaining lists at each step. MAPC with a single list of arguments is equivalent to:

```
(DE MAPC (FN L)
    (PROG (M)
     LOOP (COND [(NULL L) (RETURN NIL)])
          (SETQ M (CDR L))
          (APPLY# FN (LIST (CAR L)))
          (SETQ L M)
          (GO LOOP)))
```

Example: (MAPC (FUNCTION PRINT) '(X Y Z))

```
PRINT:          X
PRINT:          Y
PRINT:          Z
returns:        NIL
```

Example: (MAPC (FUNCTION SET) '(A B C) '(1 2 3))

This sets the values of A, B, and C to 1, 2, and 3, respectively, and returns NIL.

(MAPLIST FN L1 L2 ... LN)
(MAPL FN L1 L2 ... LN)

MAPLIST is like MAP except that instead of returning NIL, it returns the list of values returned by FN. For a single list of arguments, MAPLIST is equivalent to:

```
(DE MAPLIST (FN L)
    (PROG (M RESULT)
     LOOP (COND [(NULL L) (RETURN (REVERSE RESULT))])
          (SETQ M (CDR L))
          (SETQ RESULT
                (CONS (APPLY# FN (LIST L)) RESULT))
          (SETQ L M)
          (GO LOOP)))
```

Examples:

```
(MAPLIST (FUNCTION CAR) '(A B C D)) = (A B C D)
(MAPLIST (FUNCTION REVERSE) '(A B C D)) =
        ((D C B A) (D C B) (D C) (D))
```

(MAPCAR FN L1 L2 ... LN)
(MAPCL FN L1 L2 ... LN)

MAPCAR is like MAPLIST except that MAPCAR applies FN to the CARs of the remaining lists at each step. For a single list of arguments, MAPCAR is equivalent to:

```
(DE MAPCAR (FN L)
    (PROG (M RESULT)
     LOOP (COND [(NULL L) (RETURN (REVERSE RESULT))])
          (SETQ M (CDR L))
          (SETQ RESULT
                (CONS (APPLY# FN (LIST (CAR L)))
                      RESULT))
          (SETQ L M)
          (GO LOOP)))
```

Examples:

```
(MAPCAR (FUNCTION NCONS) '(A B C D))
    = ((A) (B) (C) (D))
(MAPCAR (FUNCTION ATOM) '((X) Y (Z)))
    = (NIL T NIL)
```

12.5.2 Other Mapping functions

(MAPATOMS FN)

Applies FN (a function of one argument) to every atomic symbol on the OBLIST and returns NIL. MAPATOMS is compiled in-line.

(EVERY FN L1 L2 ... LN)

FN, a function of n arguments, is applied to the CARs of L1 ... Ln. EVERY returns T if each application returns a non-NIL value. If some application of FN returns NIL, EVERY stops at that point and returns NIL. For example, (EVERY 'ATOM L) checks whether L is a list of atoms. EVERY is compiled in-line.

(SOME FN L1 L2 ... LN)

FN, a function of n arguments, is APPLYed to the CARs of L1 ... Ln. If all applications of FN return NIL, SOME returns NIL. If a non-NIL result is found, SOME stops at that point and returns the tail of Ln starting with the value that caused the non-NIL result. SOME is compiled in-line.

Example:

```
(SOME (FUNCTION (LAMBDA (I) (AND [LT I 6] [GT I
0])))
      '(0 -1 10 3 4 0 16))
  = (3 4 0 16)
```

(NOTEVERY FN L1 L2 ... LN)

= (NOT (EVERY FN L1 L2 ... Ln))

(NOTANY FN L1 L2 ... LN)

= (NOT (SOME FN L1 L2 ... Ln))

(SUBSET FN L)

SUBSET applies FN (a function of one argument) to each element of the list L, returning a list consisting of each element of L which causes FN to return a non-NIL value. For example, (SUBSET 'ATOM L) finds all atoms in L. SUBSET is compiled in-line.

12.5.3 Mapping by modifying

The functions MAPCON and MAPCAN produce lists by using NCONC to splice together the values returned by repeated applications of their functional argument.

MAPCON and MAPCAN are especially useful in the case where the function returns NIL. Since NIL does not affect a list if NCONC'ed to it, the output from that function does not appear in the result returned from MAPCON or MAPCAN. For example, a function to remove all the vowels from a word can be written as:

```
(READLIST
 (MAPCAN (FUNCTION
          (LAMBDA (I)
           (COND [(MEMQ I '(A E I O U)) NIL] [T (LIST I)])))
         (EXPLODE WORD)))
```

(MAPCON FN L1 L2 ... LN)

MAPCON applies the function FN to the argument lists L1 ... Ln, to the CDRs of the lists, to the CDRs of those lists, and so on, stopping on the shortest list. The values returned by FN are spliced together with NCONC and returned as the value of MAPCON. FN should always return a list or NIL.

For a single list, MAPCON is equivalent to:

```
(DE MAPCON (FN L)
    (PROG (M RESULT)
     LOOP (COND [(NULL L) (RETURN RESULT)])
          (SETQ M (CDR L))
          (SETQ RESULT
                (NCONC RESULT
                       (APPLY# FN (LIST L))))
          (SETQ L M)
          (GO LOOP)))
```

Example:
```
(MAPCON (FUNCTION COPY) '(1 2 3 4))
  = (1 2 3 4 2 3 4 3 4 4)
```

<u>(MAPCAN FN L1 L2 ... LN)</u>
<u>(MAPCONC FN L1 L2 ... LN)</u>

MAPCAN is similar to MAPCON except it calls FN with the CARs of each list instead of the whole lists.

```
(DE MAPCAN (FN L)
    (PROG (M RESULT)
     LOOP (COND [(NULL L) (RETURN RESULT)])
          (SETQ M (CDR L))
          (SETQ RESULT
                (NCONC RESULT
                       (APPLY# FN (LIST (CAR L)))))
          (SETQ L M)
          (GO LOOP)))
```

12.5.4 The MAP functions redefined

The definitions of the MAP functions given above accurately describe the order of evaluation, but the actual implementation does not use REVERSE or NCONC. Instead, it uses a machine-code version of TCONC and LCONC, more closely resembling the following definitions:

```
(DE MAPLIST (FN L)
    (PROG (M PTR)
          (SETQ M (NCONS NIL))
     LOOP (COND [(NULL L) (RETURN (CAR PTR))])
          (SETQ M (CDR L))
          (TCONC PTR (APPLY# FN (LIST L)))
          (SETQ L M)
          (GO LOOP)))
```

```
(DE MAPCON (FN L)
    (PROG (M PTR)
          (SETQ M (NCONS NIL))
     LOOP (COND [(NULL L) (RETURN (CAR PTR))])
          (SETQ M (CDR L))
          (LCONC PTR (APPLY# FN (LIST L)))
                {;; This is the only difference between
                    MAPLIST and MAPCON.}
          (SETQ L M)
          (GO LOOP)))
```

```
(DE MAPCAR (FN L)
    (PROG (M PTR)
          (SETQ M (NCONS NIL))
     LOOP (COND [(NULL L) (RETURN (CAR PTR))])
          (SETQ M (CDR L))
          (TCONC PTR (APPLY# FN (LIST (CAR L))))
          (SETQ L M)
          (GO LOOP)))


(DE MAPCAN (FN L)
    (PROG (M PTR)
          (SETQ M (NCONS NIL))
     LOOP (COND [(NULL L) (RETURN (CAR PTR))])
          (SETQ M (CDR L))
          (LCONC PTR (APPLY# FN (LIST (CAR L))))
                {;; This is the only difference between
                    MAPCAR and MAPCAN.}
          (SETQ L M)
          (GO LOOP)))
```

12.6 Searching Functions

(ASSOC X L)

ASSOC searches the list of dotted pairs L for a pair whose CAR is EQ to X. If such a pair is found it is returned as the value of ASSOC, otherwise NIL is returned. ASSOC is equivalent to:

```
(DE ASSOC (X L)
    (COND [(NULL L) NIL]
          [(EQ X (CAAR L)) (CAR L)]
          [T (ASSOC X (CDR L))]))
```

Example:
```
(ASSOC 1 '((1 . ONE) (2 . TWO))) = (1 . ONE)
```

(ASSOC# X Y)

ASSOC# is similar to ASSOC, but it uses EQUAL instead of EQ.

(SASSOC X L FN)

SASSOC searches the list of dotted pairs L for a pair whose CAR is EQ to X. If such a pair is found it is returned as the value of ASSOC, otherwise the value of FN, a function of no arguments, is returned.

```
(DE SASSOC (X L FN)
    (COND [(NULL L) (FN)]
          [(EQ X (CAAR L)) (CAR L)]
          [T (SASSOC X (CDR L) FN)]))
```

Example:
```
(SASSOC 0 '((1 . ONE) (2 . TWO))
        (FUNCTION (LAMBDA NIL 'LOSE)))
   = LOSE
```

12.7 Sorting

(INSERT X L COMPAREFN NODUPS)

INSERT destructively inserts X into the sorted list L in the proper slot using COMPAREFN as a binary comparison function. (COMPAREFN X Y) should return a non-NIL value if X either precedes Y in sorted order or X and Y are equal, and NIL if Y precedes X. If COMPAREFN is missing or NIL, LEXORDER will be used. NODUPS controls the handling of duplicate values: if NODUPS is non-NIL, X will not be inserted into L if an element equal to X is already present in L. INSERT performs a binary search to determine where to insert the new element. The value returned by INSERT is the list L with X inserted.

(MERGE L1 L2 COMPAREFN NODUPS)

MERGE returns a new list by merging the sorted lists L1 and L2. COMPAREFN and NODUPS are the same as they are in INSERT.

(SORT L COMPAREFN NODUPS)

SORT returns a new list by sorting the list L, using a binary insertion sort. COMPAREFN and NODUPS are the same as they are in INSERT.

CHAPTER 13

PROPERTY LISTS

The property list of an identifier is a list of pairs (property name, property value) associated with that identifier. The typical kinds of properties which are found in property lists are print names, values, and function definitions.

13.1 Print Names

Every identifier has a print name (PNAME) on its property list. The print name of an identifier is a list of addresses in Full-Word Space. Each word contains five ASCII characters. For example, the identifier TIME-OF-DAY would be initially represented as follows:

```
atom header -> .-----.------.---------------------------
               |     |      |
              "-1"  PNAME   .--------.--------.--------
                            |        |        |
                           "TIME-"  "OF-DA"  "Y@@@@"
```

where @ means null or ASCII 0.

13.2 Special Cells

When a value is assigned to an identifier for the first time, the property name VALUE is put on the identifier's property list, with the corresponding property value being a pointer to what is called a special cell.

The CDR of the special cell (called the value cell) holds the value of the identifier, and the address of the special cell remains constant for that identifier unless REMPROP'ed, to enable compiled functions to reference the values of SPECIAL variables directly. Global variables and all variables bound in interpreted functions also store their values in special cells.

The CAR of the special cell points to the atom header (for backtraces) unless the identifier is a SPECIAL variable that is mentioned in compiled code. In that case, the CAR must be NIL (zero), because compiled code accesses the special cells with indirect addressing, and that involves bits in the left half of the word (i.e., the CAR). (A different mechanism is use for backtracing these variables, as described in 23.6.4.) If you print the property lists of some variables, that's why you sometimes see NIL at the head of the VALUE slot, and other times see the atoms's name there.

Example: The atom T has the following form:

```
                         property list
atom header -> .-----.------.-------.------.----------
               |     |      |       |      |
              "-1"   VALUE  *----T  PNAME  .--------
                            |              |
                            NIL            "T@@@@"
```

* denotes the special cell

If we type (SETQ FOO 99), and FOO is not mentioned in compiled code, then the atom FOO has the following form:

```
                         property list
atom header -> .-----.------.--------.------.----------
               |     |      |        |      |
              "-1"   VALUE  *----99  PNAME  .--------
                            |               |
                            FOO             "FOO@@"
```

* denotes the special cell

13.2.1 Conflicting properties

When an identifier has a function on its property list (e.g., EXPR), it does not usually have a VALUE property as well, although that is possible. Several system functions, in fact, do have both, but this can cause trouble for user-defined functions and is not generally advised. See 8.3 concerning the precedence EVAL gives to properties.

13.3 Property List Functions

NOTE

All functions described in this chapter which expect an identifier as one (or more) of its arguments will give either erroneous results or an error condition if any S-expression other than an identifier is supplied.

<u>(GET I P)</u>

GET is a function which searches the property list of the identifier I looking for the property name which is EQ to P. If such a property name is found, the value associated with it is returned as the value of GET, otherwise NIL is returned. Note that there is an ambiguity if the property is found, but its value is NIL. GET is equivalent to:

```
(DE GET (I P)
  (COND [(NULL (CDR I)) NIL]
        [(EQ (CADR I) P) (CADDR I)]
        [T (GET (CDDR I) P)]))
```

<u>(GETL I L)</u>

GETL is another function which searches property lists. GETL searches the property list of the identifier I looking for the first property which is a member (MEMQ) of the list L. GETL returns the remaining property list, including the property name if any such property was found, NIL otherwise. GETL is equivalent to:

```
(DE GETL (I L)
  (COND [(NULL (CDR I)) NIL]
        [(MEMQ (CADR I) L) (CDR I)]
        [T (GETL (CDDR I) L)]))
```

(PUT I V P)
(PUTPROP I V P)

PUTPROP adds the property name P with property value V to the property list of identifier I. If the property name P is already in the property list, the old property value is replaced by the new one; otherwise the new property name P and its value V are placed on the beginning of the property list. PUTPROP returns V.

NOTE

In some LISP systems, the parameters to PUT and PUTPROP are in a different order.

(DEFPROP "I" "V" "P")

= (PROG2 (PUTPROP I V P) I)

DEFPROP is the same as PUTPROP except that it does not evaluate its arguments, and it returns I.

Example:

```
(DEFPROP POSP (LAMBDA (X) (GREATERP X 0)) EXPR)
   = POSP
```

(REMPROP I P)

REMPROP removes the property P from the property list of identifier I. REMPROP returns T if there was such a property, NIL otherwise.

13.4 Changing the value of variables

SET and SETQ are used to change the values of variables which are bound by either LAMBDA or PROG, or variables which are bound globally. (See 8.1).

(SET E V)

SET changes the value of the identifier specified by the expression E to V and returns to V. Both arguments are evaluated.

NOTE

In compiled functions, SET can be used only on globally bound and SPECIAL variables.

(SETQ "ID" V)

SETQ changes the value of ID to V and returns V. SETQ evaluates V, but does not evaluate ID.

(DEFV "ID" "VALUE")

This is like (SETQ ID VALUE), except that VALUE is not evaluated and the value returned is ID instead of VALUE. DEFV is used by the prettyprinter to print VALUE properties.

(DV "ID" "VALUE")

DV is the same as DEFV, but DV adds ID to the list ALLVALS.

ALLVALS

Any variable defined with DV is kept on the global list ALLVALS.

13.5 Defining New Functions

(DE "ID" "ARGS" "FORM1" "FORM2" ...)

DE places the list (LAMBDA ARGS FORM1 FORM2 ...) on the property list of ID under property EXPR. If ID previously had any of the properties EXPR, FEXPR, SUBR, FSUBR, LSUBR, or MACRO, then DE will return the list (ID REDEFINED). Otherwise, DE returns ID.

DE sets the global variable LASTWORD to ID.

(DF "ID" "ARGS" "FORM1" "FORM2" ...)

DF is like DE except that is defines a function with a FEXPR property. DF also sets the global variable LASTWORD to ID.

(DM "ID" "ARGS" "FORM1" "FORM2" ...)

DM is the same as DE, except that it defines a MACRO. DM also sets the global variable LASTWORD to ID.

(UNSAVE "ID")

If an existing function is redefined via DE, DF, or DM, the old definition is saved on the property list of the function name under the property UNSAVE. The old definition may be restored via the function UNSAVE.

The saving of old definitions may be disabled by setting UNSAVE to NIL. It is initially T.

Function definitions may also be saved by calling the function SAVE directly:

(SAVE "ID")

For example, if a file is to be loaded that redefines FOO, then (SAVE FOO) may be used to save its original definition, and (UNSAVE FOO) will restore it. SAVE and UNSAVE return the function name if the save/unsave was successful, NIL otherwise.

ALLFNS

The name of each function defined via DE, DF, or DM, or edited with EDITF, is kept on the global list ALLFNS. This list may be consulted after a long terminal session to see what functions have been created or modified and must therefore be saved before exiting.

13.6 Other functions

(DEFLIST "L" "DEFVAL" "PROP")
(DEFLIST "L" "PROP")

DEFLIST is useful for placing a property on a number of identifiers. L should be a list of items, each of which is either an atomic symbol A or a two-element list (A VAL). Each A will have a PROP property placed on its property list, with a value of VAL if present, or DEFVAL if only the atomic symbol was given. DEFVAL is optional, with a default value of T assumed. As an example of the use of DEFLIST, the following will give TOM and BOB ages of 15, and SAM an age of 20 (i.e., the 20 overrides the default value of 15):

```
(DEFLIST (TOM BOB (SAM 20)) 15 AGE)
```

(DEFP "AT1" "AT2" "PROP")

DEFP places the PROP property of AT2 onto AT1. For example,

```
(DEFP DO PROGN FSUBR)
```

defines DO to be the same function as PROGN. PROP can be a list of property names, in which case DEFP uses the first one found on AT2's property list.

(ADDPROP ID VALUE PROP)

ADDPROP is used to collect a number of values under a single property. Definition:

```
(DE ADDPROP (ID VALUE PROP)
    (PUTPROP ID (ENTER VALUE (GET ID PROP)) PROP))
```

(PUTLIST L VALUE PROP)

PUTLIST places VALUE as the PROP property of each element of L (which should be a list of identifiers). PUTLIST returns NIL.

(REMLIST L PROP)

REMLIST removes the PROP property from each element of L (which should be a list of identifiers). REMLIST returns NIL.

(REMPROPS ID L)

REMPROPS treats each element of L (a list of identifiers) as a property, removing that property from ID. REMPROPS returns NIL.

CHAPTER 14

FILES

14.1 File specifications

Syntax:

```
<filename-list>          ::= <device-name>
                         ::= <filename-list> <device-name>
                         ::= <ppn>
                         ::= <filename-list> <ppn>
                         ::= <filename-list> <filename>

<device-name>            ::= <identifier> :

<ppn>                    ::= ( <inum> <inum> {<sfd> ...} )

<filename>               ::= <identifier>
                         ::= ( <identifier> . <identifier> )

<sfd>                    ::= <identifier>
```

Semantics:

File specifications on the PDP-10 look like:

```
DEVICE:FILE.EXT[PROJ,PROG,A,B,C,D,E]<PROTECTION>
```

In LISP, this is written as a list:

```
(DEVICE: (PROJ PROG A B C D E) (FILE . EXT))
```

14.1.1 Device names

A device name is an identifier whose last character is a colon, e.g., DSK:. Device names can refer to physical structures (DPA2:, MTA1:), or file structures (DSKA:). System-defined names, called "pseudo-devices" or "ersatz devices," refer to particular disk areas; SYS:, for example, is actually DSK:[1,4]. "Logical devices" are defined by the ASSIGN monitor command; e.g., after the command

```
.ASSIGN DTA3 A
```

all references to A: are actually references to DTA3:. LISP permits all three kinds of devices. In addition, LISP permits an arbitrary assignment of device names to ppn's, which makes it more flexible than the operating system. Any device name may have a ppn on its property list under the name DEVPPN. For example:

```
(DEFPROP AILIBRARY: (4777Q 11Q) DEVPPN)
(DEFPROP OLDSTUFF: (12Q 24Q VERSN2) DEVPPN)
```

Thereafter, (AILIBRARY: (SETQS.LSP)) would actually refer to DSK:SETQS.LSP[4777,11], and (OLDSTUFF: MOD1) would refer to DSK:MOD1[12,24,VERSN2].

NOTE

> Except for those with the DEVPPN property, device names may be no longer than five characters, not counting the final colon.

14.1.2 File names

A filename is either an identifier which specifies a file with no extension, or a dotted pair of file name and extension.

14.1.3 PPN's and subfile directories

A standard PPN (project-programmer number) is represented as a list of two integers, e.g., (10Q 7Q).

For users on systems which support subfile directories, PPNs may now take up to 5 sfds:

```
(PROJ PROG SFD1 SFD2 SFD3 SFD4 SFD5)
```

<u>(%DEVP X)</u>

> %DEVP returns T if X is either a device name (an atomic symbol which ends in ":"), or a programmer project number (a list whose CDR is not an atomic symbol).

14.1.4 File Protection

When OUTPUT (used by DSKOUT, etc.) creates a new file, it retrieves the desired protection from the variable FILPRO. For example,

```
(SETQ FILPRO 115Q)
```

will cause a protection code of <115> to be assigned to all files created by LISP. If FILPRO is NIL (its initial value), the user's default protection code will be used.

The protection of an existing file is also returned by RENAME, *RENAME, and FILBAK when a file is successfully renamed. DSKOUT uses this feature to transfer the protection of an existing file to a new file of the same name. (That is, if FOO.LSP has protection <177> and it is rewritten with DSKOUT, the new version will still have protection <177>).

14.2 Channel Names

All I/O is done through channels, 14 of which may be active at any time. Each channel is identified by a name, which can be an INUM or a LISP identifier that does not end with a colon (to distinguish it from a device name). The channel NIL always refers to the TTY. The channel T is used when you omit a channel name. Except for NIL, a channel name should not be used for simultaneous input and output.

While up to 14 channels may be active any any given time, only one input channel and one output channel may be "selected" at a time. When an input channel is selected, all input (via READ, TYI, etc.) come from that channel. Likewise, when a channel is selected for output, all printing is done on that channel.

14.3 Input Selection and Control

(INPUT "CHANNEL" "FILESPEC1" "FILESPEC2" ...)

INPUT releases any file previously initialized on the channel, and initializes for input the first file specified by the list of file specs. INPUT returns the channel if one was specified, T otherwise. INPUT does not evaluate its arguments.

Example:
```
(INPUT CHANX DSK:  (10Q 7Q) (COMMON.MAC))
```

14.3.1 Default extensions on input

Whenever INPUT looks for a file with no specified extension (e.g., (INPUT D: X)), if it fails to find the file, it will then attempt to look for X.LSP. The extension it uses is the value of the global variable DEFAULTEXT and is initially LSP. If DEFAULTEXT is NIL, no second attempt will be made. This feature applies to all functions that read files, such as LOOKUP and RENAME.

14.3.2 Input functions

(INCH)

INCH returns the name of the currently selected input channel.

(INC CHANNEL ACTION)

INC selects the specified channel for input. If ACTION = NIL then the previously selected input file is not released, but only deselected. If ACTION is not NIL, then that file is released, making the previously selected channel available.

The input functions in Chapter 15 read from the selected input channel. When a file on the selected channel is exhausted, then the next file in the filename-list for the channel is initialized for input, until the filename-list is exhausted. Then the TTY is automatically selected for input and (ERR 'EOF) is called. The use of ERRSET around any functions which accept input therefore makes it possible to detect end-of-file. If no ERRSET is used, control returns to the top level of LISP.

INC evaluates its arguments, and returns the previously selected channel name.

To read from several files at once, separate channels should be initialized by INPUT, and INC can then select the appropriate channel to read from.

Here is an example showing the use of three I/O channels to write a merge/sort procedure where the input is in two files (FILE1 and FILE2) and the output goes into a third file (FILE3).

```
(DEFPROP FILEMERGE
 (LAMBDA (FILE1 FILE2 FILE3)
  (PROG (CHAN1 CHAN2 CHAN3 OLDINCHAN OLDOUTCHAN)
        {;; Open the I/O channels. GENSYMs won't
            conflict with any existing channel names.}
        (SETQ CHAN1
              (EVAL (LIST 'INPUT (GENSYM) 'DSK: FILE1)))
        (SETQ CHAN2
              (EVAL (LIST 'INPUT (GENSYM) 'DSK: FILE2)))
        (SETQ CHAN3
              (EVAL (LIST 'OUTPUT (GENSYM) 'DSK: FILE3)))
        (SETQ OLDINCHAN (INCH))
        (SETQ OLDOUTCHAN (OUTC CHAN3 NIL))
        (DO-MERGE FILE1 CHAN1 FILE2 CHAN2)
        {;; Close the output file.  Restore previous I/O
            files.}
        (OUTC OLDOUTCHAN T)
        (INC OLDINCHAN NIL)))
 EXPR)

(DEFPROP DO-MERGE
 (LAMBDA (FILE1 CHAN1 FILE2 CHAN2)
  (PROG (X1 X2)
        {;; READ a number from the first file.  Test for
            empty file.}
        (COND [(NULL (SETQ X1 (MERGE-READ FILE1 CHAN1)))
               (GO EMPTY2)])
     2. {;; READ from the second file.  Also test for empty
            file.}
        (COND [(NULL (SETQ X2 (MERGE-READ FILE2 CHAN2)))
               (GO EMPTY1)])
 COMPARE
        (COND [(GT X1 X2) (PRINT X2) (GO 2.)])
        (PRINT X1)
        (COND [(SETQ X1 (MERGE-READ FILE1 CHAN1))
               (GO COMPARE)])
        (PRINT X2)
 EMPTY2 (RETURN (MERGE-EMPTY FILE2 CHAN2))
 EMPTY1 (PRINT X1)
        (RETURN (MERGE-EMPTY FILE1 CHAN1))))
 EXPR)

(DEFPROP MERGE-EMPTY
 (LAMBDA (FILE CHAN)
  (PROG (X)
     1. (COND [(SETQ X (MERGE-READ FILE CHAN))
               (PRINT X)
               (GO 1.)])))
 EXPR)
```

```
(DEFPROP MERGE-READ
 (LAMBDA (FILE CHAN)
  (PROG (X)
        {;; select the channel}
        (INC CHAN NIL)
        {;; READ a number}
        (SETQ X (ERRSET (READ) NIL))
        (RETURN (COND [(EQ X '$EOF$)
                        {;; return NIL on end-of-file}]
                       [T (OR [NUMBERP (CAR (CONSP X))]
                              [ERROR (LIST "ERROR ON FILE"
                                           FILE "INPUT=" X)])
                        ]))))
 EXPR)
```

14.4 Output selection and control

(OUTPUT "CHANNEL" "FILESPEC")

OUTPUT initializes for output on the specified channel the single file specified by FILESPEC. OUTPUT does not evaluate its arguments, and returns the channel name if specified, T otherwise.

(OUTCH)

OUTCH returns the name of the currently selected output channel.

(OUTC CHANNEL ACTION)

OUTC selects the specified channel for output. The channel NIL selects the teletype. The output functions in Chapter 17 transfer output to the selected output channel.

If ACTION = NIL, then the previously selected output file is not closed, but only deselected. If ACTION is not NIL, then that file is closed. OUTC evaluates its arguments and returns the previously selected channel name.

Examples: (At the top level)

```
(OUTC (OUTPUT LPT:) T)
(OUTC NIL T)
(OUTPUT FOO DSK: BAZ)
```

14.5 Reading files: DSKIN and GETDEF

(DSKIN "FILESPEC1" "FILESPEC2" ...)

In loading a file into a LISP program, it is not normally necessary to make use of the full generality available in INC and INPUT. The function DSKIN has the same effect as doing INC and INPUT on its arguments, except that no channel name is specified and no device name is required. The channel name will always be unique, and DSK: will be supplied as a device name, if none is given.

```
Example: (DSKIN FOO DTA3: BAR (1 2) (SIMU.MAN))
         will READ the files DSK:FOO, DTA3:BAR,
         and DSK:SIMU.MAN[1,2].
```

DSKIN READs and EVALs the contents of the named files.

If the value of the symbol DSKIN is T (its default value) then DSKIN uses PRINA to print the non-NIL values of the expressions loaded. If the value of DSKIN is the atom PRINT, then the values are printed with the function PRINT, one per line. If DSKIN is set to NIL, no printing is done.

```
Example: (DSKIN (FUNCS.LSP) DTA0: (DATA.LSP))
         will read DSK:FUNCS.LSP and DTA0:DATA.LSP

         (DSKIN (667Q 2Q) (DSKLOG.LSP))
         will read DSK:DSKLOG.LSP[667,2]
```

If the value of BUILDPPLST is non-NIL, then DSKIN will construct a prettyprint command list (see 17.5) from the expressions DSKIN reads. The list is bound to an atom whose name is constructed from the first file name in the call to DSKIN. For (DSKIN PROVER THMS), the command list will be bound to the atom PROVERFNS if it is not already bound, or NEWPROVERFNS otherwise. BUILDPPLST is initially NIL.

(The BUILDPPLST feature uses the random-access input functions defined in 14.10 when LAP expressions appear in the file. In this case, the input device must be DSK:.)

(GETDEF "FILESPEC" "ID1" "ID2" ...)

GETDEF is similar to DSKIN, but only one file is accessed and only selected expressions from that file are read. In particular, all definitions of each ID are loaded, including expressions starting with DEFPROP, DE, DF, DM, LAP, DEFP, and DEFV. (This list of expression-types to be examined is stored as the value of the atom GETDEF, and may be changed if desired.) For example:

```
(GETDEF (FUNCS.LSP) FN1 FN2 FN3)
```

loads all definitions of FN1, FN2, and FN3 found in the file DSK:FUNCS.LSP. The value of each expression loaded is printed on the terminal as feedback.

GETDEF can thus be used to perform a "library search" through a collection of functions.

GETDEF doesn't INTERN any new atomic symbols unless they're contained in one of the selected expression. Otherwise, free storage would become clogged up with unused atomic symbols when scanning a large file for definitions.

14.6 Writing files: DSKOUT

(DSKOUT "FILESPEC" "E1" "E2" ...)

DSKOUT is used to create an entire output file. It sets the linelength to DSKLENGTH, and evaluates all of the expressions E1, E2, ... If an expression is atomic, then that atom is given to the function PPL instead of being evaluated directly. If there are no expressions given, e.g.,

```
(DSKOUT (FILE.EXT))
```

then DSKOUT creates the atomic symbol FILEFNS (by concatenating "FNS" to the file name), and checks to see if this atom is bound. If so, it is passed on to PPL as if the atom had appeared in the DSKOUT. If FILEFNS is unbound, it is first set to the value of

```
(SORT (APPEND ALLFNS ALLVALS))
```

and then passed to PPL. Thus an expression such as

```
(DSKOUT (FOO.LSP))
```

may be used at any time to save all functions and top-level values typed in or changed during this LISP session. At a later time FOO.LSP can be loaded via DSKIN, new functions may be defined and added to the list FOOFNS, and the file may be recreated via the same call to DSKOUT.

If the value of DSKOUT is T (its default value), the name of each function prettyprinted during the DSKOUT is printed on the TTY as feedback. If DSKOUT is set to NIL, no TTY printing is performed.

The maximum line length used by DSKOUT is stored in DSKLENGTH, and may be changed if desired (it is initially 80). The variable LPTLENGTH is equivalent to DSKLENGTH; they may be used interchangeably.

14.6.1 File Backup Mechanism

If the value of the global variable FILBAK is non-NIL and the specified output file already exists, DSKOUT will attempt to rename the file. (An error message will be printed on the TTY if the file cannot be backed up.) If the value of FILBAK is an atom whose print name is less than three characters in length, the characters are inserted into the old extension. Otherwise, the print name is used to replace the old extension. The initial value of FILBAK is Q, so all backup files will start with Q (FOO.QSP for FOO.LSP, FOO.QUZ for FOO.FUZ, etc.).

Secondary backups are also made. If a backup file already existed when an existing file was rewritten, the old backup would be lost. Thus two DSKOUTs to the same file would be enough to destroy the original version. One way to remedy this problem is to save multiple backup files, but if too many are kept, disk space is wasted; if not enough are kept, the problem is simply delayed. Our solution is to keep the newest, the next-to-newest, and the oldest files. The first time an existing file is rewritten, it will be backed up using FILBAK. The second time it is rewritten, the old backup file will be renamed with an extension of QBK before backing up the file. Subsequent rewrites will delete the backup file and back up as usual, but the QBK file will be kept. Thus, after any number of DSKOUTs to FOO.LSP, FOO.LSP will be the most recent version, FOO.QSP will be the next most recent, and FOO.QBK will be the oldest. The extension for the secondary backup is stored in the variable FILBAKBAK (initially QBK). If FILBAKBAK is NIL, no secondary backup will be maintained.

Example: If FNLIST is a list of your functions, they can be saved on a disk file, FUNCS.LSP by:

```
(DSKOUT (FUNCS.LSP) FNLIST)
```

If the file FUNCS.QSP exists and the file FUNCS.QBK does not, then FUNCS.QSP will be renamed to FUNCS.QBK. If the file FUNCS.LSP exists, it will be renamed to FUNCS.QSP.

14.7 Renaming and deleting files

The following functions enable you to manipulate files in those directories to which you have legitimate access. (The definition of access privileges is system-dependent.)

(*RENAME FILESPEC1 FILESPEC2)
(RENAME "FILESPEC1" "FILESPEC2")

*RENAME is a SUBR that renames FILESPEC1 to FILESPEC2. RENAME is the equivalent FSUBR; its arguments are not evaluated. They return the file protection of FILESPEC1 if the rename is successful and cause an error if it fails. If a device is specified in FILESPEC1 and no device is specified in FILESPEC2 the device specified in FILESPEC1 is carried over to FILESPEC2. Thus:

```
(*RENAME '((2206Q 4Q)(FOO . LSP))
         '((FOO . BAK)))
```

is equivalent to:

```
(*RENAME '((2206Q 4Q)(FOO . LSP))
         '((2206Q 4Q)(FOO . BAK)))
```

If no device is specified in either FILESPEC, the user's disk area is assumed.

(DELETE "FILESPEC1" "FILESPEC2" ...)

DELETE is an FSUBR that deletes the files in the list. The devices are optional, and a device is effective over the following FILSPEC's until a new device is encountered. If the deletion is successful, DELETE returns NIL; otherwise, it causes an error. The user's disk area is assumed if no device has been specified.

Example:
```
(DELETE FOO (FOO1 . LSP) (2206Q 4Q) (OLDFIL . COM))
```

(FILBAK FILE NEWEXT)

FILBAK is a SUBR that attempts to rename FILE with the extension of NEWEXT. FILE can be either an atom (a file name) or a list (a file specification). FILBAK returns the file protection of FILE if the renaming was successful and NIL if it fails.

Examples:
(FILBAK 'FOO 'BAK)
will rename the file FOO to FOO.BAK.

(FILBAK '(FOO . LSP) 'BAK)
will rename the file FOO.LSP to FOO.BAK

(FILBAK '((2206Q 4Q) (FOO . LSP)) 'BAK)
will rename the file FOO.LSP[2206,4] to FOO.BAK[2206,4].

(MYPPN)

MYPPN returns the user's project-programmer number in a form suitable for use by the directory and I/O functions.

Example: (MYPPN) = (300Q 2002Q)

(LOOKUP DEV FILNAM)

LOOKUP is a SUBR that determines whether the file DEV:FILNAM can be read. If it cannot be read, an error is caused. Otherwise, LOOKUP returns (LIST DEV FILNAM). If DEV is NIL, DSK: is assumed and (LIST FILNAM) is returned. If there is only one parameter, LOOKUP assumes that is the file name, and it uses DSK: as the default device. In this case, it returns (LIST FILNAM NIL).

14.8 Reading Directories

14.8.1 Low-level functions

The following functions are for reading directories. UFDINP is analogous to the function INPUT in that it opens a file on a specified channel. The channel must be selected via INC in order to be read. The file is opened in binary image mode and should not be read by the normal LISP read functions. All the functions are SUBRS and thus evaluate their arguments.

<u>(UFDINP CHANNEL PPN)</u>

UFDINP opens the directory of PPN on CHANNEL. It returns the value of CHANNEL as its result. If PPN is NIL the user's directory is assumed.

Example: (UFDINP X '(2206Q 1Q)) = X

<u>(RDFILE)</u>

RDFILE returns the next file in the directory that is open on the current input channel. It returns a file which is either an atom or an atomic dotted pair. It does an (ERR 'EOF) when it reaches the end of the file.

Example:

```
(PROG (X) (INC (UFDINP T NIL) NIL)
          (SETQ X (ERRSET (RDFILE)))
          (INC NIL NIL)
          (COND [(CONSP X) (RETURN (CAR X))]))
 = (LISP . INI)
```

<u>(RDFILENAM)</u>

RDFILENAM is similar to RDFILE, except that it doesn't intern the filename and extension. DIRF uses RDFILENAM when scanning directories so as not to clog up storage with useless atomic symbols.

14.8.2 User functions

(DIR PPN)

DIR returns a list of files from the directory of PPN. If PPN is NIL, the user's directory is assumed.

Example:

```
(DIR '(2206Q 4Q))
  =  ((INIT . LSP) (FOO .LSP) MYFILE)
```

(DIRF "FILESPEC")

Unlike the function DIR, which returns a list of all the files in a given directory, DIRF prints the name of each file in the directory which "matches" FILESPEC; it is thus quite similar in operation to the DIRECT/F monitor command. FILESPEC may be a dotted pair (FILE.EXT), where either FILE and/or EXT may be * (match anything), or simply FILE, with (FILE.*) assumed. As an example of the use of DIRF,

```
(DIRF (*.LSP))
```

prints the names of all LSP files in your directory.

(TYPE "FILESPEC1" "FILESPEC2" ...)

This function types each file on the currently selected output device. Its principal use is to type a text file on the terminal without leaving LISP, for example,

```
(TYPE LSP: (LISP.HLP))
```

As usual, device and PPN may be omitted, with DSK: assumed. Note that if more than one file is given, they are simply concatenated together. Thus TYPE could be used to create a new file which is the concatenation of FILE1 and FILE2 by doing the following:

```
(PROGN (OUTC (OUTPUT T NEWFILE))
       (TYPE FILE1 FILE2)
       (OUTC NIL T))
```

14.9 Setting and retrieving the I/O path

<u>(PATH "PROJ" "PROG" {"SFD1" "SFD2" ...})</u>

PATH sets the default directory to [PROJ,PROG,...]. All file accesses with no explicit directory given will go to this directory. A path change will hold even after you leave LISP. To change back to another path, either call PATH again or use the system program SETSRC. PATH returns NIL if it couldn't set the path; otherwise it returns the new path.

<u>(PATH)</u>

A call to PATH with no arguments returns the current path for your job. The initial path is the logged-in directory.

<u>(PATH "CHANNEL")</u>

If PATH is passed the name of an I/O channel which has been opened (via INPUT or OUTPUT), the file specification currently associated with that channel is returned. If the channel is not open, PATH returns NIL.

For the terminal (i.e., (PATH NIL)), PATH returns (TTY:). For a disk device, PATH returns a 3-element list: (device path filename). For example, if the file DSKC:TESTFN.LSP[300,2001,DEMO] were open on channel C14, then (PATH C14) would return (DSKC: (300Q 2001Q DEMO) (TESTFN . LSP)). For any other device, PATH causes an error: CAN'T GET PATH.

<u>(SCAN FLAG)</u>

SCAN sets /NOSCAN if FLAG=NIL; otherwise it sets /SCAN. (The SCAN switch determines whether sfds at higher levels than the default path are searched when looking for a file.) SCAN returns the previous setting of the SCAN switch.

14.10 Random-access input

LISP can reset the location looked at by the input channel to any byte within the file.

(USETI N)

USETI resets the byte pointer associated with the currently selected input channel so that the character at byte position N will be read next. The first character in a file is at byte position 0. (USETI has no effect if reading from the terminal.)

(UGETI)

UGETI returns the byte position of the next character to be input on the currently selected input channel.

(UGETO)

UGETO returns the byte position of the next character to be output on the currently selected output channel.

As an example of the use of the random-access input package, the following function reads an expression and then sets the input pointer back so the next READ will read the expression over again. It is thus similar to the function PEEKC, except it "peeks" at an entire expression instead of a single character:

```
(DE PEEKEXPR NIL
    (PROG (POS)
         (SETQ POS (UGETI))
         (RETURN (PROG1 (READ) (USETI POS)))))
```

14.11 DSKLOG: recording a session at the terminal

<u>(DSKLOG {"FILESPEC"})</u>

It is often useful to have an exact copy of a session at the terminal, to demonstrate, for example, how a program runs -- or doesn't run. When the function DSKLOG is called, it opens a file on channel DSKLOG, using DSK:DSKLOG.LST if no parameter was given. It then sets the global variable DSKLOG to T. Thereafter, all characters read from and sent to the TTY (channel NIL) are copied into the log file, including prompt characters and I/O from compiled routines such as the Break Package and the Editor. There is one exception: if an altmode (escape, ASCII 33Q) is typed on the terminal, a dollar sign (ASCII 44Q) will be printed in the log file.

Before returning, DSKLOG prints a startup message:

    [DSKLOG started: 4-27-79 6:54 PM]

You may suspend logging by setting DSKLOG to NIL, and resume by setting it to any non-NIL value. Setting DSKLOG to a non-NIL value when DSKLOG is <u>not</u> running will cause an error, "NO FILE OPEN ON CHANNEL 'DSKLOG'", and DSKLOG will be set to NIL again.

<u>(LOGOUT)</u>

LOGOUT terminates the log. It prints a final message:

    [DSKLOG finished: 4-27-79 6:55 PM]

It sets DSKLOG to NIL and closes the log file.

If the current output channel is NIL when DSKLOG and LOGOUT are called, as is expected, then the startup and final messages will, of course, also appear in the log file.

Example:

```
*(DSKLOG)
[DSKLOG started: 4-27-79 6:54 PM]
```

```
*(DE F(X) (COND ((LE X 1) 1) (T (* X (F (-I X]
F


*(F 3)
6


*(TRACE F$
(F)


*(F 3$
Enter F:
!     X = 3
!  Enter F:
!  !     X = 2
!  !  Enter F:
!  !  !     X = 1
!  !  F = 1
!  F = 2
F = 6
6


*(LOGOUT$

[DSKLOG finished: 4-27-79 6:55 PM]
```

Except for the very first line (the call to DSKLOG), that entire text appears in the log file.

CHAPTER 15

INPUT

15.1 Input Functions

(READ)

READ causes the next S-expression to be read from the selected input device, and it returns the internal representation of the S-expression. READ uses INTERN to guarantee that references to the same identifier are EQ.

READ will accept any S-expression which conforms to the following syntax:

Syntax:

```
<readable S-expr>        ::= <atom>
                         ::= ' <readable S-expr>
                         ::= ( <readable S-exprlist>
                                { . <readable S-expr> } )
                         ::= [ <unbalanced S-expression list> ]
                         ::= ( )

<readable S-exprlist>    ::= <readable S-expr>
                         ::= <readable S-expr>
                               <readable S-exprlist>
```

Semantics:

The delimiter "'" designates that the following readable S-expression is to be quoted. The delimiter "@" may also be used to quote expressions.

Examples:

'A   means (QUOTE A)

```
'('A B) means (QUOTE ((QUOTE A) B))
''A     means (QUOTE (QUOTE A)))
```

The delimiters "[" and "]" operate as "super-parentheses." A right bracket "]" will close all open left parentheses "(" up to the matching left bracket "[". If there is no matching left bracket, it will close the entire S-expression (as altmode does for TTY input). No syntax is given for unbalanced-S-expression-list, but it is intended to mean an S-expression-list which is lacking one or more right parentheses.

Example:

```
(COND [(ATOM X) (REVERSE(CDR Y][T(APPEND Y Z])
  = (COND ((ATOM X) (REVERSE (CDR Y))) (T (APPEND Y Z)))
```

(TYI)

TYI causes the next character to be read from the selected input device and returns the ASCII code for that character.

A function TEREAD which ignores all characters until a line-feed is seen can be defined:

```
(DE TEREAD NIL
   (PROG NIL
    L    (COND [(EQ (TYI) 12Q) (RETURN NIL)])
         (GO L)))
```

(TYILIST L "E1" "E2" ...)

TYILIST evaluates L and uses it as a "logical input channel." The expressions E1, E2, ..., are evaluated. Any input required during the evaluation comes from L. L should be a list of integers corresponding to ASCII characters; if any elements are out of range, the error message "ASCII VALUE OUT OF BOUNDS" will appear.

TYILIST returns the unused part of L. If the end of the list is reached, a final blank will be supplied. Past that, (ERR EOF) will be called.

Example:

```
*(TYILIST '(101Q 102Q 40Q 65Q 40Q 103Q 104Q)
          (SETQ X (READ))
          (SETQ Y (READ)))
(40Q 103Q 104Q)
*X
AB
*Y
5
```

<u>(READCH)</u>

READCH causes the next character to be read from the selected input device and returns the corresponding single-character identifier. READCH is equivalent to (INTERN (ASCII (TYI))).

<u>(RDNAM)</u>

RDNAM functions in the same manner as READ except that it does not INTERN the atoms that it reads. Thus an atom read by RDNAM and an atom read by READ are <u>NOT</u> EQ.

Example:

```
*(PROG () (CLRBFI) (RETURN (EQ (RDNAM) (READ))))
*FOO
*FOO
NIL
```

15.1.1 Reading Whole Lines

<u>(LINEREAD FLAG)</u>
<u>(READL FLAG)</u>

READL reads a line, returning it as a list. If some expression takes more than one line or a line terminates in a comma, space or tab, then READL continues reading until an expression ends at the end of a line.

FLAG determines whether a carriage return by itself is acceptable input. If FLAG = NIL or is missing, READL does a READ first to insure that something appears on the line. If FLAG = T and the first thing seen is a line terminator (such as carriage-return line-feed), READL simply returns NIL. Note that there may be a line terminator left in the input buffer by a previous READ, so if (READL T) is used, a (CLRBFI) should normally be done first to flush the input buffer.

READL is used by the Editor and Break Package to read in commands, and may be useful for other supervisor-type functions.

Example:

```
*(READL)
*A B (C D
*E) F G
(A B (C D E) F G)

*(READL)
*A B (C D E),
*F G
(A B (C D E) F G)
```

(READP)

READP returns T if a character can be input and NIL otherwise. READP does not pause or input a character.

(UNTYI)

UNTYI "unreads" a character (such as a character input by a TYI or a READCH), so that the next call to READ, TYI, etc., will pick up the UNTYI'ed character as the next character to be read, and returns the ASCII code for that character.

In the LISP READ routine, an atom may be terminated either by a break character (DELIM, a character which must be interpreted by READ as well as serving to terminate the atom, such as "(", ")", "[", and ".") or a separator character (IGNORE, a character used only to separate atoms, but not in itself meaningful, such as carriage-return or blank). In order to save a break character for later interpretation, the LISP READ routines use a one-character buffer. UNTYI simply stores its argument in this buffer; thus there are two problems in using UNTYI. First, if UNTYI is used several times in succession with no intervening READ's, TYI's, etc., then only the most recent character is actually "unread" -- all others are lost. Second, if there is a break character in the one-character buffer when an UNTYI is performed, the break character will be lost.

(PEEKC)

PEEKC returns the ASCII code of the next character in the input stream without reading the character, equivalent to (UNTYI (TYI)).

15.2 Input from the TTY

When input is from the TTY, READ is terminated by either an entire S-expression or by an incomplete S-expression followed by altmode. Altmode has the effect of typing a space followed by the appropriate number of right parentheses to complete the S-expression. This feature is particularly useful when an unknown number of right parentheses are needed or when in (DDTIN NIL) mode (see below).

(TTYIN "E1" "E2" ...)

TTYIN may be used to request input from the terminal instead of the currently selected input device. The current channel is deselected, the TTY is selected and the expressions E1, E2, etc., are evaluated (presumably doing some input). The previous channel is then reselected, and the value of the last expression is returned as the value of the TTYIN. TTYIN is compiled in-line.

(DDTIN X)

DDTIN is a function which selects the TTY input mode. With (DDTIN NIL), the default mode, typing a rubout to READ, READCH, or TYI will delete the last character typed, and typing control-U will delete the entire last line. Input is not seen by LISP until either altmode or carriage return is typed.

With (DDTIN T) and typing to READ, a rubout will delete the entire S-expression being read and start reading again.

(CLRBFI)

CLRBFI clears the TTY input buffer.

(TTYECHO)

TTYECHO complements the TTY echo switch. TTYECHO returns T if the echo is being turned on, and NIL if it is being turned off.

(PROMPT N)

The LISP READ routines type out a "prompt character" when they expect to read from the TTY. This character is normally a "*". PROMPT resets this prompt character. N is the ASCII code for the new prompt character.

The ASCII code for the old prompt character is returned. (PROMPT NIL) returns the current prompt character without changing it.

Example:

```
*(PROMPT 53Q)
52Q
+
```

(INITPROMPT N)

Whenever LISP is forced back to the top level (e.g., by an error or control-G), the prompt character is reset. INITPROMPT is similar to PROMPT except that it sets the top-level prompt character, and (INITPROMPT NIL) returns the ASCII code for the top-level prompt character without changing it.

15.3 READ MACROS

Read Macros allow you to specify a function to be executed each time a selected character is read during input of your data or programs. This function is generally used to produce one or more elements of the input list which are built up in some way from later characters of the input string. There are two types of Read Macros, normal Read Macros whose result is used as an element of the input list in the position where the macro character occurred, and Splice Macros whose result must be a list which is spliced sequentially into the input list.

WARNING

A read- or splice- macro character occuring inside an atom name will be recognized only if it is a DELIM-character or an IGNORE-character. See section 3.1 and Chapter 16.

15.3.1 Functions for defining Read Macros

(DRM "CHARACTER" "FUNCTION")

CHARACTER is defined as a normal Read Macro with FUNCTION being a function name or a LAMBDA expression of no arguments which will be evaluated each time CHARACTER is detected as a macro during input. FUNCTION is put on the property list of CHARACTER under the property READMACRO. If FUNCTION is NIL, then the READMACRO property is removed, and CHARACTER is defined to be a syntactic LETTER.

The value of DRM is CHARACTER.

```
Examples:       (DRM * (LAMBDA () (NCONS (READ)))
                (DRM = (LAMBDA () (REVERSE (READ)))
```

The comment function "{" (see Chapter 9) is actually defined as a Read Macro. The quote-symbols "'" and "@" are not implemented as Read Macros; they are directly coded for efficiency.

(DSM "CHARACTER" "FUNCTION")

DSM is exactly like DRM except that CHARACTER is defined as a Splice Macro.

```
Example:        (DSM : (LAMBDA () (CONS NIL (READ)))
```

15.3.2 Using Read Macros

The use of Read Macros is best described with examples. The Read Macros defined above will be used for the examples.

```
Input:        (A B C = (D E F) G H)
READ returns: (A B C (F E D) G H)

Input:        (FOO1 FOO2 *FOO3 FOO4)
READ returns: (FOO1 FOO2 (FOO3) FOO4)

Input:        (AT1 :(AT2 AT3) AT4)
READ returns: (AT1 NIL AT2 AT3 AT4)

Input:        (AA AB :AC)
READ returns: (AA AB NIL . AC)
```

A Splice Macro, in effect, places the result of the function evaluation into the input stream minus the outermost set of parentheses.

CHAPTER 16

THE LISP SCANNER

In section 3.1 we presented the "spelling rules" for LISP identifiers. In this this chapter, we describe the scanner that uses those rules, including the details of the scanner table (16.1), and a list of user functions that can change the spelling rules (16.2).

16.1 CHRTAB

The scanner (lexical analyzer) that is used by READ and TYI is implemented as a series of finite-state machines, one for each kind of lexical item (e.g., identifiers, numbers, strings). The information about each ASCII character (0-177Q) is stored in a table (CHRTAB) in the LISP interpreter; CHRTAB[0] describes ASCII 0, CHRTAB[1] describes ASCII 1, etc. The functions in this chapter access CHRTAB.

A word in CHRTAB has the following form:

Bit 0 is 0 if this character requires a slash when it appears in the name of an identifier, past the first character (e.g., 1 for "@", 1 for "7", 0 for ".", 1 for "A").

Bit 1 is 0 if this character requires a slash to be the first character of the name of an identifier (e.g., 0 for "@", 0 for "7", 0 for ".", 1 for "A").

Bits 0 and 1 are used by PRIN and ignored by PRINC.

Bits 2-5 are for scanning atoms (RATAB, read-atom table), which is the initial state of the scanner.

0: comment-beginners (~, ^Y, ^Z)
1: null character (ASCII 0)
2: delimiters

3: ignored characters
4: slash character
5: letters
6: minus sign (-)
7: dot (.)
8: digits
9: string-beginners (")
10: read macros
11: splice macros
12: plus sign (+)

Bits 6-8 are for scanning numbers (NUMTAB) and expressions after dots (DOTAB).
0: comment-beginner
1: null character
2: delimiters
3: dot (.)
4: exponent letter (E, e)
5: digits
6: octal point (Q, q)

Bits 9-10 are for scanning strings (STRTAB).
0: comment-beginner
1: null character
2: string-ender (")
3: everything else

Bits 11-13 are for scanning identifiers past the first character (IDTAB).
0: comment-beginner
1: null character
2: delimiters
3: slash character
4: letters and digits

Bits 14-16 are for scanning exponents.
0: comment-beginner
1: null character
2: delimiters
3: digits

Bits 17-19 are for scanning delimiters.
0: left parenthesis
1: right parenthesis
2: left bracket ([)
3: right bracket (]) and altmode
4: dot (.)
5: quote symbol (', @)

Bits 20-25 contain the RADIX-50 code for the character; this is used by the symbol-table functions (see 24.2).

Bit 26 is 1 if the character is a comment-ender (line-feed). (See Chapter 9.)

Bits 27-35 are unused.

16.2 Modifying CHRTAB

In the following functions, the first parameter (N) is used as an index into CHRTAB. If N is a number, it must be between 0 and 177Q; if it is outside that range, the error message "ASCII VALUE OUT OF BOUNDS" will appear. Otherwise, N must be an identifier or a string, and LISP calls CHRVAL to get the ASCII code for the first character of that identifier.

(MODCHR N X)

MODCHR returns the previous contents of CHRTAB[N], the table entry for the Nth ASCII character. If X is non-NIL, CHRTAB[N] is set to X.

WARNING

MODCHR should be used with great caution, since it possible to do arbitrary damage to the scanner. There is no backup for the scanner and no way to restore its contents automatically. If you change the left parenthesis to be a syntactic letter at the top level, for instance, there's no way to reverse that, since function calls would no longer be possible.

Most uses of MODCHR are for things like redefining the comment character. The next five functions make that easier and less risky.

(COMMENTBEGIN N)

This returns the ASCII code for the most recently defined comment-beginning character. If N is non-NIL, it also defines N as a comment-beginning character. Initially, control-Y (ASCII 31Q), control-Z (ASCII 32Q), and tilde (~, ASCII 176Q) are comment-beginners; tilde is the most recent. The print routines use the most recent comment-beginner when breaking atoms over line boundaries (see Chapter 9).

COMMENTBEGIN sets RATAB, IDTAB, and STRTAB to 0.

(COMMENTEND N)

This returns the ASCII code for the most recently defined comment-ending character. If N is non-NIL, it also defines N to be a comment-ender. Line-feed (ASCII 12Q) is the initial comment-ender. The print routines use the most recent comment-ender when breaking atoms over line boundaries (see Chapter 9).

COMMENTEND sets bit 26 of CHRTAB[N] to 1.

(STRINGBEGIN N)

This returns the most recently defined string-beginning character. If N is non-NIL, it also defines N to be a string-beginner. Double-quote (", ASCII 42Q) is the initial string-beginner.

STRINGBEGIN sets RATAB to 9.

(STRINGEND N)

This returns the most recently defined string-ending character. If N is non-NIL, it also defines N to be a string-ender. Double-quote (", ASCII 42Q) is the initial string-ender.

STRINGEND sets STRTAB to 2.

(SLASHIFY N)

This returns the most recently defined slashifier. If N is non-NIL, it also defines N to be a slashifier. ASCII 57Q (/) is the initial slashifier.

SLASHIFY sets RATAB to 4 and IDTAB to 3.

(LETTER N)

LETTER defines N's syntax class to be that of a letter, i.e., RATAB = 5, IDTAB = 4, and STRTAB = 3. LETTER returns NIL.

(DELLIM N)

DELLIM defines N's syntax class to be that of a delimiter, i.e., RATAB = 2, IDTAB = 2, and STRTAB = 3.

(IGNORE N)

IGNORE defines N's syntax class to be that of an ignored character (such as blank or comma), i.e., RATAB = 3, IDTAB = 2, and STRTAB = 3.

(LETTERP N)

LETTERP returns T if N's syntax class is that of a letter. Note: only the RATAB is tested (= 5). Note also that "+" and "-" can be used as letters, but their RATAB's are not 5.

(DELLIMP N)
(DELIM N)

DELLIMP returns T if N is a delimiter, i.e., if RATAB for N is 2.

(IGNOREP N)

IGNOREP returns T if N is an ignored character, i.e., if RATAB for N is 3.

(SETCHR N X)

SETCHR sets the RATAB index for N (bits 2-5 of CHRTAB[N]) to bits 32-35 of X and sets bit 1 of CHRTAB[N] ("slash if first character") to bit 31 of X.

DRM calls SETCHR with N = 10 (decimal) to set the RATAB index to 10 (indicating a read macro) and to indicate that the character needs to be "slashified" if used as the first character in an identifier. DSM calls SETCHR with N = 11.

SETCHR returns a 5-bit number, indicating the appropriate previous bits from CHRTAB[N]. If X is NIL, CHRTAB[N] is not changed.

(LISPSCAN)

MLISP, an ALGOL-like dialect of LISP, uses LISP's READ functions but a different scanner table. That scanner table is in effect after (MLISPSCAN) is called by the MLISP parser. When it finishes, it restores the LISP scanner table by calling (LISPSCAN). In case of serious errors that may occur while MLISP's scanner table is in effect, you can use ^C^A to call LISPSCAN. [This applies only to systems supporting MLISP.]

CHAPTER 17

OUTPUT

17.1 Basic Functions

(PRIN S)
(PRIN1 S)

PRIN causes the S-expression S to be printed on the selected output device with no preceding or following spaces. PRIN also inserts slashes ("/") before any characters in identifiers which would be syntactically incorrect otherwise (see Chapter 3). Double quotes around strings are printed.

Functions that use PRIN are PRINT, PRINA, and PRINL.

(PRINC S)

PRINC is the same as PRIN except that no slashes are inserted and double quotes around strings are not printed.

Functions that use PRINC are PRINAC, PRINLC, and PRINTC.

(TERPRI X)

TERPRI prints a carriage-return and line-feed and returns the value of X.

(PRINT S)

= (PROGN (TERPRI NIL) (PRIN S) (PRINC '/) S)
PRINT outputs a carriage return/line feed, uses PRIN to print the S-expressions S, and prints a blank. PRINT returns S.

(TYO N)

TYO prints the character whose ASCII value is N, and returns N. (TYO 101Q) prints an "A" and returns 101Q.

(TYOLIST "E1" "E2" ...)

TYOLIST evaluates the expressions E1, E2, ..., and returns a list of ASCII values of any characters that would have been output during the evaluation, including spacing characters (e.g., blanks, tabs). TYOLIST creates a "logical output channel."

```
Example:   (TYOLIST (PRINT 1) (PRINT 2) (TYO 11Q))
             = (15Q 12Q 61Q 40Q 15Q 12Q 62Q 40Q 211Q)
```

TYOLIST compiles in-line.

17.2 Spacing

(LINELENGTH N)

LINELENGTH is used to examine or change the maximum output linelength on the selected output channel. If N = NIL then the current linelength is returned unchanged; otherwise the linelength is changed to the value of N, which should be an integer. LINELENGTH returns N.

(CHRCT)

CHRCT returns the number of character positions remaining on the output line of the selected output channel.

(CHRPOS)

= (*DIF (LINELENGTH NIL) (CHRCT))
CHRPOS returns the number of the next available print position.

(TAB N)

TAB tabs to position N on the output line, doing a TERPRI if the current position is already past N. Note should be taken that TAB outputs spaces only when necessary and outputs tab characters otherwise.

(SPACES N {POS})

This function prints N spaces, using tab characters when possible. If N spaces won't fit on the current line, SPACES tabs to position POS on the next line. POS is optional and defaults to 1.

(LINES N)

This function prints N blank lines. Note that the next print position will always be at the start of a line, so (LINES 0) may be used as a "conditional TERPRI" which outputs a carriage return if not already at the start of a line.

17.3 More printing functions

(PRINA X {POS})

PRINA is like PRIN, except that if an atom won't fit on the line, a tab to position POS on the next line is performed before printing resumes. POS is optional, with a value of 1 assumed if omitted.

(PRINAC X {POS})

PRINAC is the same as PRINA, except that PRINC is used to print atoms instead of PRIN.

(TYOA CHAR {POS})

TYOA is identical to TYO, except that if there is no room for CHAR on the current line, TYOA tabs to position POS on the next line before printing CHAR. POS is optional and defaults to 1.

(MSG "ITEM1" "ITEM2" ...)

MSG provides a general message-printing facility for LISP. Each ITEM is an instruction which provides a specific formatting capability:

"abcdefg"	Print the string "abcdefg" using PRINAC
16	Print 16 blank spaces (any positive number)
(T 39)	Tab to column 39 (argument is evaluated)
T	Move to new line (TERPRI)
-16	Print 16 blank lines (any negative number)
(E EXPR)	Evaluate EXPR
other	EVAL and print using PRINA

As an example of the use of MSG, consider the following:

```
(MSG T "Value of X is:" 5 X T)
```

which is equivalent to:

```
(PROGN (TERPRI)
       (PRINAC "Value of X is:")
       (SPACES 5)
       (PRINA X)
       (TERPRI))
```

Note that MSG prints the desired message on the currently selected output device. MSG returns NIL and is compiled in-line.

(TTYMSG "ITEM1" "ITEM2" ...)

TTYMSG is identical to MSG, except printed output is directed to the terminal instead of the currently selected output device. To insure that the message will appear on the terminal even if ^O has been struck, a TALK is performed before printing. TTYMSG is compiled in-line.

(PRINL L {POS})

PRINL prints the list L without the outermost parentheses; i.e., it prints the elements of L separated by spaces. Each element is printed using PRINA. POS defaults to 1.

(PRINLC L {POS})

PRINLC is identical to PRINL, except uses PRINAC instead of PRINA to print the list elements.

(PRINTC X)

PRINTC is identical to PRINT, except that it uses PRINC instead of PRIN.

(TALK)

TALK undoes the effect of typing a control-O (which turns off output to the TTY). It may be used to insure that a message will appear on the terminal. (TALK) is automatically called by the system whenever an error condition is encountered or a prompt character is output.

17.4 Printing non-standard expressions

(PRINLEV EXPRESSION DEPTH)

PRINLEV is a printing routine similar to PRINT. PRINLEV, however, only prints to a depth of DEPTH, and is useful for printing deeply nested or circular lists. In addition, PRINLEV recognizes lists which are circular down the CDR and closes these with '...]' instead of ')'. The combination of these two features allows PRINLEV to print any circular list without an infinite loop.

PRINLEV uses TYOA, PRINA, and PRINAC, and the second parameter it passes to those functions (column for TAB) is the global variable PRINLEV, which is initially 6.

(PRINTLEV EXPRESSION DEPTH)

= (PROGN (TERPRI NIL) (PRINLEV EXPRESSION DEPTH) EXPRESSION)

Note that since the value of PRINTLEV is the value of EXPRESSION, PRINTLEV should not be used at the top level if EXPRESSION is a circular list structure, since LISP would then attempt to PRINT the circular structure which is returned as the value.

17.5 The LISP PRETTYPRINTER

The LISP prettyprint package enables you to print functions in readable form and create formatted symbolic files. Its capabilities include a "printmacro" mechanism, two levels of user commenting, and a "prettyprint command" facility for controlling the printing process.

17.5.1 Basic Functions

(PP "A1" "A2" ...)

If A is atomic, each property of A which appears on the list PRETTYPROPS is printed in readable format. (If no such properties appear, a message to that effect is printed. This message may be suppressed by setting NOPRETTYPROPS to NIL.) Each non-atomic A is simply printed by SPRINT unless its CAR is defined as a "prettyprint command," in which case the expression is evaluated. (Prettyprint commands are explained below.) A may also be a list consisting of a LAP expression followed by a sequence of LAP code; such a list will be printed in standard LAP format.

If no A's are present, the value of LASTWORD is used. LASTWORD is also set to the name of the last function printed. If the value of the global variable PP is non-NIL and output is being directed to a device other than the terminal, PP will print the name of each function printed on the terminal. This feature is used by DSKOUT to provide feedback: PP is set to the value of DSKOUT before the pretty-printer is invoked. PP is initially NIL.

(PPL "VAR1" "VAR2" ...)

Each VAR should be an atomic symbol whose value is a prettyprint list to be passed on to PP. This prettyprint list may contain atomic symbols whose properties are to be printed, prettyprint command expressions, and other expressions which are to be SPRINTed. Each VAR (except ALLFNS and ALLVALS) which is not already a member of its prettyprint list will be printed, so that if an output file is later read back in, the value will be restored. The compiler ignores prettyprint lists, and does not copy them into its output (LAP) file.

(SPRINT EXP {COL})

SPRINT is the workhorse of the prettyprint package -- it is used by PP and PPL to print expressions starting in column COL (1 if missing). The pretty-printing capabilities of SPRINT may be suppressed by setting the special variable PRETTYFLG to NIL. In this mode, SPRINT simply passes EXP to PRIN.

17.5.2 PRETTYPROPS

In its simplest form, PRETTYPROPS is a list of atomic symbols which gives the properties which PP is to print. Each atomic argument to PP which has a property on PRETTYPROPS will be printed as a DEFPROP expression. Occasionally, however, it is desirable to print certain properties in something other than DEFPROP format. This may be accomplished by putting a dotted pair of the form (PROP . FN) onto PRETTYPROPS; when an atom with a PROP property is encountered, PP simply prints a carriage return and calls FN. FN will be passed three arguments: the atom currently being printed, the value stored under the property PROP, and the atom PROP itself. The function can then print anything it wishes before returning to PP, at which time another carriage return will be printed. For example, the functions PP-VALUE and PP-RMACS are provided by the pretty-print package to print VALUE and READMACRO properties in special form.

PRETTYPROPS is initialized to (SPECIAL EXPR FEXPR MACRO (VALUE . PP-VALUE) PRINTMACRO (READMACRO . PP-RMACS)).

17.5.3 Prettyprint Commands

Prettyprint commands may be used as arguments to PP or in PPL prettyprint lists to perform a variety of special formatting tasks. A prettyprint command is simply an expression whose CAR is a function name with a non-NIL PPCOM property. Such expressions are evaluated when encountered by PP, thus providing a mechanism for "grabbing control" during the prettyprint process. The user may define his own prettyprint commands, or may use the following functions supplied by the system. Note that in addition to appearing as prettyprint commands in PPL lists, these expressions may be used in other contexts as well.

Prettyprint command lists are automatically constructed by DSKIN when BUILDPPLST is set to T (see 14.5).

<u>(*PG*)</u>

PG outputs a form feed; it may be used to place various sections of a large symbolic file on different pages.

<u>(F: "FN1" "FN2" ...)</u>

F: prettyprints any functional attributes of each FN, ignoring all other properties. F: simply sets PRETTYPROPS to (EXPR FEXPR MACRO) and passes its arguments on to PP, so each FN may be anything which can normally be used as an argument to PP (including another prettyprint command). PRETTYPROPS is restored after printing is completed.

<u>(P: "PROPS" "X1" "X2" ...)</u>

PRETTYPROPS is set to PROPS, the X's are passed on to PP, and PRETTYPROPS is restored. For example, F: could be defined as

```
(P: (EXPR FEXPR MACRO) FN1 FN2 ...)
```

<u>(V: "X1" "X2" ...)</u>

V: can be used for printing values. Each X may be either an atomic symbol VAR or a list of the form (VAR VAL). Each VAR will be printed as a DEFV expression, with a value of VAL if given, or the current value of the variable if only the variable name was given. Unbound variables are printed with a value of NIL.

<u>(MBD: "FN" "X1" "X2" ...)</u>

MBD: passes the X's on to PP in such a way that they will be prettyprinted inside of an expression starting with FN. For example, to prettyprint F1 and F2 inside of a PROGN expression (perhaps so they will not be compiled), you could use:

```
(MBD: PROGN F1 F2)
```

<u>(FORMS: "X1" "X2" ...)</u>

Each X is passed directly to SPRINT. FORMS: may be used to print atoms and prettyprint command expressions which would normally be handled specially by PP.

<u>(E: "E1" "E2" ...)</u>

The E's are simply evaluated. For example, the inclusion of the following in a prettyprint list could be used to change the base in the middle of a print:

```
(E: (SETQ BASE 10.))
```

17.5.4 Printmacros

SPRINT normally operates by formatting the expression being printed using indentation to produce "pretty" output. It is occasionally desirable to have certain subexpressions printed in some special format for increased readability. Such a capability is provided via the use of <u>printmacros</u>. Any function may be flagged as a printmacro by placing the macro definition on the property list of the atom under the indicator PRINTMACRO. Whenever an atom with such a property appears as the first element in a list being prettyprinted, SPRINT takes special action, depending on the value of the PRINTMACRO property:

1. If the value is a string and the expression is a list of exactly two elements, the string is simply PRINCed and the CADR of the original expression is SPRINTed. This serves as an inverse for READMACROs like the quote sign (where 'X is read as (QUOTE X)). For example,

```
(DEFPROP QUOTE "'" PRINTMACRO)
(DEFPROP THV "$?" PRINTMACRO)
```

(The QUOTE printmacro is in fact already present in LISP.)

2. If the value is the atom BRACKETS, then the expression is printed by SPRINT in the normal way, except that each top-level non-atomic argument will be printed with brackets [...] instead of the usual parentheses (...). This gives the user one more method of producing more readable output. COND, SELECTQ, AND, OR, and CATCH are initialized as printmacros of this type. To disable the use of brackets for these functions, simply REMPROP the PRINTMACRO property from their property lists.

3. If the value of the PRINTMACRO property is neither a string nor the atom BRACKETS, it is assumed to be a true printmacro function (or, more typically, the <u>name</u> of a function). This function will be passed the expression being printed as its only argument, and may print it in any format it wishes (calling SPRINT recursively if desired). If the printmacro function decides that the expression should be printed in normal form by SPRINT (i.e., if it is a "conditional" printmacro), it may simply print nothing and return the atom SPRINT. SPRINT will then print the expression as if no printmacro property were present (lest the printmacro be called again). If the printmacro function returns anything else, SPRINT assumes that it has printed the entire expression, and simply proceeds.

   As an example of a printmacro function, one might do the following in lieu of defining QUOTE as a string printmacro:

```
(DEFPROP QUOTE
 (LAMBDA (E)
       {;; Is it of the form (QUOTE XXX) ?}
       (COND [(AND [CONSP (CDR E)] [NULL (CDDR E)])
              {;; Yes. Print the quote sign ...}
              (PRINC "'")
              {;; ... and SPRINT the argument.}
              (SPRINT (CADR E) (CHRPOS))]
             [T {;; No (bizarre). Give it back to SPRINT.}
                'SPRINT]))
 PRINTMACRO)
```

In other words, if the expression is of the form (QUOTE XXX) print it as 'XXX; otherwise print it in normal list form.

To make the writing of printmacro functions easier, several auxiliary formatting functions are provided:

(PP-FORMAT E N FLAG)

Prints the expression E with the first N+1 elements (the function name and N arguments) printed on one line. FLAG specifies how the remaining arguments are to be printed: if FLAG = NIL (standard format), all remaining arguments are printed under the first argument; if FLAG = MISER, the remaining arguments are placed under the function name; if FLAG = LABELS, all non-atomic arguments are printed under the first argument, with atoms placed to the left as labels. Note, however, that if the entire expression will fit on one line, and is less than PPMAXLEN characters long (initially 65), it will be printed on one line.

(PP-MISER E)

= (PP-FORMAT E N 'MISER)
where N is the value of (GET (CAR E) 'PP-MISER) if present, or 1 if there is no PP-MISER property. This is the system printmacro function used for LAMBDA, DEFPROP, FUNCTION, and *FUNCTION (the last two with N = 0).

(PP-LABELS E)

= (PP-FORMAT E N 'LABELS)
where N is the value of (GET (CAR E) 'PP-LABELS) if present, or 1 if there is no PP-LABELS property. This is the system printmacro function used for PROG.

(PP-SPECIAL E)

= (PP-FORMAT E N FLAG)
where N is the value of (GET (CAR E) 'PP-SPECIAL) if present, or 1 if there is no PP-SPECIAL property. FLAG is either NIL or MISER, depending on how deeply nested the expression E is. This is the printmacro function used for system functions which have one or two arguments which should be printed on the same line as the function name, regardless of whether MISER format is necessary for the remaining arguments (such as SETQ and DE).

CHAPTER 18

ERRORS AND NON-STANDARD CONTROL FLOW

18.1 LISP errors

LISP errors are processed by five functions:

<u>(*RSET X)</u>

<u>(ERRSET E "ERRSW")</u>

<u>(ERR X)</u>

<u>(ERROR M)</u>

<u>(INITFN FN)</u>

The processing depends on four things:

1. The type of error. There are four types; Chapter 26 lists the error messages and their types. Type-1 errors are "correctable" by means of the Break Package. These include unbound atoms, undefined functions, too many arguments, and undefined PROG tags. All other errors are classified as "serious." Most errors are of type 2; e.g., dot context error, integer overflow, zero divisor, file protection error. A type-3 error occurs when a storage area is exhausted. Illegal memory references are type-4 errors.

2. RSTSW. This is an internal flag, not a LISP variable, that is set to the value of X when (*RSET X) is called. Its initial value is T. *RSET returns the previous value of the RSTSW.

3. ERRSW. This is an internal flag, not a LISP variable, that is set to ERRSET's second parameter (unevaluated), and redefined every time ERRSET is called: previous values are saved on the stack. The ERRSW is initially T and defaults to T if omitted in a call to ERRSET.

4. USERERRORX. This is a LISP variable, initially NIL, which the user may redefine (via SETQ) to be the name of an error-processing function.

18.1.1 Printing of error messages

When an error occurs, the associated error message will be printed unless (1) the current ERRSW is NIL or (2) it is a type-1 error and the RSTSW is 'ERRORX. The message is sent to the current output channel if the current ERRSW is 0 (zero); otherwise, it goes to the terminal.

<u>(ERROR M)</u>

The function (ERROR M) generates a type-2 error. The message M will be printed unless the ERRSW is NIL or M is NIL. If M is a non-NIL atom, is is printed with PRINTC. If it is a list, each element is printed with PRINTC.

18.1.2 Breaking

After the message is (or is not) printed, a break will occur unless the ERRSW is NIL or the RSTSW is NIL or the error is of type 3 (storage exhausted). The break is done with the function (ERRORX ERRTYP), where ERRTYP is NIL for type-1 errors, and T for types 2 and 4. ERRORX is defined as:

```
(DE ERRORX (ERRTYP)
   (COND [(AND USERERRORX [USERERRORX ERRTYP])]
         [T (... call the Break Package ...)]))
```

(The Break Package is described in Chapter 21.) By defining USERERRORX as the name of a function, you can decide whether to call the Break Package; if so, the function should return NIL, as the definition above indicates.

If ERRORX returns a value, either from USERERRORX or by the RETURN command to the Break Package, that value will effectively "correct" the error; i.e., it will be used as if no error had occurred.

18.1.3 ERR

If a break does not occur, (ERR NIL) is called.

(ERR X)

X is evaluated, and should be an atom.

ERR unwinds the stack to previous calls of ERRSET, restoring the ERRSW each time. If there were no calls to ERRSET, then ERR unwinds all the way to the top level and calls the INITFN, if defined; it does not "return" a value at all.

If X is the atom ERRORX, or if the error is of type 3, then ERR keeps unwinding the stack until it finds an ERRSET on the stack whose second parameter (the ERRSW) was the atom ERRORX, at which point that ERRSET returns X.

If X is not ERRORX, then ERR will stop unwinding the stack at the most recent ERRSET. That ERRSET will return X.

(ERR X) can also be called directly from LISP.

When you type the error-character defined by the function ERRCH (see Chapter 1), then (ERR 'ERRORX) will be called. The initial error-character is BELL (control-G).

(INITFN FN)

INITFN selects the function of no arguments (FN) as the initialization function that is evaluated after a LISP error has returned to the top level. INITFN returns the previously selected initialization function. If FN is NIL, then no initialization function will be called. The default is (INITFN NIL).

18.2 Functions for Controlling Evaluation

(CATCH "EXPR" {"LABEL"})
(CATCH "EXPR" {("L1" "E11" ...)} {("L2" "E21" ...)} ...)
(THROW VALUE {"LABEL"})

CATCH and THROW provide a more convenient method of programming transfers to a higher level in the control hierarchy than ERRSET/ERR, which (as the names imply) were originally designed for error handling rather than planned (programmed) transfers.

CATCH simply evaluates EXPR, and if no THROWs are executed during that evaluation, CATCH returns the value of EXPR. If a THROW is evaluated and the CATCH has no LABEL, then the CATCH is immediately exited with VALUE as its value (regardless of whether the THROW had a LABEL or not). An unlabeled CATCH will thus catch a value thrown by any THROW. THROW always binds its value to the atom THROW.

If the CATCH has a LABEL, it will catch values thrown only by a THROW with the same label; other THROWs are passed on in search of a higher-level CATCH with a matching label.

Finally, a single CATCH can catch a variety of different THROWs via a SELECTQ-like mechanism as shown above. Each L is either a LABEL or a list of LABELs; if a THROW LABEL matches an L or a member of an L, the corresponding E's are evaluated and the value of the last one is returned as the value of the CATCH. If no labels match, the THROW is passed on in search of a higher-level CATCH.

Note that a missing THROW LABEL is equivalent to a LABEL of NIL, and may be caught as such.

CATCH and THROW are compiled in-line.

```
(DF THROW (L)
  (SETQ THROW (EVAL (CAR L)))
  (SETQ CATCH (CADR L))
  (ERR 'THROW))
```

```
(DF CATCH (L)
  (COND
   [(OR [%CATCH (ERRSET (EVAL (CAR L)))]
         [NULL (SETQ L (CDR L))])
    THROW]
   [(ATOM (CAR L))
    (COND [(EQ CATCH (CAR L)) THROW] [T (ERR 'THROW)])]
   [T (APPLY# 'SELECTQ
               (CONS 'CATCH (APPEND L '((ERR 'THROW)))))]))

(DE %CATCH (V)
  (COND [(CONSP V) (SETQ THROW (CAR V)) (FREE V) T]
        [(NEQ V 'THROW) (ERR V)]))
```

CHAPTER 19

THE LISP EVALUATION CONTEXT STACK

19.1 The Contents of the Context Stack

Whenever a form is given to EVAL, it is pushed onto the Special Pushdown List in the form of what is called an EVAL-blip. This information is used for backtraces. An EVAL-blip entry has NIL in the left half (see SPDLFT) and the form being evaluated in the right half (see SPDLRT).

Variable bindings are also saved on the Special Pushdown List. The left side of the entry contains a pointer to the special cell, which is a CONS-cell. The right side contains the value which was saved (or UNBOUND if there was no previous value).

The only other items on the Special Pushdown List are used by the LISP interpreter, and always have a non-NIL atom in the left half.

Thus, if the left half is NIL, the item is an EVAL-blip. If the left half is a CONS-cell, then the item is a variable binding. Otherwise, the item is internal information for the interpreter.

In the user's programs, stack pointers are always represented as INUMs. This allows the program to modify them with the standard arithmetic functions so that a program can either step up the stack (toward the most recent EVAL-blip) by incrementing the pointer, or step down the stack (toward the top level of the interpreter) by decrementing the pointer.

All of the functions in this chapter take INUM's for the pointer arguments. The actual pointer to the stack element requires an offset from the beginning of the stack. To obtain a true LISP pointer, call the function STKPTR (with an INUM argument also). For example, if you wish to do an

RPLACA or RPLACD on an element of the stack, you must get a pointer via STKPTR.

19.2 Examining the Context Stack

(SPDLPT)

The value of SPDLPT is a stack pointer to the current top of the stack. (Returns an INUM).

(SPDLFT P)

The value of SPDLFT is the left side of the stack item pointed to by the stack pointer P.

(SPDLRT P)

The value of SPDLRT is the right side of the stack item pointed to by the stack pointer P.

(STKPTR P)

The value of STKPTR is a true LISP pointer to the stack item at position P.

(NEXTEV P)

If the stack pointer P is a pointer to an EVAL-blip, the value of NEXTEV is P. Otherwise, NEXTEV searches down the stack, starting from P, and returns a stack pointer to the first EVAL-blip it finds. If NEXTEV cannot find an EVAL-blip it returns NIL.

```
(DE NEXTEV (P)
  (DO WHILE (AND [GE P 0] [SPDLFT P]) (DECR P))
  (COND [(GE P 0) P]))
```

(PREVEV P)

PREVEV is similar to NEXTEV except that it moves up the stack instead of down it.

```
(DE PREVEV (P)
  (PROG (TOP)
        (SETQ TOP (SPDLPT))
        (DO WHILE (AND [LE P TOP] [SPDLFT P])
            (INCR P))
        (COND [(LE P TOP) (RETURN P)])))
```

(STKCOUNT NAME P PEND)

The value of STKCOUNT is the number of EVAL-blips with a STKNAME of NAME occurring between stack positions P-1 and PEND, where PEND < P.

```
(DE STKCOUNT (NAME P PEND)
  (PROG (C)
        (SETQ C 0)
        (DO WHILE
            (AND P
                 [SETQ P (NEXTEV (SUB1 P))]
                 [LE PEND P])
            (COND [(EQ NAME (STKNAME P)) (INCR C)]))
        (RETURN C)))
```

(STKNAME P)

If position P is not an EVAL-blip, the value of STKNAME is NIL. If position P is an EVAL-blip and the form is atomic, then the value of STKNAME is that atom. If the form is non-atomic, STKNAME returns the CAR for the form, i.e., the name of the function.

```
(DE STKNAME (P)
  (COND [(NULL P) NIL]
        [(SPDLFT P) NIL]
        [(ATOM (SETQ P (SPDLRT P))) P]
        [T (CAR P)]))
```

(STKNTH N P)

The value of STKNTH is a stack pointer to the Nth EVAL-blip starting at position P. If N is positive, STKNTH moves up the stack, and if N is negative, STKNTH moves down the stack.

```
(DE STKNTH (N P)
  (PROG (FLAG)
        (COND [(MINUSP N)
               (SETQ N (MINUS N))
               (SETQ FLAG T)])
        (DO WHILE (AND P [NEQ N 0])
            (SETQ P
                  (COND [FLAG (NEXTEV (SUB1 P))]
                        [T (PREVEV (ADD1 P))]))
            (DECR N))
        (RETURN P)))
```

(STKSRCH NAME P FLAG)

The value of STKSRCH is a stack pointer to the first EVAL-blip with a STKNAME of NAME. The direction of the search is controlled by FLAG. If FLAG is NIL, STKSRCH moves down the stack from P. Otherwise STKSRCH moves up the stack from P. STKSRCH never returns P for its value (unless P isn't a number); i.e., it steps once before checking for NAME.

```
(DE STKSRCH (NAME P FLAG)
  (COND
   [(NUMBERP P)
    (DO WHILE
        (AND [SETQ P
                   (COND [FLAG (PREVEV (ADD1 P))]
                         [T (NEXTEV (SUB1 P))])]
             [NEQ (STKNAME P) NAME])
        NIL)])
  P)
```

(FNDBRKPT P)

The value of FNDBRKPT is a stack pointer to the beginning of the EVAL-block that P is in. The beginning of a EVAL-block is defined as an EVAL-blip which does not contain the next higher EVAL-blip within it. This function is used by the backtrace functions.

19.3 Controlling Evaluation Context

(OUTVAL P V)

OUTVAL adjusts P to an EVAL-blip and returns from that position with V.

(SPREDO P)

SPREDO adjusts P to an EVAL-blip and re-evaluates from that point.

(SPREVAL P V)

SPREVAL evaluates its argument V in its local context to get a form, and then it returns to the context specified by P and evaluates the form in that context, returning from that context with the value. This is very similar to SPREDO except that the EVAL-blip on the stack is changed.

NOTE

OUTVAL, SPREDO and SPREVAL all use NEXTEV to adjust P to an EVAL-blip.

(EVALV A P)

The value of EVALV is the value of the atom A evaluated as of position P. If A is not an atom then it must be the special cell of an atom. By using the special cell instead of the atom, SPECIAL variables can be handled properly. EVALV is similar to EVAL with two arguments, but is more efficient.

(RETFROM FN VAL)

. RETFROM returns VAL from the most recent call to the function FN with the value VAL. For RETFROM to work, there must be an EVAL-blip for FN. The only way to be sure to get an EVAL-blip in compiled code is to explicitly evaluate a quoted expression which calls the function, e.g., (EVAL '(FUNC A B)).

```
(DE RETFROM (FUN VAL)
  (PROG (A)
        (COND [(SETQ A (STKSRCH FUN (SPDLPT)))
               (OUTVAL A VAL)]
              [T (ERROR
                   (LIST FUN
                         "NO EVAL BLIP - RETFROM"))])
  ))
```

CHAPTER 20

STORAGE

LISP has several different areas of memory for storing data. They can independently vary in size, and are adjustable either at runtime or before you start LISP.

20.1 Summary of Storage Allocation Areas

TOP OF CORE

EXPANDED CORE I/O buffers, LOADER, programs loaded with (LOAD NIL)
SPECIAL PUSHDOWN LIST interpreted and SPECIAL variables
REGULAR PUSHDOWN LIST function calls, non-SPECIAL parameters to compiled code
BIT TABLES mark-bits for the garbage collector
FULL WORD SPACE strings, PNAMEs, FIXNUMs, FLONUMs
FREE STORAGE CONS-cells and atom headers
BINARY PROGRAM SPACE arrays, blocks, LAP code, programs loaded with (LOAD T)
LISP INTERPRETER

BOTTOM OF CORE

20.2 Storage Allocation

When you run LISP with a core specification (e.g., ".R LISP 50"), LISP types "ALLOC? (Y OR N)". If you type "N" or space (for no), then the system uses the standard allocations. If you type "Y" (for yes) then the system allows you to specify for each area either an octal number followed by a space designating the number of words to be added to that area, or a space designating an increase of zero words. If you type an altmode (escape), it will supply zero as the answer to all the remaining questions. If you type RUBOUT, it will type XXX and allow you to retype the answer to that question.

Example: (user input is underlined)

```
ALLOC? (Y OR N) Y              (no blank or crlf)
FULL WORD SP. = 200        (200 followed by a blank)
BIN. PROG. SP. = 2000
REG. PDL. =                   (blank, meaning 0)
SPEC. PDL. = 1000
```

Any remaining storage is divided between the spaces as follows:

> 1/16 for full word space,
> 1/64 for each push down list,
> the remainder to free storage and bit tables.

20.3 Binary program space

Binary Program Space (BPS) is a contiguous block of storage. The global variable BPEND marks the highest location in BPS; the global variable BPORG marks the lowest available location in BPS. The LISP assembler increments BPORG when reading LAP code (see Chapter 23).

The LISP high segment also has space where compiled code can be stored. (HGHORG NIL) returns the address of the first free location in the high segment, analogous to BPORG. (HGHEND) returns the last free location in the high segment, analogous to BPEND. HGHORG and HGHEND are described in Chapter 25.

20.4 Storage information

(PATOM X)

The value of PATOM is T if X is an atom or X is a pointer outside of free storage, NIL otherwise.

(FSCNT)

The available words in Free Storage are linked together on the Free Storage List. FSCNT returns the length of that list, i.e., the number of available words.

(FWCNT)

The available words in Full-Word Space are linked together on the Fullword List. FWCNT returns the length of that list, i.e., the number of available words.

(FRECOR)

FRECOR calls (GC) and then returns a list indicating how much storage remains in the high segment, in Binary Program Space, in Free Storage, and in Full Word Space.

```
(DE FRECOR NIL
  (GC)
  (LIST (CONS (*DIF (HGHEND) (HGHORG NIL)) 'HBPS)
        (CONS (*DIF BPEND BPORG) 'BPS)
        (CONS (FSCNT) 'FS)
        (CONS (FWCNT 'FWS))))
```

(CORE "E1" "E2" ...)

CORE calls FRECOR, evaluates the expressions E1, E2, ..., and calls FRECOR again, returning a list of the amounts of storage consumed by the expressions. CORE is analogous to TIMER (see Chapter 25).

```
(DF CORE (L)
  (PROG (A)
        (SETQ A (FRECOR))
        (APPLY# 'PROGN L)
        (RETURN
         (MAPCAR (FUNCTION
                   (LAMBDA (X Y)
                    (CONS (*DIF (CAR X) (CAR Y))
                          (CDR X))))
                 A
                 (FRECOR)))))
```

20.5 Reallocation of Storage

It is possible to expand core without leaving LISP.

<u>(REALLOC FWS BPS RPDL SPDL FS)</u>

REALLOC's arguments specify increments (in words) to be added to each of the five major allocation areas: fullword space, binary program space, the regular pushdown list, the special pushdown list, and free storage. After calling (EXCISE) and expanding core as necessary and reallocating storage, REALLOC returns control directly to the top level of LISP, calling the INITFN, if any.

For those of us who can't remember the order of the arguments to REALLOC, there are these functions:

<u>(EXPFWS FWS)</u>

= (REALLOC FWS 0 0 0 0)

<u>(EXPBPS BPS)</u>

= (REALLOC 0 BPS 0 0 0)

<u>(EXPFS FS)</u>

= (REALLOC 0 0 0 0 FS)

(EXCISE)

EXCISE contracts core to its length after the most recent REALLOCation or most recent last START: all storage in Expanded Core is released. All open I/O channels are cleared, and the terminal is selected for both input and output.

EXCISE does a RESET monitor call. Among its other effects, RESET releases all files without closing them. For input files, the effect is the same as if they had been closed, but output files that are still open are deleted. If an output file was superseding (overwriting) an older file with the same name, the older file is retained.

20.6 Garbage Collection

All LISP systems have a function known as the garbage collector. This function analyzes the entire state of list structure which is pointed to by either the OBLIST, the regular pushdown list, the special pushdown list, list arrays, and a few other special cells. By recursively marking all words in Free Storage and Full-Word Space that are pointed to in this manner, it is possible to determine which words are not pointed to and are therefore garbage. Such words are collected together on their respective available-storage lists.

The garbage collector is called automatically when either Free Storage or Full-Word Space has been exhausted.

(GC)

GC calls the garbage collector. It always returns NIL.

(GCGAG X)

GCGAG sets an internal flag to the value of X, and returns the previous setting of the flag. When any garbage collection occurs, then the following is printed if the flag is non-NIL:

either	FREE STORAGE EXHAUSTED
or	FULL WORD SPACE EXHAUSTED
or	nothing
followed by	x FREE STORAGE, y FULL WORDS AVAILABLE

where x and y are numbers in octal.

(SPEAK)
(CONSCOUNT)

SPEAK returns the total number of CONSes which have been executed.

(GCTIME)

GCTIME returns the number of milliseconds LISP has spent garbage collecting.

20.7 Running out of storage

If full word space or free storage is exhausted, a garbage collection will occur, but it may not return any storage. Binary program space is not garbage-collected, nor are the pushdown lists. When any of these run completely out of space, a type-3 error occurs (see Chapter 18): the Break Package is bypassed, and the stack is unwound until an (ERRSET ... ERRORX) is found, at which point NIL (not ERRORX) is returned as the value of the ERRSET. If no such ERRSET is found, LISP goes back to top level, invoking the INITFN.

20.8 Releasing storage directly

(FREE X)

FREE returns the word X to the Free Storage List and returns NIL.

(FREELIST X)

FREELIST returns all of the words on the top level of the list X to the Free Storage List and returns NIL. FREELIST takes repeated CDRs until it reaches NIL.

WARNING

FREE and FREELIST can catastrophically destroy the garbage collector by creating a circle in the Free Storage List if they are used to return words that are still in use (pointed to by some cell). Do not use these functions unless you are certain what you are doing. They are only useful in rare cases where a small amount of working storage is needed by a routine that is called quite often.

CHAPTER 21

THE BREAK PACKAGE

21.1 Introduction

Debugging a collection of LISP functions involves isolating problems within particular functions and determining when and where incorrect values are being generated and transmitted. In the UCI LISP system, there are six facilities to help you monitor your program.

One of these is the function ERRORX, which takes control whenever an error occurs in a program, as described in Chapter 18.

The second facility is the control-C trapping mechanism, which allows you to interrupt your computation temporarily and examine its progress, as described in Chapter 1.

The next three facilities, BREAK, TRACE and BREAKIN, allow you to modify selected function definitions temporarily so that you can follow the flow of control in your programs. All of these facilities use the same system function, BREAK1, as the user interface.

The final debugging facililty is TRACEV, which allows you to trace assignments (SET and SETQ) to selected variables.

BREAK, BREAKIN, TRACE and TRACEV together are called _the Break Package_. BREAK and TRACE can be used on compiled and system functions as well as EXPR's, FEXPR's, and MACRO's. BREAKIN can be used only with interpreted functions. TRACEV can be used only with interpreted and SPECIAL variables.

BREAK modifies the definition of a function FN, so that if a break condition (which you specify) is satisfied, the process is halted temporarily on a call to FN. You can then interrogate the state of the machine, perform any computations, and continue or return from the call.

TRACE modifies a definition of a function FN so that whenever FN is called, its arguments (or some other values you specify) are printed. The value that FN returns is also printed.

BREAKIN allows you to insert a breakpoint <u>inside</u> a function definition. When the breakpoint is reached and a break condition (which you specify) is satisfied, then a temporary halt occurs and you can again investigate the state of the computation.

TRACEV modifies the definitions of SET and SETQ so that whenever any specified variable is assigned a new value, a message is printed, giving the name of the variable and its new value.

The two examples that follow illustrate some of these facilities. In the first example, we trace the function FACTORIAL. TRACE redefines FACTORIAL so that it calls BREAK1 in such a way that it prints some information, in this case the arguments and value of FACTORIAL, and then goes on with the computation. When an error occurs on the fifth recursion, BREAK1 reverts to interactive mode, and a full break occurs. The situation is then the same as though we had originally performed (BREAK FACTORIAL) instead of (TRACE FACTORIAL), and we can evaluate various LISP forms and direct the course of the computation. In this case, we examine the variable N, instruct BREAK1 to change L to 1, and continue. The > command, following an UNBOUND ATOM or UNDEFINED FUNCTION error, tells BREAK1 to use the next expression instead of the atom which caused the error. The > command here does a destructive replacement of 1 for L, and saves an edit step by correcting the typo in the function definition. The rest of the tracing proceeds without incident. The function UNTRACE restores FACTORIAL to its original definition.

```
*(DE FACTORIAL (N)
     (COND ((ZEROP N) L)
           (T (TIMES N (FACTORIAL (SUB1 N))))))

 FACTORIAL

 *(TRACE FACTORIAL)

 (FACTORIAL)

 *(FACTORIAL 4)
 ENTER FACTORIAL:
 !     N = 4
 !  ENTER FACTORIAL:
 !  !     N = 3
 !  !  ENTER FACTORIAL:
 !  !  !     N = 2
 !  !  !  ENTER FACTORIAL:
 !  !  !  !     N = 1
 !  !  !  !  ENTER FACTORIAL:
 !  !  !  !  !     N = 0
 L
 UNBOUND VARIABLE - EVAL

 (L BROKEN)

 1:N

 0

 1:> 1

 !  !  !  !  FACTORIAL = 1
 !  !  !  FACTORIAL = 1
 !  !  FACTORIAL = 2
 !  FACTORIAL = 6
 FACTORIAL = 24
 24

 *(UNTRACE FACTORIAL)

 (FACTORIAL)

 *(FACTORIAL 4)

 24
```

In the second example, we have written Ackermann's function. We use BREAK to place a call to BREAK1 around the body of the function. We indicate that ACK is to be broken when M equals N, and that before the break occurs, the arguments to ACK are to be printed. While calculating (ACK 2 1), ACK is called twice when M = N. During the first of these breaks, we print out a backtrace of the function names and variable bindings. We continue the computation with the command GO, which causes the value of (ACK 1 1), 3, to be printed before the break is released. The second break is released with an OK, which does not print the result of (ACK 1 1). Finally, (UNBREAK T) restores the latest broken or traced function to its original definition.

```
*(DE ACK (M N)
     (COND ((ZEROP M) (ADD1 N))
           ((ZEROP N) (ACK (SUB1 M) 1))
           (T (ACK (SUB1 M) (ACK M (SUB1 N))))))

 ACK

 *(BREAK (ACK (EQ N M) (ARGS)))

 (ACK)

 *(ACK 2 1)
    M = 1
    N = 1

 (ACK BROKEN)

 1:BKFV

 ACK
     M = 2
     N = 0
 ACK
     M = 2
     N = 1
 ACK

 1:GO

 3

    M = 1
    N = 1

 (ACK BROKEN)

 1:OK

 5

 *(UNBREAK T)

 (ACK)
```

21.2 TRACE and BREAK

TRACE and BREAK use the function BREAK0 to modify function definitions such that calls to those functions will first call BREAK1, the most important part of the Break Package. Traced and broken functions can be prettyprinted and edited without any special effort.

BROKENFNS is a list of the functions currently broken. TRACEDFNS is a list of the functions currently traced.

21.2.1 Tracing/breaking compiled functions

When BREAK0 breaks a SUBR or an FSUBR, it prints a message of the form (fname ARGUMENT LIST?). You should respond with a list of identifiers (the names of the formal parameters) for the function being broken. The identifiers in this list are actually bound during the calls to the broken function, so make sure that they do not conflict with other variables. For LSUBRs, the atom N? is automatically used as the name of the parameter. FSUBRs take only one formal parameter, and BREAK0 checks to see that you specify a list with just one name.

The identifier lists that you supply are saved from one call to the next, so they need only be supplied once for each function. The list is stored on the property list of the function name, under the property ARGS. A function which wishes to break a compiled function under program control without user interaction can thus specify an identifier list by placing it under the ARGS property.

21.2.2 Parameters to TRACE

(TRACE "E1" "E2" ...)

For each expression E, TRACE does the following:

1. If E is an atom (TRACE FN) or a 1-element list (TRACE (FN)), FN is taken to be the name of a function, and the function will be traced each time it is called. (See the example at the beginning of the chapter.)

In this case, TRACE calls (BREAK0 FN T ((TRACE) //BREAK1 (UNTRACE)).

2. If E is of the form (FN TEST), the function FN will be traced unless TEST evaluates to NIL. E.g., (TRACE (FACTORIAL (GE N 10))).

   In this case, TRACE calls (BREAK0 FN TEST ((TRACE) //BREAK1 (UNTRACE))).

3. If E is of the form (FN1 IN FN2), the function FN1 will be traced only if called from within FN2.

   In this case, TRACE calls (BREAK0 (FN1 IN FN2) T ((TRACE) //BREAK1 (UNTRACE))).

4. If E is of the form (FN TEST V1 V2 ...), then unless TEST evaluates to NIL, FN will be traced, and the variables (or forms) V1, V2, ..., will be evaluated and printed.

   In this case, TRACE calls (BREAK0 FN TEST ((TRACE) (?= V1 V2 ...) (UNTRACE))).

5. Finally, if E is of the form ((FN1 IN FN2) TEST V1 V2 ...), then if FN1 is called from within F2 and TEST doesn't evaluate to NIL, F1 will be traced and the variables V1, V2, ..., evaluated and printed.

   In this case, TRACE calls (BREAK0 (FN1 IN FN2) TEST ((TRACE) (?= V1 V2 ...) (UNTRACE))).

Examples:

```
(TRACE FOO)
(TRACE *TIMES (SELECTQ IN DOIT))
(TRACE (EVAL IN FOO))
(TRACE (TRY T M N X (*PLUS N M)))
```

21.2.3 LASTWORD

LASTWORD is the variable used by TRACE, BREAK, EDITF, EDITP, and PP when no parameter is given. If the value of LASTWORD is 'FOO, then (TRACE) is equivalent to (TRACE FOO). LASTWORD is <u>set</u> by TRACE, BREAK, EDITF, EDITP, PP, DE, DF, and DM. Thus, after (DE BAZ (X Y Z) ...), typing (PP) would be the same as typing (PP BAZ); after (PP A B C), typing (BREAK) would be the same as typing (BREAK C).

21.2.4 TRACE Output

TRACE uses the global variable #%INDENT to keep track of its position on the line. It prints a parameter X by calling (%PRINFN X). %PRINFN is a global variable, initially set to 'PLEV. PLEV is defined:

```
(DE PLEV (X) (PRINTLEV X %LOOKDPTH))
```

%LOOKDPTH is a global variable initially set to 6.

TRACE can therefore prettyprint parameters by:

```
(SETQ %PRINFN 'PRETPRIN)
(DE PRETPRIN (FORM)
     (SPRINT FORM (*PLUS 10 #%INDENT)))
```

TRACE output may be directed either to the currently selected output channel or to the terminal. If the global variable TRACE is NIL (its default setting), trace output is directed to the terminal; otherwise, trace output is directed to the current output channel.

21.2.5 UNTRACE

<u>(UNTRACE "FN1" "FN2" ...)</u>

UNTRACE takes a list of functions modified by TRACE and restores them to their original state. Its value is the list of functions that were "untraced."

(UNTRACE T) will untrace the function most recently traced (the CAR of TRACEDFNS).

(UNTRACE) will untrace <u>all</u> of the functions currently traced (i.e., all those on TRACEDFNS).

If one of the functions is not traced, UNTRACE returns a value of (fn NOT BROKEN) for that function and no changes are made to fn.

21.2.6 BREAK

(BREAK "E1" "E2" ...)

BREAK, like TRACE, calls BREAKO. It differs from TRACE only in the third parameter it passes to BREAKO.

(BREAK FN) calls (BREAKO FN T NIL)

(BREAK (FN1 IN FN2)) calls (BREAKO (FN1 IN FN2) T NIL)

(BREAK FN TEST V1 V2 ...)
calls (BREAKO FN TEST (V1 V2 ...))

```
(DF BREAK (L)
  (MAPCAR
   (FUNCTION
    (LAMBDA (FN)
     (COND [(ATOM FN)
             (SETQ FN (BREAKO FN T NIL))
             (COND [(ATOM FN) (SETQ LASTWORD FN)])
             FN]
            [(EQ (CADR FN) 'IN) (BREAKO FN T NIL)]
            [(CDR FN)
             (BREAKO (CAR FN) (CADR FN) (CDDR FN))]
            [T (CONS FN '(?))])))
   (OR L [LIST LASTWORD])))
```

Examples:

```
     (BREAK FOO)
     (BREAK ((GET IN FOO) T (GO)))
     (BREAK (SETQ (EQ N 1)
            ((PRINT (QUOTE N=1)))(?= M)))
```

21.2.7 UNBREAK

(UNBREAK "E1" "E2" ...)

UNBREAK takes a list of functions modified by BREAK or BREAKIN and restores them to their original state. Its value is the list of functions that were "unbroken."

(UNBREAK T) will unbreak the function most recently broken (the CAR of BROKENFNS).

(UNBREAK) will unbreak <u>all</u> of the functions currently broken (i.e., all those on BROKENFNS).

If one of the functions is not broken, UNBREAK returns a value of (fn NOT BROKEN) for that function and no changes are made to fn.

NOTE

If a function is both traced and broken, either UNTRACE or UNBREAK will restore the original function definition.

21.3 BREAKIN

(BREAKIN "E1" "E2" "E3" "E4")

BREAKIN enables you to insert a break (i.e., a call to BREAK1) at a specified location in a LISP function. For example, if FOO calls FIE, inserting a break in FOO before the call to FIE is similar to breaking FIE. However, BREAKIN can be used to insert breaks before or after PROG labels, SETQ expressions, or even the evaluation of a variable. This is because BREAKIN operates by calling the editor and actually inserting a call to BREAK1 at a specified point *inside* the function.*

You specify where the break is to be inserted by a sequence of editor commands. These commands are preceded by BEFORE, AFTER, or AROUND, which BREAKIN uses to determine what to do once the editor has found the specified point, i.e., put the break BEFORE that point, AFTER that point, or AROUND that point. For example, (BEFORE COND) will insert a break before the first occurrence of COND, (AFTER COND 2 1) will insert a break after the predicate in the first COND clause, (AFTER BF (SETQ X &)) after the *last* place X is set. (BEFORE TTY:), (AROUND TTY:) or (AFTER TTY:) permit you to type in commands to the editor, locate the correct point, and verify it using the editor P command. Upon exit from the editor with OK, the break is inserted. (A STOP command typed to TTY: produces the same effect as an unsuccessful edit command in the original specification, e.g., (BEFORE CONDD). In both cases, the editor aborts, and BREAKIN types (NOT FOUND).)

For BREAKIN BEFORE or AFTER, the break expression is NIL, since the value of the break is usually not of interest. For BREAKIN AROUND, the break expression will be the indicated form. When in the break, you can use the EVAL command to evaluate that form and see its value, before allowing the computation to proceed. For example, if you inserted a break after a COND predicate, e.g., (AFTER (EQUAL X Y)), you would be powerless to alter the flow of computation if the predicate were not true, since the break would not be reached. However, by breaking (AROUND (EQUAL X Y)), you can evaluate the break expression, (EQUAL X Y), see its value, and evaluate something

---

* BREAKIN requires the editor.

else.

The message typed for a BREAKIN break identifies the location of the break as well as the function, e.g.,

```
((FOO (AFTER COND 2 1)) BROKEN)
```

BREAKIN is a FEXPR which has a maximum of four arguments. The first argument is the function to be broken in. The second argument is a list of editor commands, preceded by BEFORE, AFTER, or AROUND, which specifies the location inside the function at which to break. If there is no second argument, a value of (BEFORE TTY:) is assumed. The third and fourth arguments are the break condition and the list of commands to be performed before the interactive break occurs, (BRKWHEN and BRKCOMS for BREAK1) respectively. If there is no third argument, a value of T is assumed for BRKWHEN, causing a break each time the BREAKIN break is executed. If the fourth argument is missing, a value of NIL is assumed. For example,

```
(BREAKIN FOO (AROUND COND))
```

inserts a break around the first call to COND in FOO.

It is possible to insert multiple break points, with a single call to BREAKIN by using a list of the form ((BEFORE ...) ... (AROUND ...)) as the second argument. It is also possible to BREAK or TRACE a function which has been modified by BREAKIN, and conversely to BREAKIN a function which is broken or traced. UNBREAK restores functions which have been broken in.

Examples:

```
(BREAKIN FOO (AROUND TTY:) T (?= M N) ((*PLUS X Y)))
(BREAKIN FOO2 (BEFORE SETQ) (EQ X Y))
```

21.4 BREAKO

<u>(BREAKO FN WHEN COMS)</u>

BREAKO is an EXPR. It sets up a break on the function FN by redefining FN as a call to BREAK1 with BRKEXP a form equivalent to the definition of FN, and WHEN, FN, and COMS as BRKWHEN, BRKFN, and BRKCOMS, respectively (see BREAK1). BREAKO also adds FN to the front of the list BROKENFNS. Its value is FN.

If FN is non-atomic and of the form (fn1 IN fn2), BREAKO first calls a function which changes the name of fn1 wherever it appears inside of fn2 to that of a new function, fn1-IN-fn2, which is initially defined as fn1. Then BREAKO proceeds to break on fn1-IN-fn2 exactly as described above. This procedure is useful for breaking on a function that is called from many places, but where you're only interested in the call from a specific function, e.g., (RPLACA IN FOO), (PRINT IN FIE). fn2 must be a LISP (non-compiled) function in this case. If fn1 is not found in fn2, BREAKO returns the value (fn1 NOT FOUND IN fn2).

If FN is non-atomic and not of the form above, BREAKO is called for each member of FN using the same values for WHEN and COMS specified in this call to BREAKO. This distributivity permits you to specify complicated break conditions without excessive retyping, e.g.,

```
(BREAKO '(FOO1 ((PRINT PRIN1) IN (FOO2 FOO3)))
        '(EQ X T)
        '((EVAL) (?= Y Z) OK))
```

will break on FOO1, PRINT-IN-FOO2, PRINT-IN-FOO3, PRIN1-IN-FOO2, and PRIN1-IN-FOO3.

If FN is non-atomic, the value of BREAKO is a list of the individual values.

21.5 BREAK1

The heart of the debugging package is a function called BREAK1. BREAK and TRACE redefine functions in terms of BREAK1. When an error occurs, control is passed to BREAK1.

Whenever LISP types a message of the form (-- BROKEN) followed by "n:", you are then talking to BREAK1, and you are "in a break." BREAK1 allows you to interrogate the state of the world and affect the course of the computation. It uses the prompt character ':' to indicate it is ready to accept input for evaluation, in the same way as the top level of LISP uses '*'. The n before the ':' is the level number that indicates how many levels of BREAK1 are currently open. If you type an expression for evaluation, the value will be printed out, followed by another ':'. You may also type in one of the commands that are specifically recognized by BREAK1. (For a summary of commands, see Table I).

Once inside BREAK1, you can do anything you could do at the top level of LISP. For example, you can define new functions or edit existing ones, set breaks, or trace functions. You may evaluate an expression, see that the value was incorrect, call the editor, change a function, and evaluate the expression again, all without leaving the break.

It is important to emphasize that once a break occurs, you are in complete control of the flow of the computation, and the computation will not proceed without specific instruction from you. The computation will continue only when you type one of the commands that leaves the break (GO, OK, RETURN, FROM?=, EX). If you want to abort the computation, this also can be done (using ^ or ^^).

BREAK1 is just another LISP function, not a special system feature like the interpreter or the garbage collector. It has arguments and returns a value, the same as any other function. A call to BREAK1 has the form:

(BREAK1 BRKEXP BRKWHEN BRKFN BRKCOMS BRKTYPE)

> BRKWHEN is a LISP function that is evaluated to determine if a break will occur. If BRKWHEN returns NIL, BRKEXP is evaluated and returned as the value of the BREAK1. Otherwise a break occurs.
>
> BRKFN is the name of the function being broken and is used to print an identifying message.
>
> BRKCOMS is a list of command lines (as returned by READL) which are executed as if they had been typed

in from the terminal. The command lines on BRKCOMS are executed before commands are accepted from the terminal, so that if one of the commands on BRKCOMS causes a return, a break occurs without the need for interaction with the terminal.

BRKTYPE identifies the type of the break. It is used primarily by the error package; you should always use NIL for this argument.

The value returned by BREAK1 is called "the value of the break." You can specify this value explicitly by using the RETURN command described below. In most cases, however, the value of the break is given implicitly, via a GO or OK command, and is the result of evaluating the break expression, BRKEXP.

BRKEXP is, in general, an expression equivalent to the computation that would have taken place had no break occurred. In other words, you can think of BREAK1 as a fancy EVAL, which permits interaction before and after evaluation. The break expression then corresponds to the argument to EVAL. For BREAK and TRACE, BRKEXP is a form equivalent to that of the function being traced or broken. For errors, BRKEXP is the form which caused the error. For ^C^B and ^C^H breaks, BRKEXP is the next form to be evaluated.

21.5.1 What you can do in a break

21.5.1.1 Break Commands - Once in a break, in addition to evaluating expressions, you can perform certain useful actions by typing atoms recognized as "break commands." The following commands can be typed in or may be put on the list BRKCOMS. Table I is a summary of these commands.

<u>GO</u>

GO releases the break and allows the computation to proceed. BREAK1 evaluates BRKEXP, its first argument, prints the value, and returns it as the value of the break. BRKEXP is the expression set up by the function that called BREAK1. For BREAK or TRACE, BRKEXP is equivalent to the body of the definition of the broken function. For the error package, BRKEXP is the expression in which the error occurred. For ^C^B and ^C^H breaks, it is the next form to be evaluated.

<u>OK</u>

OK is the same as GO except that the value of BRKEXP is not printed.

EVAL

EVAL causes BRKEXP to be evaluated. The break is maintained and the value of the evaluation is printed and bound on the variable !VALUE. Typing GO or OK will not cause reevaluation of BRKEXP following EVAL but another EVAL will. EVAL is a useful command when you're not sure whether the break will produce the correct value, and you want to be able to do something about it if it is wrong.

RETURN form

The form is evaluated and its value is returned as the value of the break. For example, you might use the EVAL command and follow this with RETURN (REVERSE !VALUE).

FROM?= form

This permits you to release the break and return to a previous context with form to be evaluated. For details see context commands.

> [or ->] expr

This command is useful for UNBOUND ATOM or UNDEFINED FUNCTION errors. It replaces the expression containing the error with expr. (Expr is not evaluated.)

```
FOO1
UNDEFINED FUNCTION
(FOO1 BROKEN)
1:> FOO
```

changes FOO1 to FOO and continues the computation. Expr need not be atomic, e.g.,

```
FOO
UNBOUND ATOM
(FOO BROKEN)
1:> (QUOTE FOO)
```

For UNDEFINED FUNCTION errors, you can specify a function and its first argument, e.g.,

```
MEMBERX
UNDEFINED FUNCTION
(MEMBERX BROKEN)
1:> MEMBER X
```

Note that in the some cases the form containing the offending atom will not be on the stack (notably, after calls to APPLY) and in these cases the function definition will not be changed. In most cases, however, > will correct the function definition.

USE x FOR y

This causes all occurrences of y in the form on the stack at LASTPOS to be replaced by x. (For error breaks, unless a F command has been used, this form is the one in which the error occurred.) Note: The change is done with RPLACA and is permanent.

^ (up-arrow)

^ calls ERR and aborts the break. This is a useful way to unwind to a previous break. All other errors, including those encountered while executing the GO, OK, EVAL, and RETURN commands, maintain the break.

^^ (two up-arrows)

This returns control directly to the top level of LISP, invoking the INITFN.

ARGS

ARGS prints the names and the current values of the arguments of BRKFN. In most cases, these are the arguments of the broken function.

21.5.1.2 Context Commands - All information pertaining to the evaluation of forms in LISP is kept on the stack (the Special Pushdown List). (See Chapter 19.) Whenever a form is evaluated, that form is placed on the stack. Whenever a variable is bound, the old binding is saved on the stack. The context (the bindings of free variables) of a function is determined by its position in the stack. When a break occurs, it is often useful to explore the contexts of other functions on the stack. BREAK1 allows this by means of a context pointer, LASTPOS, which is a pointer into the stack. BREAK1 permits commands to move the context pointer and to evaluate atoms or expressions as of its position in the stack. For the purposes of this document, when moving through the stack, "backward" is considered to be toward the top level or, equivalently, towards the older function calls on the stack.

F [or &] arg1 arg2 ... argN

F resets LASTPOS, which establishes a context for the commands ?=, USE, EX, FROM?=, and the backtrace commands described below. LASTPOS is initialized to the function just before the call to BREAK1.

F takes the rest of the input line as its list of arguments. F first resets LASTPOS to the function call just before the call to BREAK1, and then for each atomic argument, F searches backward for a call to that atom. The following atoms are treated specially:

F [or &]

When used as the first argument, this causes LASTPOS not to be reset above BREAK1 but continues searching from the previous position of LASTPOS.

Numbers

If negative, this moves LASTPOS back (i.e., towards the top level) that number of calls; if positive, forward.

_ (left arrow)

Search forward instead of backward for the next atom.

Example:

If the stack looks like

```
BREAK1          (13)
FOO             (12)
SETQ            (11)
COND            (10)
PROG             (9)
FIE              (8)
COND             (7)
FIE              (6)
COND             (5)
FIE              (4)
COND             (3)
PROG             (2)
FUM              (1)
```

then

```
F FIE COND     will set LASTPOS to to (7)
F & COND       will then set LASTPOS to (5)
F FUM _ FIE    will stop at (4)
F & 2          will then move LASTPOS to (6)
F              will reset LASTPOS to (12)
```

If F cannot successfully complete a search for argN or if argN is a number and F cannot move the number of functions asked, "argN?" is typed. In either case, LASTPOS is restored to its value before the F command was entered.

NOTE

It is possible to move past BRKEXP (i.e., into the break package functions) when searching or moving forwards.

When F finishes, it types the name of the function at LASTPOS.

F can be used on BRKCOMS, in which case the remainder of the list is treated as the list of arguments. E.g., (F FOO FIE FOO).

<u>EDIT</u> arg1 arg2 ... argN

EDIT uses its arguments to reset LASTPOS in the same manner as the F command. The form at LASTPOS is then given to the LISP Editor. This command can save you the trouble of calling EDITF and the finding the expression that you need to edit.

?= arg1 arg2 ... argN

This is a multi-purpose command. Its most common use is to interrogate the values of the arguments of the broken function. (ARGS is also useful for this purpose.) E.g., if FOO has three arguments (X Y Z), then typing ?= to a break of FOO, will produce:

```
n:?=
X =   value of X
Y =   value of Y
Z =   value of Z
```

?= takes the rest of the input line as its arguments. If the argument list to ?= is NIL, as in the above case, it prints all of the arguments of the function at LASTPOS. If you type

```
?= X (CAR Y)
```

you will see the value of X and the value of (CAR Y). The difference between using ?= and typing X and (CAR Y) directly into BREAK1 is that ?= evaluates its input as of LASTPOS; typing them directly will evaluate them at the level of the break. This provides a way of examining variables or forms as of a particular point on the stack. For example,

```
F FOO FOO
?= X
```

will allow you to examine the value of X in an earlier call to FOO.

?= also recognizes numbers as referring to the correspondingly numbered argument. Thus

```
F FIE
?= 2
```

will print the name and value of the second argument of FIE (providing FIE is not compiled).

?= can also be used on BRKCOMS, in which case the remainder of the list on BRKCOMS is treated as the list of arguments. For example, if BRKCOMS is ((EVAL) (?= X (CAR Y)) GO)), BRKEXP will be evaluated, the values of X and (CAR Y) printed, and then the function exited with its value being printed.

FROM?= {FORM}

FROM?= exits from the break by unwinding the stack back to LASTPOS. If FORM is NIL or missing, re-evaluation continues with the form on the stack at LASTPOS. If FORM is not NIL, the function call on the stack at LASTPOS is replaced by FORM and evaluation continues with FORM. FORM is evaluated in the context of LASTPOS. There is no way of recovering the break once the stack has been undone. Among other things, FROM?= allows you to return a particular value as the value of any function call on the stack. To return 1 as the value of the previous call to FOO:

```
F FOO
FROM?= 1
```

Since form is evaluated after it is placed on the stack, a value of NIL can be returned by using (QUOTE NIL).

EX {POS}

EX exits from the break and re-evaluates the form at POS. POS is optional and defaults to LASTPOS. EX is equivalent to FROM?= NIL.

FIX {POS}

FIX is a combination of EDIT and EX. It first calls the editor on the form at POS (or the form just before the call to BREAK1 if POS is missing), and then re-evaluates from that point when the editor returns.

21.5.1.3 Backtrace Commands - The backtrace commands print information about function calls on the stack. The information is printed in the reverse order that the calls were made. All backtraces start at LASTPOS.

BKF

BKF gives a backtrace of the names of functions that are still pending.

BKE

BKE gives a backtrace of the expressions which called functions still pending; i.e., it prints the function calls themselves, instead of only the names as in BKF.

BK

BK gives a full backtrace of all expressions still pending.

All of the backtrace commands may be suffixed by a 'V' and/or followed by an integer. If the integer is included, it specifies how many blocks are to be printed. (Blocks end at explicit function calls; there may be several embedded expressions within a single block.) By using the integer feature in conjunction with the F command, which moves LASTPOS, you can display any contiguous part of the backtrace. If a 'V' is included, variable bindings are printed along with the expressions in the backtrace.

Example:

BKFV
would print the names and variable bindings of the functions called before LASTPOS.

BKV 5
would print everything (expressions and variables) for 5 blocks before LASTPOS.

The output of the backtrace commands deserves some explanation. Expressions are printed by PRINLEV with a depth of %BKTRDPTH, which is initially 3. Previous calls to the Break Package appear as **BREAK**. Calls to the editor appear as **EDITOR**. /#/ is a notation which represents "the previous expression." For example, (SETQ FIE (FOO)) would appear in a BK backtrace as

```
(FOO)
(SETQ FIE /#/)
```

21.5.2 Breakmacros

Whenever an atomic command is encountered by BREAK1 that it does not recognize, either via BRKCOMS or the terminal, it uses ASSOC to search the list BREAKMACROS to see if the atom has been defined as a break macro. The form of BREAKMACROS definitions is:

```
(... (atom args ttyline1 ttyline2 ... ttylineN) ... )
```

ATOM is the command name. ARGS is the argument(s) for the macro. The arguments of a breakmacro are assigned values from the remainder of the command line in which the macro is called. If ARGS is atomic, it is assigned the remainder of the command line as its value. If ARGS is a list, the elements of the rest of the command line are assigned to the variables, in order. If there are more variables in ARGS then items in the rest of the command line, a value of NIL is filled in. Extra items on the command line are ignored. The TTYLINEs are the body of the breakmacro definition and are lists of break commands or forms to be evaluated. If the atom is defined as a macro (i.e., is found on BREAKMACROS), BREAK1 assigns values to the variables in ARGS, substitutes these values for all occurrences of the variables in TTYLINEs and appends the TTYLINEs to the front of BRKCOMS. When BREAK1 is ready to accept another command, if BRKCOMS is non-NIL it takes the first element of BRKCOMS and processes it exactly as if it had been a line input from the terminal. This means that a macro name can be defined to expand to any arbitrary collection of expressions that you type in. If the command is not contained in BREAKMACROS, it is treated as a function or variable as before.

Example: a command PARGS to print the arguments of the function at LASTPOS could be defined by evaluating:

```
(NCONC BREAKMACROS '((PARGS NIL (?=))))
```

A command FP which finds a place on the stack and prints the form there can be defined by:

```
(NCONC BREAKMACROS
   '(FP X (F . X) ((PRINT (SPDLRT LASTPOS)))))
```

21.6 TRACEV

<u>(TRACEV "VAR1" "VAR2" ...)</u>

TRACEV provides a value-tracing facility for uncompiled LISP code. Each time one of the VARs has its value changed via SET or SETQ, a message showing the new value is printed. Note that initial variable bindings in LAMBDA expressions and PROGs, and variables bound within compiled functions, will not be traced.

The global variable TRACEVFNS is the list of variables currently being traced.

<u>(UNTRACEV "VAR1" "VAR2" ...)</u>

Each variable will have its value tracing turned off.

(UNTRACEV T) may be used to untrace the most recently-traced variable (the CAR of TRACEVFNS).

(UNTRACEV) turns off <u>all</u> value tracing (i.e., all those on TRACEVFNS).

21.7 Break Package Command Summary

Table I
Break Package Command Summary

Command	Action
GO	Evaluates BRKEXP, prints its value, and continues with this value
OK	Same as GO but no print of value
EVAL	Re-evaluate BRKEXP and print its value. Its value is bound to !VALUE
RETURN xx	Evaluate xx and continue with its value
^	Escape one level of BREAK1
^^	Escape to the top level
> [->] expr	After an error, use expr for the erring atom
FROM?= {FORM}	Continues by re-evaluating form at LASTPOS
EX {POS}	Same as FROM?= NIL. POS defaults to LASTPOS.
USE x FOR y	Substitutes x for y in form at LASTPOS (destructively)
F [&] A1..An	Resets LASTPOS (stack context)
EDIT A1..An	Resets LASTPOS and gives the form at LASTPOS to the LISP Editor
FIX {POS}	Same as EDIT then EX
?= F1..Fn	Evaluates forms F1..Fn as of LASTPOS
ARGS	Prints arguments of the broken function
BKF	Backtrace Function Names
BKE	Backtrace Function Calls
BK	Backtrace Expressions

Note: All the backtrace commands can be combined with a 'V' or followed by an integer. The 'V' will cause the values of variables to be printed. The integer will limit the trace to that number of function calls. For example, BK 3, BKEV, BKFV 5 and BKEV are all legitimate commands.

CHAPTER 22

THE LISP STRUCTURE EDITOR

22.1 Introduction

The LISP editor is a valuable software tool that allows rapid, convenient modification of list structures. Most often it is used to edit function definitions (even while the function itself is running) via the function EDITF, e.g., (EDITF FOO). However, the editor can also be used to edit the value of a variable, via EDITV, to edit special properties of an atom, via EDITP, or to edit an arbitrary expression, via EDITE.

The editor is a set of <u>LISP programs</u>. Some of these programs, like the pattern-matcher, are sufficiently general to be used as stand-alone functions.

The editor is also a <u>command-language interpreter</u> and has its own "top level." The syntax of editor commands will be described in 22.2. The editor can even call itself in a useful and non-trivial way to permit even greater flexibility in the command language.

Finally, the editor can be viewed as a <u>programming language</u> in its own right. While most users will tend to stay at the command level, others will find it useful to write their own programs, called editmacros, and extend the range of editing commands available to them. Some of the current commands, in fact, are implemented as editmacros. The programming language and some of the other advanced features of the editor appear in 22.13.

22.1.1 Integration with LISP

The simplest way to get into the editor is by calling one of the top-level functions, such as EDITF (see 22.17), but there are other ways. One of the commands available in the Break Package is EDIT, which will pass an item on the runtime stack to the editor, to be changed in place. BREAKIN also uses the editor to permit you to place calls to the Break Package at particular points inside functions (see 21.3).

There are also several ways of getting to LISP from inside the editor. The simplest is to use the command E followed by some expression, which will simply be passed to EVAL. Other editor functions call for evaluation of specific parameters before proceeding (see 22.13).

22.1.2 Safety featurafety features

The editor has two kinds of checkpoint mechanisms. The first provides a way of getting back to some previous place in the structure. The second mechanism, the UNDO command, provides a way of reversing the effect of any change made to the structure and thereby encourages experimentation with new commands. The UNDO facility can even be used between one editing session and the next, permitting tentative decisions during debugging.

The editor is also very tolerant of command errors, such as referring to the third element of a two-element list. Editor errors do not cause breaks or even go through the ERROR machinery but are direct calls to ERR indicating that a command is in some way faulty. What happens next depends on the context in which the command was being executed. For example, there are conditional commands which branch on errors. In most situations, though, an error will cause the editor to type the faulty command followed by a ? and wait for more input. A command error cannot change the structure being edited. To avoid further confusion, when an error occurs, all commands on the line beyond the one which caused the error (and all commands that may have been typed ahead while the editor was computing) are forgotten.

22.1.3 Basics

The editor starts out with some S-expression to work on, whether passed directly to it (EDITE) or indirectly through a property list. At any time, its attention is focused on some particular subexpression, called the current expression. The editor keeps a list containing the current expression, the expression in which it is embedded, the expression in which that is embedded, and so on, all the way to the top-level expression. This list is called the edit chain, and it is stored on the global variable L.

The graph notation (see Chapter 2) is extended here slightly: nodes below a certain depth may appear as &, and stars (*) in the graph indicate elements in the edit chain. The lowest, rightmost star indicates the current expression. If the current expression is an atom, it will be marked with the symbols "*=".

```
*(EDITE '(A B (C D) (E (F]      ~Call the editor directly
EDIT:

#~ The # is the editor's prompt character.
#~ Print commands: P for PRINT (to depth of 2)
#~                 PP for PRETTYPRINT
#~                 ? for PRINT to depth 100

#P
(A B (C D) (E &))

#?
(A B (C D) (E (F)))
```

The graph for that is:

```
*--.--.-------.---------
|  |  |       |
A  B  .--.--  .--.----
      |  |    |  |
      C  D    E  .--
                 |
                 F
```

```
#~ Moving commands: 1 means go to first element (CAR)
#~                  2 means go to second element (CADR), etc.
#~                  0 means go back in the edit chain by one li
#~                  ^ means go all the way back to the top
#~ Simple commands may be combined on one line

#2 P
B
```

```
*--.----.-------.---------
|  |    |       |
A  *=B  .--.--  .--.----
        |  |    |  |
        C  D    E  .--
                   |
                   F
```

```
#0 P
(A B (C D) (E &))

*--.--.-------.---------
|  |  |       |
A  B  .--.--  .--.----
      |  |    |  |
      C  D    E  .--
                 |
                 F


#3 P
(C D)

*--.--.-------.---------
|  |  |       |
A  B  *--.--  .--.----
      |  |    |  |
      C  D    E  .--
                 |
                 F


#2 P
D

*--.--.---------.---------
|  |  |         |
A  B  *--.----  .--.----
      |  |      |  |
      C  *=D    E  .--
                   |
                   F


#^ P
(A B (C D) (E &))

*--.--.-------.---------
|  |  |       |
A  B  .--.--  .--.----
      |  |    |  |
      C  D    E  .--
                 |
                 F
```

```
#4 2 1 P
F

*--.--.-------.-----------
|  |  |       |
A  B  .--.--  *--.------
      |  |    |  |
      C  D    E  *----
                 |
                 *=F


#0 0 P
(E (F))

*--.--.-------.---------
|  |  |       |
A  B  .--.--  *--.----
      |  |    |  |
      C  D    E  .--
                 |
                 F


#^ P
(A B (C D) (E &))

*--.--.-------.---------
|  |  |       |
A  B  .--.--  .--.----
      |  |    |  |
      C  D    E  .--
                 |
                 F


#~ Some basic searching: F x means find x
#F (C D)

#P
(C D)

*--.--.-------.---------
|  |  |       |
A  B  *--.--  .--.----
      |  |    |  |
      C  D    E  .--
                 |
                 F


#^ P
(A B (C D) (E &))
```

```
#~ Notice that if you're searching for an atom and that
#~ atom is the CAR of some node, then F will leave you one node
#~ above it.

#F C

#P
(C D)

*--.--.-------.---------
¦  ¦  ¦       ¦
A  B  *--.--  .--.----
      ¦  ¦    ¦  ¦
      C  D    E  .--
                 ¦
                 F


#~ F starts the search in the current expression, but if it doesn't
#~ find what it's looking for, it'll go through the rest of the tree
#~ in PRINT-order.

#F E

#P
(E (F))

*--.--.-------.---------
¦  ¦  ¦       ¦
A  B  .--.--  *--.----
      ¦  ¦    ¦  ¦
      C  D    E  .--
                 ¦
                 F


#~ If it fails to find it at all, it says so. No harm done: the
#~ edit chain is the same.

#F XXX
XXX  ?

*--.--.-------.---------
¦  ¦  ¦       ¦
A  B  .--.--  *--.----
      ¦  ¦    ¦  ¦
      C  D    E  .--
                 ¦
                 F
```

```
#^ P
(A B (C D) (E &))

*--.--.-------.---------
|  |  |       |
A  B  .--.--  .--.----
      |  |    |  |
      C  D    E  .--
                 |
                 F
```

```
#~ Some commands combine moving and searching to specify the
#~ location where the editing is to take place.

#~ Some brief examples of INSERT, DELETE, REPLACE, and MOVE.
#~ INSERT, REPLACE, and MOVE cannot be combined with other
#~ commands unless they are enclosed in parentheses. DELETE
#~ by itself means "delete the current expression." When enclosed
#~ in parentheses, it takes a "location specification" as a parameter.


#INSERT X AFTER B

#P
(A B X (C D) (E &))

*--.--.--.-------.---------
|  |  |  |       |
A  B  X  .--.--  .--.----
         |  |    |  |
         C  D    E  .--
                    |
                    F


#~ The inserted material is spliced in.
#INSERT X1 X2 X3 AFTER X

#P
(A B X X1 X2 X3 (C D) (E &))

*--.--.--.---.---.---.-------.---------
|  |  |  |   |   |   |       |
A  B  X  X1  X2  X3  .--.--  .--.----
                     |  |    |  |
                     C  D    E  .--
                                |
                                F


#~ THRU can be used to specify a part of a list.

#(DELETE (X1 THRU X3))

#P
(A B X (C D) (E &))

*--.--.--.-------.---------
|  |  |  |       |
A  B  X  .--.--  .--.----
         |  |    |  |
         C  D    E  .--
                    |
                    F
```

```
#~ Any change can be reversed with UNDO.

#UNDO
DELETE Undone

#P
(A B X X1 X2 X3 (C D) (E &))

*--.--.--.---.---.---.-------.---------
|  |  |  |   |   |   |       |
A  B  X  X1  X2  X3  .--.--  .--.----
                     |  |    |  |
                     C  D    E  .--
                                |
                                F


#REPLACE X WITH Y

#P
(A B Y X1 X2 X3 (C D) (E &))

*--.--.--.---.---.---.-------.---------
|  |  |  |   |   |   |       |
A  B  Y  X1  X2  X3  .--.--  .--.----
                     |  |    |  |
                     C  D    E  .--
                                |
                                F


#MOVE X2 TO BEFORE Y

#P
(A B X2 Y X1 X3 (C D) (E &))

*--.--.---.--.---.---.-------.---------
|  |  |   |  |   |   |       |
A  B  X2  Y  X1  X3  .--.--  .--.----
                     |  |    |  |
                     C  D    E  .--
                                |
                                F
```

```
#MOVE X1 TO AFTER E

#P
(A B X2 Y X3 (C D) (E &) X1)

*--.--.---.--.---.-------.----------.---
|  |  |   |  |   |       |          |
A  B  X2  Y  X3  .--.--  .--.----   X1
                 |  |    |  |
                 C  D    E  .--
                            |
                            F


#UNDO
MOVE Undone

#MOVE X1 TO N C  ~ Here, N means NCONC

#P
(A B X2 Y X3 (C D X1) (E &))

*--.--.---.--.---.-----------.---------
|  |  |   |  |   |           |
A  B  X2  Y  X3  .--.--.---  .--.----
                 |  |  |     |  |
                 C  D  X1    E  .--
                                |
                                F


#~ The OK command brings us back to LISP.

#OK
(A B X2 Y X3 (C D X1) (E (F)))

*
```

22.2 Syntax of editor commands

The editor uses # as its prompt character, and it uses LINEREAD for all its input.

22.2.1 Commands vs. functions

Editor commands are atoms. They take no parameters and can be combined on one line. Examples are: PP (prettyprint), 3 (move to the CADDR), DELETE (remove the current expression.

Calls to editor functions are parenthesized lists where the CAR of the list specifies the name of the function. Be warned that some names are used for both editor commands and editor functions, and the actions are not always related. For example, the command 3 means "move to the CADDR," but the function call (3) means "delete the CADDR." Editor functions may also be combined on a single line. However, if a call to an editor function is the only thing on a command line and the name of that function is not also the name of an editor command, the parentheses may be omitted.

F, BF, and E are exceptions. Unparenthesized, they denote editor commands but they take a single parameter. Parenthesized, they denote editor functions.

Examples:

P 2	Print the current expression, then move to the CADR (second element).
(P 2)	Print the CADR of the current expression.
2 P	Move to the CADR, then print it.
(2 P)	Replace the CADR of the current expression with the atom P.
(MOVE X TO 1 1)	Find X, and move it to the CAR of the CAR of the current expression.
MOVE X TO 1 1	Exactly the same as the previous command
(MOVE X TO 1) 1	Find X, move it to the CAR, and move to its CAR.
F X 2	Find X, and move to its CADR.
F (X 2)	Find the list (X 2).
(F X 2)	Find the second occurrence of X.

22.2.2 Literals versus pointers

Some editor functions treat their parameters as literals. (A 2), for example, means insert the number 2 after the current expressions.

Other functions treat their parameters as editor commands that point to the actual parameters. (DELETE 2), for example, means delete the second element of the current expression. These parameters are called location specifications, described in 22.6. Any part of a location specification that isn't a known editor command is searched for. (DELETE FOO) means search for FOO and delete the current expression there; it is identical to (DELETE (F FOO)). If you want to delete the next occurence of the atom P, you must say (DELETE (F P)), since the P in (DELETE P) would treat P as the edit command for printing.

22.2.3 Keywords and parameters

Some functions use keywords, such as "TO" and "AFTER" in MOVE X TO AFTER Y. The first occurence of the keywords act as parameter boundaries. In this example, X and Y are the parameters. In MOVE X Y Z TO AFTER A B C, the lists (X Y Z) and (A B C) are the parameters.

If you want to use a keyword as a literal parameter in a position where it would normally be interpreted as a keyword, you can embed it in an F command (e.g., MOVE (F TO) TO AFTER 3) if it's part of a location specification, or you can use a sequence of "basic" command that don't use keywords.

22.2.4 Exceptions

When the command scanner encounters a command that is neither built-in nor defined as a macro, it calls an internal function, EDITDEFAULT, to determine what action to take. If the command is part of a location specification, EDITDEFAULT treats the command as though it had been preceded by an F.

If the command is atomic and typed in directly, the procedure followed is as given below.

1. The names of editor functions are kept on the list EDITCOMSL (see footnote). If the command is one of them and there is additional input on the same teletype line, then the entire line is treated as a call to that editor function. Thus, REPLACE X WITH

Y is treated as (REPLACE X WITH Y). If the command is on the list EDITCOMSL but there is no additional input on the teletype line, an error is generated. Example:

```
#MOVE

MOVE ?
#
```

2. The commmands __P, _P, UPP, NXP, BKP, !NXP, UNDOP, and REDOP are interpreted as abbreviations for two commands, i.e., __ P, _ P, UP P, NX P, etc.

3. Otherwise, EDITDEFAULT generates an error.

EDITCOMSL = '(: A AFTER B BEFORE BELOW BI BIND BO CHANGE COMS COMSQ EMBED EXTRACT F= FOR FS I IF INSERT LC LCL LI LO LP LPQ M MAKEFN MBD MOVE MV N NTH ORF ORR R REPLACE RI RO S SECOND SURROUND SW THIRD THRU TO XTR).

22.3 Moving around inside an expression

At any given moment, the editor's attention is centered on some substructure of the expression being edited. This substructure is called <u>the current expression</u>, and it is what you see when you give the editor a print command (P, PP, or ?). Initially, the current expression is the top-level one, i.e., the entire expression being edited. Thus:

```
#PP
(LAMBDA (S) (COND [(ATOM S) 0] [T (ADD1 (LR (CDR S)))]))

*-------.----.------------
¦       ¦    ¦
LAMBDA  .--  .-----.--.--
        ¦    ¦     ¦  ¦
        S    COND  &  &
```

22.3.1 Moving down

<u>1</u>
<u>2</u>
...
<u>-1</u>
<u>-2</u>
...

A positive integer n is interpreted by the editor as a command to descend into the nth element from the beginning of the current expression. A negative integer -n is a command to descend into the nth element from the end of the current expression.

```
#3 P
(COND (& 0) (T &))

*-------.----.----------------------
¦       ¦    ¦
LAMBDA  .--  *-----.-------.-------
        ¦    ¦     ¦       ¦
        S    COND  .--.--  .--.--
                   ¦  ¦    ¦  ¦
                   &  0    T  &
```



```
#-1 P
(T (ADD1 &))

*-------.----.------------------------------
|       |    |
LAMBDA  .--  *-----.-------.-------------
        |    |     |       |
        S    COND  .--.--  *--.----------
                   |  |    |  |
                   &  0    T  .-----.--
                              |     |
                              ADD1  &
```

The specified element becomes the <u>new</u> current expression and it is added to the edit chain (indicated by stars in the graph). These commands generate an error if the specified element is out of range.

The node above the new expression is stored in LASTAIL and is used by the UP command.

22.3.2 Moving back up

22.3.2.1 Back to the top: ^ -

<u>^</u>

The command ^ (up-arrow) ascends through the entire chain of expressions to the top-level expression, which then becomes the current expression. In other words, ^ removes all links except the first one.

```
#^ P
(LAMBDA (S) (COND & &))

*-------.----.------------
|       |    |
LAMBDA  .--  .-----.--.--
        |    |     |  |
        S    COND  &  &
```

22.3.2.2 Back one link: 0 -

<u>0</u>

The command 0 is used to go back up the edit chain by one link. It removes the last link of the chain, thereby making the <u>previous</u> link be the current expression. The 0 command generates an error if the current expression is the top-level expression.

```
#-1 -1 -1 P
(ADD1 (LR &))

*-------.----.------------------------------------
|       |    |
LAMBDA  .--  *-----.-------.----------------------
        |    |     |       |
        S    COND  .--.--  *--.-------------------
                   |  |    |  |
                   &  0    T  *-----.--------
                              |     |
                              ADD1  .---.--
                                    |   |
                                    LR  &
```

```
#0 P
(T (ADD1 &))

*-------.----.----------------------------------
|       |    |
LAMBDA  .--  *-----.-------.----------------
        |    |     |       |
        S    COND  .--.--  *--.-----------
                   |  |    |  |
                   &  0    T  .-----.--
                              |     |
                              ADD1  &
```

22.3.2.3 Ascending the CAR: UP -

<u>UP</u>

UP makes the old current expression be the first element of the new current expression. If the current expression happens to be the first element in the next higher expression, then UP is exactly the same as 0. Otherwise, UP modifies the edit chain so that the new current expression is a (proper) tail of the next higher expression.

Perhaps the easiest way to understand UP is to think of it as ascending a CAR-link. If the current expression isn't a CAR, UP does nothing.

```
#UP P
... (T &))

*-------.----.---------------------
|       |    |
LAMBDA  .--  *-----.-------*-------
        |    |     |       |
        S    COND  .--.--  .--.--
                   |  |    |  |
                   &  0    T  &
```

```
#UP P
... (T &))

*-------.----.---------------------
|       |    |
LAMBDA  .--  *-----.-------*-------
        |    |     |       |
        S    COND  .--.--  .--.--
                   |  |    |  |
                   &  0    T  &
```

The ... is used by the editor to indicate that the current expression is a tail of the next higher expression as opposed to being an element (member) of the next higher expression.

UP gives the editor a nearby *pou sto*, a place to stand, from which it can make changes in the current expression that would be otherwise impossible, such as inserting elements in front of the current expression.

For more details on UP, see 22.15.3.

!0

The command 0 usually corresponds to going back to the next higher left parenthesis, but not if the previous line is a CDR (tail). For example,

```
#0 2 P
((ATOM S) 0)

*-------.----.---------------------------------
|       |    |
LAMBDA  .--  *-----.-------------.--------
        |    |     |             |
        S    COND  *---------.--  .--.--
                   |         |    |  |
                   .-----.--  0    T  &
                   |     |
                   ATOM  S


#UP P
... (& 0) (T &))

*-------.----.-----------------------
|       |    |
LAMBDA  .--  *-----*-------.-------
        |    |     |       |
        S    COND  .--.--  .--.--
                   |  |    |  |
                   &  0    T  &


#1 P
((ATOM S) 0)

*-------.----.---------------------------------
|       |    |
LAMBDA  .--  *-----*--------------.--------
        |    |     |              |
        S    COND  *---------.--  .--.--
                   |         |    |  |
                   .-----.--  0    T  &
                   |     |
                   ATOM  S


#0 P
... (& 0) (T &))

*-------.----.-----------------------
|       |    |
LAMBDA  .--  *-----*-------.-------
        |    |     |       |
        S    COND  .--.--  .--.--
                   |  |    |  |
                   &  0    T  &
```

If you want to go back to the next higher level (left parenthesis), regardless of any intervening tails, use the command !0 ("bang-zero.") !0 does repeated 0's until it reaches a point where the current expression is not a tail of the next higher expression. In graph terms, !0 goes all the way to the left.

```
#1 P
((ATOM S) 0)

*-------.----.-------------------------------
|       |    |
LAMBDA  .--  *-----*---------------.-------
        |    |     |               |
        S    COND  *----------.--  .--.--
                   |          |    |  |
                   .-----.--  0    T  &
                   |     |
                   ATOM  S
```

```
#!0 P
(COND (& 0) (T &))

*-------.----.------------------------
|       |    |
LAMBDA  .--  *-----.-------.--------
        |    |     |       |
        S    COND  .--.--  .--.--
                   |  |    |  |
                   &  0    T  &
```

22.3.3 Moving over

22.3.3.1 Next on this level: NX -

NX

Suppose we are currently looking at the (ATOM S) in our expression. We could get to the 0 in the COND typing 0 and then 2 or -1, or we can use the command NX, which does both operations.

```
#F ATOM P
(ATOM S)

*-------.----.-------------------------------
|       |    |
LAMBDA  .--  *-----.---------------.-------
        |    |     |               |
        S    COND  *----------.--  .--.--
                   |          |    |  |
                   *-----.--  0    T  &
                   |     |
                   ATOM  S

#NX P
0

*-------.----.----------------------------------
|       |    |
LAMBDA  .--  *-----.-----------------.-------
        |    |     |                 |
        S    COND  *----------.----  .--.--
                   |          |      |  |
                   .-----.--  *=0    T  &
                   |     |
                   ATOM  S

#NX
NX  ?
```

NX effectively does an UP followed by a 2 (up, over, and down), thereby making the current expression be the next expression. NX generates an error if the current expression is the last one in a list. (!NX, described below, will handle this case.)

(NX n)

This is equivalent to n NX commands, except that if an error occurs, the edit chain is not changed.

22.3.3.2 Previous on this level: BK -

BK

BK is like NX, except makes the expression immediately before the current expression become current (up, back over, and down). BK generates an error if the current expression is the first expression in a list.

```
#BK P
(ATOM S)

*--------.---.--------------------------------
|        |   |
LAMBDA   .-- *------.---------------.-------
         |   |      |               |
         S   COND   *----------.--  .--.--
                    |          |    |  |
                    *-----.--  O    T  &
                    |     |
                    ATOM  S

#BK
BK  ?
```

(BK n)

This is equivalent to n BK commands, except if an error occurs, the edit chain is not changed.

(NX -n) is equivalent to (BK n), and vice versa.

Both NX and BK operate by performing a !0 followed by an appropriate number, so that there won't be an extra tail above the new current expression, as there would be if NX operated by performing an UP followed by a 2.

22.3.3.3 Next on any level: !NX -

!NX

!NX makes the current expression be the next expression at a higher level: it goes through any number of right parentheses to get to the next expression.

```
#!NX P
(T (ADD1 &))

*-------.----.----------------------------------
|       |    |
LAMBDA  .--  *------.-------.---------------
        |    |      |       |
        S    COND   .--.--  *--.-----------
                    |  |    |  |
                    &  0    T  .-----.--
                               |     |
                               ADD1  &
```

!NX operates by going back up the edit chain (0) until it reaches a stage where the current expression is not the last expression (nor a tail) of the next higher expression, and then it does a NX. Thus !NX always goes through at least one unmatched right parenthesis, and the new current expression is always on a different level. !NX and NX always produce different results.

22.3.4 Jumping

Whenever an editor command or function causes a jump larger than a single ascent or descent, the edit chain is saved in UNFIND, and the edit command < restores that chain. UNFIND is reset by ^, _, __, !NX, < itself, <P, and all the commands that involve a search: F, BF, LC, ::, BELOW, etc.

Exception

UNFIND is not reset when the current edit chain is the top level expression, since you can always return there by using the ^ command.

The edit chain is also saved, on a different list, whenever a print command is given. The edit command <P restores the chain from that list.

Finally, you may make an explicit checkpoint at any time with the MARK command. The edit chain is saved in MARKLIST and is restored with the commands _ and __.

< or \

< restores the current expression to the expression before the last "big jump." For example, if you typed F COND, and then F CAR, < would take you back to the COND. Another < would take you back to the CAR.

<P or \P

<P restores the edit chain to its state as of the last print command, either by P, ?, or PP. If the edit chain has not been changed since the last print, <P restores it to its state as of the printing before that one; i.e., two chains are always saved.

Thus if you type P followed by 3 2 1 P, <P will take you back to the first P, as 0 0 0 would. Another <P would then take you back to the second P. You can use <P to flip back and forth between two current expressions.

MARK

MARK adds the current edit chain to the front of the list MARKLIST.

_

_ (left-arrow) makes the new edit chain be (CAR MARKLIST). It generates an error if MARKLIST is NIL, i.e., if no MARKS have been performed, or if all the marks have been erased.

__

__ (2 left-arrows) is similar to _ but it also erases the MARK; i.e., it performs (SETQ MARKLST (CDR MARKLST)).

If you did not mark a particular expression, you may still be able to return there by using < or <P.

22.4 Commands that print

P

P prints the current expression with PRINTLEV, using the value of the global variable EDITPLEV for the depth. EDITPLEV is initially 2. P will print comments as *COMMENT* unless the global variable COMMENTFLG is T.

P;

This is the same as P, but with COMMENTFLG = T.

PP

PP prettyprints the current expression.

PP;

PP; prettyprints the current expression, but with COMMENTFLG = T.

(P m)

This prints mth element of current expression.

(P 0)

This is the same as P.

(P m n)

This prints mth element of current expression to a depth of n.

(P 0 n)

This prints current expression to a depth of n.

P1
P2 etc.

P1 is the same as (P 0 1), P2 is the same as (P 0 2), etc.

?

Same as (P 0 100)

Both (P m) and (P m n) use the general NTH command to obtain the corresponding element, so that m does not have to be a number. E.g., (P COND 3) will work.

All printing functions print to the teletype, regardless of the primary output file. No printing function ever changes the edit chain. All record the current edit chain for use by <P (see 22.3.4).

22.5 Search commands

The forward- and backward-search functions can match a variety of patterns in addition to simple, explicit S-expressions. The F command starts searching in the current expression; if no match is found there, F will look through the entire remaining structure *in the order in which the expression is printed*. The B command does the same, but in reverse order. The pattern matcher, EDIT4E, is also available as a separate function.

All of the commands below set LASTAIL for use by UP (see 22.3.2.3), set UNFIND for use by < (see 22.3.4), and do not change the edit chain or perform any CONSes if they are unsuccessful or aborted.

22.5.1 Forward search

22.5.1.1 F -

F pattern

F starts a search for the next occurrence of pattern. Note that when F and BF are used as commands (i.e., unparenthesized), they use the next single item of input as the pattern. If the pattern is omitted, the previous F or BF pattern is used.

F first tests whether the pattern is an element of the current expression by doing

```
(MEMQ pattern current-expression)
```

If that fails, F proceeds with a full recursive search through the current expression. Thus if the current expression is

```
(PROG NIL LP (COND [... (GO LP1)]) ... LP1 ...)
```

then F LP1 will find the PROG label LP1, not the LP1 inside the GO expression, even though the latter appears first (in print order) in the current expression.

If the target expression is not found in the current expression, then F automatically ascends and searches those portions of the higher expressions that would appear after the current expression if the expression were PRINTed.

If the search is successful, the new current expression will be the <u>structure</u> where the expression was found. If the search is for an atom, e.g., F X, the current expression will be the structure containing the atom X. If the search is for a list, e.g., F (NULL X), the current expression will be the list itself. The chain will be the same as one resulting from the appropriate sequence of ascent and descent commands. (See also 22.5.4.)

If the search is not successful, an error occurs, and neither the current expression nor the chain is changed.

F is never a no-op. If it is successful, then the current expression after the search will never be the same as the current expression before the search. Thus F X repeated without intervening commands that change the edit chain can be used to find successive instances of X.

22.5.1.2 Variations on F -

<u>FP</u> pattern

This is the same as "F pattern P".

<u>(F pattern N)</u>

This is the same as F, except the MEMQ check is not performed.

<u>(F pattern T)</u>

This is similar to F, except that it may succeed without changing edit chain, and it does not perform the MEMQ check.

Thus if the current expression is (COND ...), F COND will look for the next COND, but (F COND T) will "stay here."

(F pattern n)

This finds the nth place that pattern matches. Equivalent to (F pattern T) followed by (F pattern N) repeated n-1 times. Each time the pattern successfully matches, n is decremented by 1, and the search continues, until n reaches 0. Note that the pattern does not have to match with n identical expressions; it just has to match n times. Thus if the current expression is (FOO1 FOO2 FOO3), then (F FOO@ 3) will find FOO3. (See 22.5.4.)

If the pattern does not match successfully n times, an error is generated and the edit chain is unchanged (even if the pattern matched n-1 times).

(F pattern) or
(F pattern NIL)

These match only elements at the top level of the current expression. The search will not descend into the current expression, nor will it go outside of the current expression. It may succeed without changing the edit chain.

For example, if the current expression is

(PROG NIL (SETQ X (COND A B)) (COND C) ...)

then F (COND --) will find (COND A B), whereas (F (COND --)) will find (COND C).

(FS pattern[1] ... pattern[n])

Equivalent to "F pattern[1] F pattern[2] ... F pattern[n]", so that if F pattern[m] fails, the edit chain is left at place where pattern[m-1] matched.

(F= expression x)

Equivalent to (F (== . expression) x). This searches for a structure EQ to the expression. (See 22.5.4.)

(ORF pattern[1] ... pattern[n])

Equivalent to
(F (*ANY* pattern[1] ... pattern[n]) N). This searches for an expression that is matched by either pattern[1] or pattern[2] or ... or pattern[n].

22.5.2 Backward search

22.5.2.1 BF -

BF pattern

BF (backwards find) searches in reverse print order, beginning with expression immediately before the current expression, unless the current expression is the top-level expression, in which case BF searches the entire expression, in reverse order.

If pattern is omitted, the previous F or BF pattern is used.

BF uses the same pattern-matching routine as F, but the searching begins at the end of each list, and descends into each element before attempting to match that element. If unsuccessful, the search continues with the next previous element, etc., until the front of the list is reached, at which point BF ascends and backs up, etc.

For example, if the current expression is

```
(PROG NIL (SETQ X (SETQ Y (LIST Z)))
          (COND [(SETQ W ...) ...]) ...)
```

then F LIST followed by BF SETQ will leave the current expression as (SETQ Y (LIST Z)), as will F COND followed by BF SETQ.

22.5.2.2 Variations on BF -

BFP pattern

Same as BF pattern, followed by a P.

(BF pattern T)

The search always includes current expression, i.e., starts at end of current expression and works backward, then ascends and backs up, etc.

Thus in the previous example, where F COND followed by BF SETQ found (SETQ Y (LIST Z)), F COND followed by (BF SETQ T) would find the (SETQ W ...) expression.

(BF pattern) or
(BF pattern NIL)

Same as BF pattern.

22.5.3 Where you are after a search

After searching successfully for an atom, F does an UP. This feature makes the basic editing commands (A, B, and :) and the higher-level editing commands (INSERT, CHANGE, REPLACE, and DELETE) form-oriented. For example, if you type F SETQ, and then DELETE, or simply (DELETE SETQ), you will delete the entire SETQ expression, whereas (DELETE X) if X is a variable, deletes just the variable X. In both cases, the operation is performed on the corresponding form and in both cases is probably what you intended.

Similarly, if you type (INSERT (RETURN Y) BEFORE SETQ), you mean before the SETQ expression, not before the atom SETQ.* A consequence of this procedure is that a pattern of the form (SETQ Y --) can be viewed as simply an elaboration and further refinement of the pattern SETQ. Thus (INSERT (RETURN Y) BEFORE SETQ) and (INSERT (RETURN Y) BEFORE (SETQ Y --)) perform the same operation, assuming the next SETQ is of the form (SETQ Y --)). In fact, this is one of the motivations behind making the current expression after F SETQ, and F (SETQ Y --) be the same.

Occasionally, however, you may have a data structure in which no special significance or meaning is attached to the position of an atom in a list, as LISP attaches to atoms that appear as CAR of a list, versus those appearing elsewhere in a list. In general, you may not even know whether a particular atom is at the head of a list or not. Thus, when you write (INSERT expression AFTER FOO), you may mean after the atom FOO, whether or not it is CAR of a list. By setting the variable UPFINDFLG to NIL (initially, and usually, set to T), you can suppress the implicit UP that follows searches for atoms, and thus achieve the desired effect. With UPFINDFLG = NIL, the current expression after F FOO, for example, will be the atom FOO. In this case, the A, B, and : operations will operate with respect to the atom FOO. If you want the operation to refer to the list which FOO heads, simply use instead the pattern (FOO --).

22.5.4 Definition of pattern matching

The search expression given to F or BF need not be a literal S-expression. Instead, it can be a pattern, that is, an expression with symbols that have particular meaning to the pattern matcher.

<u>&</u>
<u>--</u> (2 minus-signs)

The symbol & can be used anywhere within the pattern to match any <u>single</u> element of a list, and -- can be used to match with any <u>segment</u> of a list. Thus, F (NULL &) can be used to find (NULL X), and F (CDR --) or F (CDR & &), but not F (CDR &), to find (CDR X Y).

& and -- can be nested arbitrarily deeply in the pattern. For example, if there are many places where the variable X is set, F SETQ may not find the desired expression, nor may F (SETQ X &). It may be necessary to use F (SETQ X (LIST --)). However, the usual technique in such a case is to pick out a unique atom which occurs prior to the desired expression and perform two F commands. This homing-in process seems to be more convenient than

----

* There is some ambiguity in (INSERT expr AFTER functionname), since you might want to make expr be the function's first argument. Similarly, the you cannot write (REPLACE SETQQ WITH SETQ) to change the name of the function. In these cases, you must write (INSERT expr AFTER functionname 1), and (REPLACE SETQQ 1 WITH SETQ).

ultra-precise specification of the pattern.

<u>@</u>

Any atom ending in @ (at-sign) in a pattern will match with the first atom or string that contains the same initial characters. For example, F VER@ will find VERYLONGATOM. @ can also be nested inside of the pattern, e.g., F (SETQ VER@ (CONS --)).

If the search is successful, the editor will print = followed by the atom which matched with the @-atom.

```
#F (SETQ VER@ &)
=VERYLONGATOM
#
```

All of the editor commands that search use the same pattern-matching routine, EDIT4E. (This routine is available to the user directly, and is described in 22.17.) The specifications of the match are as follows:

1. A pattern PAT matches with X if PAT is EQ to X (or EQSTR if strings).

2. PAT matches with X if PAT is the atom &.

3. PAT matches with X if PAT is a number and EQUAL to X.

4. If (CAR PAT) is the atom *ANY* and (CDR PAT) is a list of patterns, then PAT matches X if and only if one of the patterns in (CDR PAT) matches X.

5. If PAT is a literal atom or string and (NTHCHAR PAT -1) is the atom @, then PAT will match any literal atom or string which has the same initial characters as PAT; e.g. VER@ matches VERYLONGATOM as well as "VERYLONGSTRING".

6. If (CAR PAT) is the atom --, then PAT will match X if:

   A. (CDR pat) = NIL, i.e., PAT = (--). For example, (A --) matches (A), (A B C), and (A . B).

      In other words, -- can match any tail of a list.

B. (CDR PAT) matches with some tail of X. For example, (A -- (&)) will match (A B C (D)), but not (A B C D) or (A B C (D) E). However, note that (A -- (&) --) will match (A B C (D) E).

In other words, -- will match any interior segment of a list.

7. If (CAR PAT) is the atom ==, then PAT will match X if and only if (CDR PAT) is EQ to X. (This pattern is for use by programs that call the editor as a subroutine, since any non-atomic expression in a command typed in by the user obviously cannot be EQ to existing structure.)

8. Otherwise if X is a list, PAT will match X if (CAR PAT) matches (CAR X), and (CDR PAT) matches (CDR X).

When searching, the pattern-matching routine is called only to match with <u>elements</u> (members) of the structure, unless the pattern begins with :::, in which case CDR of the pattern is matched against <u>tails</u> of the structure. In this case, the tail does not have to be a proper tail; (::: A --) will match with the element (A B C) as well as with CDR of (X A B C), since (A B C) is a tail of (A B C). Thus if the current expression is (A B C (B C)),

```
#F (B --)
#P
(B C)
#0 F (::: B --)
#P
... B C (B C))
#F (::: B --)
#P
(B C)
#
```

22.5.5 The search algorithm

Searching begins with the current expression and proceeds in print order. Searching usually means finding the next instance of this pattern, and consequently a match is not attempted that would leave the edit chain unchanged, although there is a variation of the F command that can succeed and leave the current expression unchanged. At each step, the pattern is matched against the next element in the expression currently being searched, unless the pattern begins with :::, in which case it is matched against the corresponding tail of the expression. If the pattern is EQ to a tail of the expression, that also defines a successful match, so that a search for FOO will find the FOO in (FIE . FOO). The only exception to this occurs when PATTERN is NIL, e.g., F NIL. In this case, the pattern will not match a null tail, since most lists end in NIL, but it will match a NIL element.

If the match is not successful, the search operation is recursive first in the CAR direction and then in the CDR direction. If the element under examination is a list, the search descends into that list before attempting to match other elements (or tails) at the same level. (There is also a variation of the F command that attempts matches only at the top level of the current expression, neither descending into elements nor ascending to higher expressions.)

However, at no point is the total recursive depth of the search (sum of number of CARs and CDRs descended into) allowed to exceed the value of the variable MAXLEVEL. At that point, the search of that element or tail is abandoned, exactly as though the element or tail had been completely searched without finding a match, and the search continues with the next element or tail for which the recursive depth is below MAXLEVEL. This feature is designed to enable you to search circular list structures (by making MAXLEVEL small), as well as protecting you from accidentally encountering a circular list structure in the course of normal editing. MAXLEVEL is initially set to 300. If a successful match is not found in the current expression, the search automatically ascends to the next higher expression, and continues searching there, starting with the next expression after the expression it just finished searching. If there is still no match, it ascends again, etc. This process continues until the entire edit chain has been searched, at which point the search fails, generating an error. If the search fails, the edit chain is not changed (nor are any CONSes performed.)

If the search is successful, i.e., if an expression is found that matches the pattern, the edit chain is set to the value it would have had had the user reached that expression via a sequence of integer commands.

If the matching expression is a list, it will become the final link in the edit chain, the new current expression. If the matching expression is an atom, the current expression will be the tail beginning with that atom*;

----

* Exception: in situations where match is with Y in (X . Y), where Y is atomic and not NIL, the current expression will be (X . Y).

i.e., that atom will be the first element in the new current expression. In other words, the search effectively does an UP.

22.6 Location specifications

22.6.1 Specifying a single structure

The explicit move-commands can be combined with the search-commands to produce a more general method of specifying a position, called a location specification. A location specification is a list of edit commands that are executed in the normal fashion with two exceptions:

1. All commands not recognized by the editor are interpreted as though they had been preceded by F. Normally such commands would cause errors. For example, the location specification (COND 2 3) specifies the 3rd element in the first clause of the next COND. (You could always write (F COND 2 3) for (COND 2 3) if you were not sure whether or not COND was the name of an atomic command.)

2. If an error occurs while evaluating one of the commands in the location specification, and the edit chain had been changed during the course of executing the location specification, the location operation will continue. In other words, the location operation keeps going unless it reaches a state where it detects that it is looping, at which point it gives up. Thus, if (COND 2 3) is being located, and the first clause of the next COND contained only two elements, the execution of the command 3 would cause an error. But the search would then continue by looking for the next COND. However, if a point were reached where there were no more CONDs, then the first command, COND, would cause the error; the edit chain would not have been changed, and so the entire location operation would fail, and cause an error.

NOTE

Throughout this chapter, the meta-symbol $ is used to denote a location specification. Thus $ is a list of commands interpreted as described above. $ can also be atomic, in which case it is interpreted as (LIST $).

If $ is NIL (empty), the corresponding operation is performed here (on the current edit chain); e.g., (REPLACE WITH (CAR X)) is equivalent to (: (CAR X)). For added readability, HERE is also permitted: (INSERT (PRINT X) BEFORE HERE) will insert (PRINT X) before the current expression (but not change the edit chain).

Note also that $ does not have to specify a location within the current expression. It is perfectly legal to ascend to INSERT, REPLACE, or DELETE. For example (INSERT (RETURN)

AFTER ^ PROG -1) will go to the top, find the first PROG, and insert a (RETURN) at its end, and not change the current edit chain.

(LC . $)

LC is simply the explicit call to the location operation; e.g., (LC COND 2 3) will perform the search described above.

(LCL . $)

LCL is the same as LC except that the search is confined to current expression. (The edit chain L is re-bound during the search so it looks as if the editor were called on just the current expression.) For example, to find a COND containing a RETURN, one might use the location specification (COND (LCL RETURN) <) where the < would reverse the effects of the LCL command, and make the final current expression be the COND.

(SECOND . $)

This is the same as (LC . $) followed by another (LC . $) except that if the first succeeds and second fails, no change is made to the edit chain.

(THIRD . $)

This is similar to SECOND.

<u>(_ pattern)</u>

The function _ (left-arrow) goes back up the edit chain (via $\overline{0}$) looking for a link in the chain that matches pattern. If pattern is atomic, it is matched with the first element of each link, otherwise with the entire link.

If pattern is of the form (IF expression), then the expression is evaluated at each link, and if its value is NIL, or the evaluation causes an error, the ascent continues.

For example:

```
#PP
(PROG NIL
      (COND [(NULL (SETQ L (CDR L)))
             (COND [FLG (RETURN L)])]
            [(NULL (CDR (MEMB (CAR L) (CADR L))))
             (GO LP)]))
#F CADR
#(_ COND)
#P
(COND (& &) (& &))
#
```

Note that this command differs from BF in that it does not search <u>inside</u> each link, it simply ascends. Thus in the previous example, F CADR followed by BF COND would find (COND [FLG (RETURN L)]), not the higher COND.

If no match is found, an error is generated and the edit chain is unchanged.

<u>(BELOW com x)</u>

BELOW goes back up the edit chain looking for a link specified by com; then it comes x links back down the chain. x is evaluated, e.g., (BELOW com (*PLUS A B)). If omitted, x defaults to 1.

For example, (BELOW COND) will cause the COND <u>clause</u> containing the current expression to become the new current expression. Thus if the current expression is as shown above, F CADR followed by (BELOW COND) will make the new expression be

```
((NULL (CDR (MEMB (CAR L) (CADR L)))) (GO LP))
```

and is therefore equivalent to 0 0 0 0.

BELOW operates by evaluating x and then executing com, or (_ com) if com is not a recognized edit command, and measuring the length of the edit chain at that point. If that length is m and the length of the current edit chain is n, then BELOW ascends n-m-y links where y is the value of x. BELOW generates an error if com causes an error, i.e., if it can't find the higher link, or if n-m-y is negative.

The BELOW command is useful for locating a substructure by specifying something it contains. For example, suppose you are editing a list of lists, and you want to find a sublist that contains a FOO (at any depth). You can use F FOO (BELOW <).

(NEX x)

Same as (BELOW x) followed by NX.

For example, if you are deep inside of a SELECTQ clause, you can advance to the next clause with (NEX SELECTQ).

NEX

Same as (NEX _).

The atomic form of NEX is useful if you will be performing repeated executions of (NEX x). By simply MARKing the chain corresponding to x (see 22.3.4), you can use NEX to step through the sublists.

(NTH $)

This is a generalized NTH command. It effectively performs "(LCL . $) (BELOW <) UP".

In other words, NTH locates $, using a search restricted to the current expression, and then backs up to the current level, where the new current expression is the tail whose first element contains, however deeply, the expression that was the terminus of the location operation. For example:

```
#P
(PROG (& &) LP (COND & &) (EDITCOM &)
               (SETQ UNFIND UF) (RETURN L))
#(NTH UF)
#P
... (SETQ UNFIND UF) (RETURN L))
#
```

If the search is unsuccessful, NTH generates an error and the edit chain is not changed.

Note that (NTH n) is just a special case of (NTH $), and in fact, no special check is made for numbers.

(pattern :: . $)

This is equivalent to
"(F pattern N) (LCL . $) (_ pattern)".
For example, (COND :: RETURN) finds a COND that contains a RETURN at any depth. If the current expression is

```
(PROG NIL (COND [(NULL L)
                 (COND [FLG (RETURN L)])]) ...)
```

then (COND :: RETURN) will make (COND [FLG (RETURN L)]) be the current expression. Note that it is the innermost COND that is found, because this is the first COND encountered when ascending from the RETURN. In other words, (pattern :: $) is not <u>always</u> equivalent to "(F pattern N) (LCL . $) <".

Note that $ is a location specification, not just a pattern. Thus (RETURN :: COND 2 3) can be used to find the RETURN which contains a COND whose first clause contains (at least) three elements. Note also that since $ permits any edit command, the user can write commands of the form (COND :: (RETURN :: COND)), which will locate the first COND that contains a RETURN that contains a COND.

22.6.2 Specifying a segment: TO and THRU

XTR, EXTRACT, EMBED, DELETE, REPLACE, and MOVE will operate on a <u>segment</u> of a list if you use the TO or THRU command in their location specifications.

<u>($1 THRU $2)</u>

THRU does "(LC . $1) UP (BI 1 $2) 1". The BI (see 22.10.4) groups the segment into a single element, and the 1 makes the final current expression be that element.

For example, if the current expression is

(A (B (C D) (E) (F G H) I) J K)

then following (C THRU G), the current expression will be

((C D) (E) (F G H))

<u>($1 TO $2)</u>

TO is the same as THRU except that the last element is not included: after the BI, an (RI 1 -2) is performed.

<u>($1 TO)</u>
<u>($1 THRU)</u>

These are the same as ($1 THRU -1): they specify the segment from $1 through the end of the list.

If both $1 and $2 are numbers, and $2 is greater than $1, then $2 counts from the beginning of the current expression, the same as $1. In other words, if the current expression is (A B C D E F G), (3 THRU 4) means (C THRU D), not (C THRU F). In this case, the corresponding BI command is (BI 1 $2-$1+1).

22.6.2.1 Examples -

THRU and TO are not very useful commands by themselves, and are not intended to be used "solo," but in conjunction with XTR, EXTRACT, EMBED, DELETE, REPLACE, and MOVE, causing these functions to use the specified segment as their parameter. Example:

```
#P
(PROG NIL (SETQ A &) (RPLACA & &) (PRINT &) (RPLACD & &))
#(MOVE (3 THRU 4) TO BEFORE 5) P
(PROG NIL (PRINT &) (SETQ A &) (RPLACA & &) (RPLACD & &))
#
```

Note that when specifying $2 in the MOVE, 5 was used instead of 6. This is because the $2 is located _after_ $1 is. The THRU location groups items together and thus changes the numeric location of the following items.

```
#P
(PROG NIL (PRIN1 &) (PRIN1 &) (SETQ IND &) (SETQ VAL &)
          (PRINT &))
#MOVE (5 THRU 7) TO BEFORE 3
#P
(PROG NIL (SETQ IND &) (SETQ VAL &) (PRINT &) (PRIN1 &)
          (PRIN1 &))
#(DELETE (SETQ THRU PRI@))
= PRINT
#P
(PROG NIL (PRIN1 &) (PRIN1 &))
#
```

```
#P
... LP (SELECTQ & & &) (SETQ Y &) OUT (SETQ FLG &) (RETURN Y))
#(MOVE (1 TO OUT) TO N HERE) P
... OUT (SETQ FLG &) (RETURN Y) LP (SELECTQ & & &) (SETQ Y &))
#PP
(PROG (TEMP1 TEMP2)
      (COND [(NOT (MEMQ REMARG LISTING))
             (SETQ TEMP1 (ASSOC REMARG NAMEDREMARKS))
             (SETQ TEMP2 (CADR TEMP1))]
            [T (SETQ TEMP1 REMARG)])
      (NCONC LISTING REMARG)
      (RETURN (CONS TEMP1 TEMP2)))
#(EXTRACT (SETQ THRU CADR) FROM COND) PP
(PROG (TEMP1 TEMP2)
      (SETQ TEMP1 (ASSOC REMARG NAMEDREMARKS))
      (SETQ TEMP2 (CADR TEMP1))
      (NCONC LISTING REMARG)
      (RETURN (CONS TEMP1 TEMP2)))
```

```
#P
(VAL (RPLACA DFPRP &) (RPLACD & &) (RPLACA VARS &) (RETURN &))
#(MOVE (2 TO) TO N (_ PROG))
#(N (GO VAR))
#P
(VAL (GO VAR))
#
```

22.6.3 Specifying a copy:

A, B, :, INSERT, REPLACE, and CHANGE are among the functions that take literal parameters, but they make a special case for expressions of the form (## com[1] ... com[n]). The com's are editor commands, and the actual parameter used is a copy of the expression that is current after executing those commands. (The execution does not affect the edit chain for the command in which this form appears.)

The ##-form resembles a location specification, but the com's must be valid editor commands: there is no default search for unrecognized items. Of course, by using LC, you can produce the effect of a location specification; e.g., (## (LC . $)).

The form (##) specifies a copy of the current expression.

For example,

```
(INSERT (## F COND -1 -1)) AFTER 3)
```

will make a copy of the last form (-1) in the last clause

(-1) of the next COND (F), and insert it after the third element of the current expression. This is very different from

```
(INSERT F COND -1 (## -1) AFTER 3)
```

which inserts the atom F, the atom COND, the number -1, and a copy of the current expression's last element (## -1) after the third element of the current expression, because INSERT treats it first parameter literally unless that parameter is a ##-form.

22.7 Insertion

22.7.1 Basic commands

<u>(-1 e1 ... en)</u>

This inserts e1 ... en before the first element in the current expression.

<u>(-2 e1 ... en)</u>

This inserts e1 ... en before the second element of the current expression. (Likewise for -3, -4, etc.)

<u>(N e1 ... en)</u>

N (for NCONC) attaches e1 ... en at the <u>end</u> of the current expression.

<u>(B e1 ... en)</u>

B (for BEFORE) inserts e1 ... en before the current expression; it is equivalent to "UP (-1 e1 ... en).

<u>(A e1 ... en)</u>

A (for AFTER) inserts e1 ... en after the current expression; it does an UP and then either a (-2 e1 ... en) or an (N e1 ... en), if the current expression is the last one in the next higher expression.

If the current expression is a tail, then B and A work as if the current expression were the first element in that tail. Thus if the current expression were

```
... (PRINT Y) (PRINT Z))
```

then (B (PRINT X)) would insert (PRINT X) before (PRINT Y), leaving the current expression

```
... (PRINT X) (PRINT Y) (PRINT Z))
```

The parameters e1 ... en are treated literally, but the A and B functions recognize ##-forms (see 22.6.3).

22.7.2 INSERT

The INSERT function uses a location specification to indicate where the insertion should occur. The edit chain is the same after INSERT as before, but UNFIND is set to what the edit chain was after the insertion was performed, so that < can restore it.

<u>(INSERT e1 ... en BEFORE . $)</u>

This is equivalent to "(LC . $) (B e1 ... en)".

<u>(INSERT e1 ... en AFTER . $)</u>

This is equivalent to "(LC . $) (A e1 ... en)".

Since INSERT uses A and B, it recognizes ##-forms that appear in e1 ... en; otherwise it treats e1 ... en literally.

22.7.3 Examples

```
#P
(A B C D E)

*--.--.--.--.--
¦  ¦  ¦  ¦  ¦
A  B  C  D  E


#(-1 X Y) P      ~ Insert X Y before the first element
(X Y A B C D E)

*--.--.--.--.--.--.--
¦  ¦  ¦  ¦  ¦  ¦  ¦
X  Y  A  B  C  D  E


#(N (X Y)) P     ~ Attach the list (X Y) to the end
(X Y A B C D E (X Y))

*--.--.--.--.--.--.--.-------
¦  ¦  ¦  ¦  ¦  ¦  ¦  ¦
X  Y  A  B  C  D  E  .--.--
                     ¦  ¦
                     X  Y
```

```
#4 P               ~ Move to the 4th element
B

*--.--.--.----.--.--.--.-------
|  |  |  |    |  |  |  |
X  Y  A  *=B  C  D  E  .--.--
                       |  |
                       X  Y


#(A (B1 B2)) P  ~ Insert (B1 B2) after B. (A does an UP.)
... B (B1 B2) C D E (X Y))

*--.--.--*--.---------.--.--.--.-------
|  |  |  |  |         |  |  |  |
X  Y  A  B  .---.---  C  D  E  .--.--
            |   |              |  |
            B1  B2             X  Y


#(B (A1 A2)) P           ~ Insert (A1 A2) before the B.
... (A1 A2) B (B1 B2) C D E (X Y))

*--.--.--*---------.--.---------.--.--.--.-------
|  |  |  |         |  |         |  |  |  |
X  Y  A  .---.---  B  .---.---  C  D  E  .--.--
         |   |        |   |              |  |
         A1  A2       B1  B2             X  Y


#^ P                     ~ Back to the top.
(X Y A (A1 A2) B (B1 B2) C D E (X Y))

#INSERT Z AFTER Y        ~ Use loc. spec.

#P
(X Y Z A (A1 A2) B (B1 B2) C D E (X Y))

*--.--.--.--.---------.--.---------.--.--.--.-------
|  |  |  |  |         |  |         |  |  |  |
X  Y  Z  A  .---.---  B  .---.---  C  D  E  .--.--
            |   |        |   |              |  |
            A1  A2       B1  B2             X  Y
```

```
#INSERT A1A AFTER A1

#P
(X Y Z A (A1 A2) A1A B (B1 B2) C D E (X Y))

*--.--.--.--.---------.----.--.---------.--.--.--.-------
|  |  |  |  |         |    |  |         |  |  |  |
X  Y  Z  A  .---.---  A1A  B  .---.---  C  D  E  .--.--
            |   |             |   |              |  |
            A1  A2            B1  B2             X  Y

#~ Remember that F A1 leaves the current expression ABOVE
#~ an atomic CAR (see 22.2.?).


#UNDO           ~ Let's try it again
INSERT Undone

#P
(X Y Z A (A1 A2) B (B1 B2) C D E (X Y))

#E (SETQ UPFINDFLG NIL) ~ ... but with UPFINDFLG off.
NIL

#INSERT A1A AFTER A1

#P
(X Y Z A (A1 A1A A2) B (B1 B2) C D E (X Y))

*--.--.--.--.-------------.--.---------.--.--.--.-------
|  |  |  |  |             |  |         |  |  |  |
X  Y  Z  A  .---.----.--- B  .---.---  C  D  E  .--.--
            |   |    |       |   |              |  |
            A1  A1A  A2      B1  B2             X  Y
#~ Aha!


#UNDO   ~ But we can do it without setting UPFINDFLG to NIL.
INSERT Undone

#E (SETQ UPFINDFLG T)   ~ Turn it back on
T

#INSERT A1A AFTER A1 1  ~ Just use a better loc. spec.!

#P
(X Y Z A (A1 A1A A2) B (B1 B2) C D E (X Y))
```

```
*--.--.--.--.--------------.--.---------.--.--.--.--------
|  |  |  |  |              |  |         |  |  |  |
X  Y  Z  A  .---.----.---  B  .---.---  C  D  E  .--.--
            |   |    |        |   |              |  |
            A1  A1A  A2       B1  B2             X  Y
```

22.8 Deletion

All the functions in this section, except for DELETE itself, are special cases of the replacement functions, which are discussed in the next section.

22.8.1 Basic commands

<u>(1)</u>

This deletes the first element from the current expression (c-e) by doing (RPLACA c-e (CADR c-e)) and (RPLACD c-e (CDDR c-e)), and will therefore cause an error if c-e is an atom or a one-element list. In this case, use the DELETE command.

<u>(2)</u>

This deletes the second element from the current expression, and will fail if the current expression is not a list of at least two elements. (Likewise for (3), (4), ...).

<u>DELETE</u>
<u>(:)</u>

DELETE and (:) are equivalent; they delete the current expression (or its first element, if the current expression is a tail).

DELETE first tries to delete the current expression with "UP (1)". This works in most cases. However, if after performing UP, the new current expression contains only one element, the command (1) will not work. Therefore DELETE starts over with "BK UP (2)". For example, if the current expression is (COND ((MEMQ X Y)) (T Y)), and the user type "-1 DELETE", the "BK UP (2)" method is used, and the new current expression will be ... ((MEMQ X Y)))

However, if the next higher expression contains only one element, BK will not work. In this case, DELETE does "UP (: NIL)". That is, it REPLACES the higher expression with NIL. For example, if the current expression is (COND ((MEMQ X Y)) (T Y)) and the user types "F MEMQ DELETE", the new current expression will be ... NIL (T Y)) and the original expression would now be (COND NIL (T Y)). The rationale behind this is that deleting (MEMB X Y) from ((MEMB X Y)) changes a list of one element to a list of no elements, i.e., () or NIL. Note that "2 DELETE" would delete ((MEMB X Y)); it would not replace it with NIL.

If the current expression is a tail, then these functions work as if the current expression were the first element in that tail.

22.8.2 DELETE

(DELETE . $)

This is equivalent to "(LC . $) DELETE". The current edit chain is not changed, unless the current expression is no longer a part of the expression being edited (see examples), but UNFIND is set to what the edit chain was after the DELETE was performed.

22.8.3 Examples

```
#P
(X Y Z A (A1 A1A A2) B (B1 B2) C D E F (X Y))

*--.--.--.--.--------------.--.---------.--.--.--.--.-------
|  |  |  |  |              |  |         |  |  |  |  |
X  Y  Z  A  .---.----.---  B  .---.---  C  D  E  F  .--.--
            |   |    |        |   |                 |  |
            A1  A1A  A2       B1  B2                X  Y


#4 P                ~ Move to the 4th element
A

*--.--.--.----.--------------.--.---------.--.--.--.--.-------
|  |  |  |    |              |  |         |  |  |  |  |
X  Y  Z  *=A  .---.----.---  B  .---.---  C  D  E  F  .--.--
              |   |    |        |   |                 |  |
              A1  A1A  A2       B1  B2                X  Y


#DELETE             ~ Delete it. Note that it does an UP first.

#P
```

```
... (A1 A1A A2) B (B1 B2) C D E F (X Y))

*--.--.--*-------------.--.---------.--.--.--.--.-------
|  |  |  |             |  |         |  |  |  |  |
X  Y  Z  .---.----.--- B  .---.---  C  D  E  F  .--.--
         |   |    |       |   |                 |  |
         A1  A1A  A2      B1  B2                X  Y


#DELETE          ~ Here the UP has no effect.

#P
... B (B1 B2) C D E F (X Y))

*--.--.--*--.---------.--.--.--.--.-------
|  |  |  |  |         |  |  |  |  |
X  Y  Z  B  .---.---  C  D  E  F  .--.--
            |   |                 |  |
            B1  B2                X  Y


#F B2 P
... B2)

*--.--.--*--.---------.--.--.--.--.-------
|  |  |  |  |         |  |  |  |  |
X  Y  Z  B  *---*---  C  D  E  F  .--.--
            |   |                 |  |
            B1  B2                X  Y


#(1)             ~ Let's try this way of deleting.
(1)  ?

#~ Won't work: there's only one element in the list.
#DELETE          ~ But DELETE command will do it.

#P               ~ Note where the current expression is.
(B1)

*--.--.--*--.-----.--.--.--.--.-------
|  |  |  |  |     |  |  |  |  |
X  Y  Z  B  *---  C  D  E  F  .--.--
            |                 |  |
            B1                X  Y
```

```
#^ P                ~ Back to the top
(X Y Z B (B1) C D E F (X Y))

*--.--.--.--.-----.--.--.--.--.-------
|  |  |  |  |     |  |  |  |  |
X  Y  Z  B  .---  C  D  E  F  .--.--
            |                 |  |
            B1                X  Y


#(DELETE B1 THRU D) P   ~ Bad syntax (no parens)
B1  ?

#(DELETE (B1 THRU D)) P ~ They needn't be on the same level.
(X Y Z B E F (X Y))

*--.--.--.--.--.--.-------
|  |  |  |  |  |  |
X  Y  Z  B  E  F  .--.--
                  |  |
                  X  Y


#DELETE (Y THRU Z)      ~ This form requires parentheses.
DELETE  ?

#(DELETE (Y THRU Z)) P
(X B E F (X Y))

*--.--.--.--.-------
|  |  |  |  |
X  B  E  F  .--.--
            |  |
            X  Y


#(DELETE X -1) P        ~ Using a longer loc. spec.
(X B E F (X))

*--.--.--.--.----
|  |  |  |  |
X  B  E  F  .--
            |
            X
```

```
#DELETE            ~ Can't delete top level.
DELETE  ?

#1 P               ~ Move to the CAR.
X

*----.--.--.--.------
|    |  |  |  |
*=X  B  E  F  .----
              |
              X


#(1)               ~ Can't delete an atom this way.
(1)  ?

#DELETE            ~ But this works.

#P
(B E F (X))

*--.--.--.----
|  |  |  |
B  E  F  .--
         |
         X
```

22.9 Replacement

22.9.1 Basic commands

<u>(1 e1 ... en)</u>

This replaces the first item in the current expression with e1 ... en. The new items are spliced in, so that e1 will be the first element in the current expression, e2 the second, and so on. This functions generates an error if the current expression is an atom.

<u>(2 e1 ... en)</u>

This replaces the second element of the current expression with e1 ... en, as above. It will fail if the current expression is not a list of at least two elements. (Likewise for (3 e1 ... en), (4 e1 ... en), etc.)

<u>(: e1 ... en)</u>

This replaces the entire current expression by e1 ... en. It is equivalent to "UP (1 e1 ... en)", so that if the current expression is a tail, it replaces its first element.

The parameters e1 ... en are treated literally, but the : function recognizes ##-forms (see 22.6.3).

22.9.2 REPLACE and its synonyms

<u>(REPLACE $ WITH e1 ... en)</u>
<u>(REPLACE $ BY e1 ... en)</u>
<u>(INSERT e1 ... en FOR . $)</u>
<u>(CHANGE $ TO e1 ... en)</u>

These are all equivalent to "(LCL . $) (: e1 ... en)".

22.9.3 Substitution: R

(R x y)

R replaces all instances of x by y in the current expression, e.g., (R CAADR CADAR). It generates an error if there is not at least one instance.

R is, in effect,

(DSUBST y x current-expression)

Actually, R computes the second argument to DSUBST by performing (F x T). The second argument is then the current expression at that point, or if that current expression is a list and x is atomic, then the first element of that current expression. Thus x can be the S-expression (or atom) to be substituted for, or can be a pattern which specifies that S-expression (or atom).

For example, if the current expression is (LIST FUNNYATOM1 FUNNYATOM2 (CAR FUNNYATOM1)), then (R FUN@ FUNNYATOM3) will substitute FUNNYATOM3 for FUNNYATOM1 throughout the current expression. Note that FUNNYATOM2, even though it would have matched with the pattern FUN@, is NOT replaced.

Similarly, if (LIST (CAR X) (CAR Y)) is the first expression matched by (LIST --), then

(R (LIST --) (LIST (CAR Y) (CAR Z)))

is equivalent to

(R (LIST (CAR X) (CAR Y)) (LIST (CAR Y) (CAR Z)))

Both will replace all instances of (LIST (CAR X) (CAR Y)) by (LIST (CAR Y) (CAR Z)).

Note that other forms beginning with LIST will not be replaced, even though they would have matched with (LIST --). To change all expressions of the form (LIST --) to (LIST (CAR Y) (CAR Z)), use (LP (REPLACE (LIST --) WITH (LIST (CAR Y) (CAR Z)))). The LP function is described in 22.13.4.

22.9.4 Switching elements: SW

(SW n m)

SW switches the nth and mth elements of the current expression.

For example, if the current expression is

(LIST (CONS (CAR X) (CAR Y)) (CONS (CDR Y)))

then (SW 2 3) will modify it to be

(LIST (CONS (CDR X) (CDR Y)) (CONS (CAR X) (CAR Y)))

The relative order of n and m is not important: (SW 3 2) and (SW 2 3) are equivalent.

SW uses the generalized NTH command to find the nth and mth elements. Thus in the previous example, (SW CAR CDR) would produce the same result.

22.9.5 Examples

```
#P
(B E F (X))
```

```
*--.--.--.----
|  |  |  |
B  E  F  .--
         |
         X
```

```
#(2 (E1 E2)) P            ~ Replace the 2nd element.
(B (E1 E2) F (X))
```

```
*--.---------.--.----
|  |         |  |
B  .---.---  F  .--
   |   |        |
   E1  E2       X
```

```
#(3 F1 F2 F3) P         ~ Replace the 3rd element (splicing).
(B (E1 E2) F1 F2 F3 (X))


*--.---------.---.---.---.----
|  |         |   |   |   |
B  .---.---  F1  F2  F3  .--
   |   |                 |
   E1  E2                X


#4 P                    ~ Move to the 4th element.
F2


*--.---------.---.-----.---.----
|  |         |   |     |   |
B  .---.---  F1  *=F2  F3  .--
   |   |                   |
   E1  E2                  X


#(: F2A F2B) P                  ~ Replace it (goes UP first).
... F2A F2B F3 (X))


*--.---------.---*----.----.---.----
|  |         |   |    |    |   |
B  .---.---  F1  F2A  F2B  F3  .--
   |   |                       |
   E1  E2                      X


#(: (F2AA F2AB)) P              ~ Replace THAT (already UP).
... (F2AA F2AB) F2B F3 (X))


*--.---------.---*-------------.----.---.----
|  |         |   |             |    |   |
B  .---.---  F1  .-----.-----  F2B  F3  .--
   |   |         |     |                |
   E1  E2        F2AA  F2AB             X
```

```
#REPLACE 0 E1 2 WITH NEWE2        ~ Loc. Spec.

#P
... (F2AA F2AB) F2B F3 (X))


*--.------------.---*-------------.----.---.----
|  |            |   |             |    |   |
B  .---.------  F1  .-----.-----  F2B  F3  .--
   |   |            |     |                |
   E1  NEWE2        F2AA  F2AB             X


#CHANGE -1 TO X                   ~ Change last element.

#P
... (F2AA F2AB) F2B F3 X)


*--.------------.---*-------------.----.---.--
|  |            |   |             |    |   |
B  .---.------  F1  .-----.-----  F2B  F3  X
   |   |            |     |
   E1  NEWE2        F2AA  F2AB


#(N X X X) P                      ~ Add some more X's.
... (F2AA F2AB) F2B F3 X X X X)


*--.------------.---*-------------.----.---.--.--.--.--
|  |            |   |             |    |   |  |  |  |
B  .---.------  F1  .-----.-----  F2B  F3  X  X  X  X
   |   |            |     |
   E1  NEWE2        F2AA  F2AB


#R X x                    ~ Change to lower case x.

#P
... (F2AA F2AB) F2B F3 x x x x)
```

```
*--.------------.---*------------.----.---.--.--.--.--
|  |            |   |            |    |   |  |  |  |
B  .---.------  F1  .-----.----- F2B  F3  x  x  x  x
   |   |            |     |
   E1  NEWE2        F2AA  F2AB


#^ P                          ~ Move back to the top.
(B (E1 NEWE2) F1 (F2AA F2AB) F2B F3 x x x x)


*--.------------.---.------------.----.---.--.--.--.--
|  |            |   |            |    |   |  |  |  |
B  .---.------  F1  .-----.----- F2B  F3  x  x  x  x
   |   |            |     |
   E1  NEWE2        F2AA  F2AB


#R F@ Y                       ~ Replacement, with pattern match.
= F1

#P                            ~ Only F1 was replaced.
(B (E1 NEWE2) Y (F2AA F2AB) F2B F3 x x x x)


*--.------------.--.------------.----.---.--.--.--.--
|  |            |  |            |    |   |  |  |  |
B  .---.------  Y  .-----.----- F2B  F3  x  x  x  x
   |   |           |     |
   E1  NEWE2       F2AA  F2AB


#LP (REPLACE F@ WITH Y)       ~ Different matches.
= F2AA
= F2B
= F3
3 Occurrences

#P
(B (E1 NEWE2) Y Y Y Y x x x x)


*--.------------.--.--.--.--.--.--.--.--
|  |            |  |  |  |  |  |  |  |
B  .---.------  Y  Y  Y  Y  x  x  x  x
   |   |
   E1  NEWE2
```

```
#(SW 6 7) P                  ~ Switch.
(B (E1 NEWE2) Y Y Y x Y x x x)


*--.------------.--.--.--.--.--.--.--.--
¦  ¦            ¦  ¦  ¦  ¦  ¦  ¦  ¦  ¦
B  .---.------  Y  Y  Y  x  Y  x  x  x
   ¦   ¦
   E1  NEWE2


#(SW x Y) P                  ~ Using NTH-function
(B (E1 NEWE2) x Y Y Y Y x x x)


*--.------------.--.--.--.--.--.--.--.--
¦  ¦            ¦  ¦  ¦  ¦  ¦  ¦  ¦  ¦
B  .---.------  x  Y  Y  Y  Y  x  x  x
   ¦   ¦
   E1  NEWE2


#SW 1 -1                     ~ Swap first and last.

#P
(x (E1 NEWE2) x Y Y Y Y x x B)


*--.------------.--.--.--.--.--.--.--.--
¦  ¦            ¦  ¦  ¦  ¦  ¦  ¦  ¦  ¦
x  .---.------  x  Y  Y  Y  Y  x  x  B
   ¦   ¦
   E1  NEWE2
```

22.10 Restructuring commands

22.10.1 The MOVE command

(MOVE $1 TO fn . $2)

The MOVE command allows the user to specify (1) the expression to be moved, (2) the place it is to be moved to, and (3) the operation to be performed there, e.g., insert it before, insert it after, replace, etc. $1 and $2 are both location specifications.

fn is BEFORE, AFTER, or the name of an editor function (such as : or N). MOVE performs (LC . $1) and obtains the current expression there (or its first element, if it is a tail), called EXPR. MOVE then goes back to original edit chain, performs (LC . $2), performs (fn EXPR), and then goes back to $1 and deletes EXPR. The edit chain is not changed. UNFIND is set to what the edit chain was after (fn EXPR) was performed.

For example, if the current expression is (A B C D), then (MOVE 2 TO AFTER 4) will make the new current expression be (A C D B). Note that 4 was executed with the original edit chain, and that the second element had not yet been removed.

22.10.1.1 Examples of MOVE - As the following examples taken from actual editing will show, the MOVE command is an extremely versatile and powerful feature of the editor.

```
#?
(PROG (L) (EDLOC (CDDR C)) (RETURN (CAR L)))
#MOVE 3 TO : CAR
#?
(PROG (L) (RETURN (EDLOC (CDDR C))))
#
```

```
#P
... (SELECTQ OBJPR & &) (RETURN &) LP2 (COND & & ))
#(MOVE 2 TO N 1)
#P
... (SELECTQ OBJPR & & (RETURN &)) LP2 (COND & &))
#
```

```
#P
((NULL X) (COND & &))
#(-2 (GO DELETE)) P            ~ Insert a statement.
((NULL X) (GO DELETE) (COND & &))
#(MOVE 3 TO N (_ PROG))        ~ Move the COND to the end
#                              ~ of the surrounding PROG.
#P
((NULL X) (GO DELETE))
#< P    ~ The edit chain was saved during the MOVE. Go there.
(PROG (&) (COND & & &) (COND & & &) (COND & &))
#(INSERT DELETE BEFORE -1)     ~ Add a label.
#P
(PROG (&) (COND & & &) (COND & & &) DELETE (COND & &))
#
```

Note that in the last example, the user could have added the PROG label DELETE and moved the COND in one operation by performing (MOVE 3 TO N (_ PROG) (N DELETE)). Similarly, in the next example, in the course of specifying $2, the location where the expression was to be moved to, the user also performs a structure modification, via (N (T)), thus creating the structure that will receive the expression being moved.

```
#P
((CDR &) (SETQ CL &) (EDITSMASH CL & &))
#(MOVE 3 TO N 0 (N (T)) -1]
#P
((CDR &) (SETQ CL &))
#< P
(T (EDITSMASH CL & &))
#
```

If $2 is NIL or (HERE), the current position specifies where the operation is to take place. In this case, UNFIND is set to where the expression that was moved was originally located, i.e., $1. For example:

```
#P
(TENEX)
#(MOVE ^ F APPLY TO N HERE)    ~ Go to the top, find APPLY.
#P
(TENEX (APPLY & & ))
#
```

```
#P
(T (PRIN1 C-EXP))
#(MOVE BF PRIN1 TO N HERE)     ~ Look back for a PRIN1.
#P
(T (PRIN1 C-EXP) (PRIN1 &))
```

```
#
```

Finally, if $1 is NIL, the MOVE command allows the user to specify some place the current expression is to be moved to. In this case, the edit chain is changed, and is the chain where the current expression was moved to; UNFIND is set to where it was.

```
#P
(SELECTQ OBJPR (&) (PROGN & &))
#(MOVE TO BEFORE LOOP)
#P
...(SELECTQ OBJPR & &) LOOP (RPLACA DFPRP &)
      (RPLACD DFPRP &))
#
```

22.10.2 Embedding

The MBD and EMBED functions replace the current expression with one containing it as a subexpression.

(MBD X)

If X is a list, MBD substitutes a fresh copy of the current expression for each instance of the atom * in X, and replaces the current expression with the result of that substitution.

If X is an atom, this is the same as (MBD (X *)).

(MBD e1 ... en)

This is the same as (MBD (e1 ... en *)).

MBD leaves the edit chain so that the larger expression is the new current expression.

If the current expression initially is a tail, embedding works exactly the same as though the current expression were the first element in that tail. Thus if the current expression were ... (PRINT Y) (E)), then (MBD (SETQ X)) would replace it with (SETQ X (PRINT Y)).

<u>(EMBED $ IN . X)</u>
<u>(EMBED $ WITH . X)</u>
<u>(SURROUND $ IN . X)</u>
<u>(SURROUND $ WITH . X)</u>

These are all equivalent to "(LC . $) (MBD . X)". The edit chain is not changed, but UNFIND is set to the edit chain after the MBD was performed.

Examples of EMBED and SURROUND syntax:

```
(EMBED PRINT IN SETQ X)
(EMBED 3 2 IN RETURN)
(EMBED COND 3 1 IN (OR * (NULL X)))
(SURROUND NUMBERP WITH (AND * (MINUSP X)))
```

22.10.2.1 Examples of embedding -

```
#P
(PRINT Y)
```

```
*------.--
|      |
PRINT  Y
```

```
#(MBD (COND ((NULL X) *) ((NULL (CAR Y)) *) (T (GO LP] PP
(COND [(NULL X) (PRINT Y)]
      [(NULL (CAR Y)) (PRINT Y)]
      [T (GO LP)])

#F PRINT P
(PRINT Y)
```

```
*-----.-------------------------.-------.-------
|     |                         |       |
COND  *----------.-----------   .--.--  .--.--
      |          |              |  |    |  |
      .-----.--  *------.--     &  &    T  &
      |     |    |      |
      NULL  X    PRINT  Y
```

```
#MBD SETQ X

#P
(SETQ X (PRINT Y))
```

```
*-----.-----------------------------------------.-------.-------
|     |                                         |       |
COND  *----------.----------------------        .--.--  .--.--
      |          |                              |  |    |  |
      .-----.--  *-----.--.------------         &  &    T  &
      |     |    |     |  |
      NULL  X    SETQ  X  .------.--
                          |      |
                          PRINT  Y
```

```
#!NX F PRINT P
(PRINT Y)
```

```
*-----.-------.-----------------------.-------
|     |       |                       |
COND  .--.--  *----------.----------  .--.--
      |  |    |          |            |  |
      &  &    .-----.--  *------.--   T  &
              |     |    |      |
              NULL  &    PRINT  Y
```

```
#MBD RETURN

#P
(RETURN (PRINT Y))
```

```
*-----.-------.-----------------------------------.-------
|     |       |                                   |
COND  .--.--  *----------.----------------------  .--.--
      |  |    |          |                        |  |
      &  &    .-----.--  *-------.-----------     T  &
              |     |    |       |
              NULL  &    RETURN  .------.--
                                 |      |
                                 PRINT  Y
```

```
#^ PP

(COND [(NULL X) (SETQ X (PRINT Y))]
      [(NULL (CAR Y)) (RETURN (PRINT Y))]
      [T (GO LP)])
```

22.10.3 Extraction

Extraction involves replacing the current expression with one of its subexpressions (from any depth).

<u>(XTR . $)</u>

XTR replaces the original current expression with the expression that is current after performing (LCL . $).

For example, if the current expression is (COND ((NULL X) (PRINT Y))), then (XTR PRINT) or (XTR 2 2) will replace the (COND ...) with the (PRINT Y) it contained.

If the current expression after (LCL . $) is a tail of a higher expression, its first element is used. For example, if the current expression is (COND ((NULL X) Y) (T Z)), then (XTR Y) will replace the COND with Y.

If the extracted expression is a list, then after XTR has finished, the current expression will be that list. Thus, in the first example, the current expression after the XTR would be (PRINT Y).

If the extracted expression is not a list, the new current expression will be a tail whose first element is that non-list. Thus, in the second example, the current expression after the XTR would be ... Y followed by whatever had followed the COND.

If the current expression initially is a tail, extraction works exactly the same as though the current expression were the first element in that tail. Thus if the current expression is ... (A B C) D), then (XTR C) will replace (A B C) with C, leaving ... C D) as the current expression.

(EXTRACT $1 FROM $2)

EXTRACT is "(LC . $2) (XTR . $1)". The current edit chain is not changed, but UNFIND is set to the edit chain after the XTR was performed.

Example: If the current expression is

(PRINT (COND ((NULL X) Y) (T Z)))

then following

(EXTRACT Y FROM COND)

the current expression will be (PRINT Y).

(EXTRACT 2 -1 FROM COND), (EXTRACT Y FROM 2), and (EXTRACT 2 -1 FROM 2) will all produce the same result.

22.10.4 Commands that "move parentheses"

The commands presented in this section permit modification of the list structure itself, as opposed to modifying components thereof. Their effect can be described as inserting or removing a single left or right parenthesis, or a pair of left and right parentheses. Of course, there will always be the same number of left parentheses as right parentheses in any list structure, since the parentheses are just a notational guide to the structure provided by PRINT. Thus, no command can insert or remove just one parenthesis, but this is suggestive of what actually happens.

In all six commands, n and m are used to specify an element of a list, usually of the current expression. In practice, n and m are usually positive or negative integers with the obvious interpretation. However, all six commands use the generalized NTH command (see 22.6.1) to find their elements, so that nth element means the first element of the tail found by performing (NTH n). In other words, if the current expression is

(LIST (CAR X) (SETQ Y (CONS W Z)))

then (BI 2 CONS), (BI X -1), and (BI X Z) all specify the exact same operation.

All six commands generate an error if the element is not found, i.e., if the NTH fails. All are, of course, UNDO-able.

<u>(BI n m)</u>

BI (Both In) inserts a left parenthesis before the nth element and a right parenthesis after the mth element in the current expression. It generates an error if the mth element is not contained in the nth tail; i.e., the mth element must be "to the right" of the nth element.

<u>(BI n)</u>

This is the same as (BI n n).

All the examples here will use the same initial expression.

```
#P
(A B (C D E) F G)
```

```
*--.--.----------.--.--
¦  ¦  ¦          ¦  ¦
A  B  .--.--.--  F  G
      ¦  ¦  ¦
      C  D  E
```

```
#(BI 2 4) P
(A (B (C D E) F) G)
```

```
*--.-------------------.--
¦  ¦                   ¦
A  .--.----------.--   G
   ¦  ¦          ¦
   B  .--.--.--  F
      ¦  ¦  ¦
      C  D  E
```

```
#UNDO
BI Undone
```

<u>(BO n)</u>

BO (Both Out) removes both parentheses from the nth element. It generates an error if nth element is not a list.

```
#P
(A B (C D E) F G)

#(BO 3) P
(A B C D E F G)


*--.--.--.--.--.--.--
¦  ¦  ¦  ¦  ¦  ¦  ¦
A  B  C  D  E  F  G


#UNDO
BO Undone
```

<u>(LI n)</u>

LI (Left In) inserts a left parenthesis before the nth element (and a matching right parenthesis at the end of the current expression). It is equivalent to (BI n -1).

```
#P
(A B (C D E) F G)

#(LI 2) P
(A (B (C D E) F G))


*--.--------------------
¦  ¦
A  .--.----------.--.--
   ¦  ¦          ¦  ¦
   B  .--.--.--  F  G
      ¦  ¦  ¦
      C  D  E
```

```
#UNDO
LI Undone
```

(LO n)

LO (Left Out) removes a left parenthesis from the nth element. All elements following the nth element are deleted. It generates an error if the nth element is not a list.

```
#P
(A B (C D E) F G)

#(LO 3) P
(A B C D E)


*--.--.--.--.--
¦  ¦  ¦  ¦  ¦
A  B  C  D  E


#UNDO
LO Undone
```

(RI n m)

RI (Right In) inserts a right parenthesis after the mth element of the nth element. The rest of the nth element is brought up to the level of the current expression.

Another way of thinking about RI is to read it as "move the right parenthesis at the end of the nth element IN to after the mth element."

```
#P
(A B (C D E) F G)

#(RI 3 1) P
(A B (C) D E F G)
```

```
*--.--.----.--.--.--.--
|  |  |    |  |  |  |
A  B  .--  D  E  F  G
      |
      C
```

```
#UNDO
RI Undone
```

<u>(RO n)</u>

RO (Right Out) removes the right parenthesis from the nth element, moving it to the end of the current expression. All elements following the nth element are moved inside the nth element. It generates an error if nth element is not a list.

Another way of thinking about RO is to read it as "move the right parenthesis at the end of the nth element OUT to the end of the current expression."

```
#P
(A B (C D E) F G)

#(RO 3) P
(A B (C D E F G))
```

```
*--.--.----------------
|  |  |
A  B  .--.--.--.--.--
      |  |  |  |  |
      C  D  E  F  G
```

22.10.5 More examples of restructuring

```
#P
(T (COND &) (EDITSMASH CL & &) (COND &))
#(-2 (GO REPLACE))
#(MOVE (COND TO) TO N PROG (N REPLACE))
#P
(T (GO REPLACE))
#< P
(PROG (&) (COND & & &) (COND & & &) DELETE (COND & &) REPLACE
(COND &) (EDITSMASH CL & &) (COND &))
#
```

```
#PP
(LAMBDA(CLAUSALA X)
 (PROG (A D)
       (SETQ A CLAUSALA)
  LP   (COND ((NULL A) (RETURN NIL)))
       (SERCH X A)
       (RUMARK (CAR A))
       (NOTICECL (CAR A))
       (SETQ A (CDR A))
       (GO LP)))
#(EXTRACT (SERCH THRU NOT@) FROM PROG) P
= NOTICECL
(LAMBDA (CLAUSALA X) (SERCH X A) (RUMARK &) (NOTICECL &))
#(EMBED (SERCH TO) IN (MAP [FUNCTION (LAMBDA (A) *] CLAUSALA]
#PP
(LAMBDA(CLAUSALA X)
 (MAP (FUNCTION
       (LAMBDA(A)
        (SERCH X A)
        (RUMARK (CAR A))
        (NOTICECL (CAR A))))
      CLAUSALA))
```

22.11 The UNDO mechanism

22.11.1 UNDO and !UNDO

UNDO

This undoes the most recent structure modification command that has not yet been undone, and prints the name of that command, e.g., DELETE UNDONE. The edit chain is then exactly what it was before the "undone" command had been performed. If there are no commands to undo, UNDO types NOTHING SAVED.

The availability of UNDO should give you confidence to experiment with any and all editing commands, no matter how complex, because you can always reverse the effect of the command.

!UNDO

!UNDO ("bang-undo") undoes all modifications performed during this call to the editor. As each command is undone, its name is printed. If there is nothing to be undone, !UNDO prints NOTHING SAVED.

22.11.2 The UNDO-list

Each command that causes structure modification automatically adds an entry to the front of UNDOLST. The entry contains the information required to restore all pointers that were changed by the command.

??

This command prints the entries on UNDOLST. The entries are listed in the reverse order of their execution, i.e., the most recent entry first. For example:

```
#P
(CONS (T &) (& &))
#(1 COND) (SW 2 3) P
(COND (& &) (T &))
#??
SW (1 --)
#
```

22.11.3 UNDO UNDO

Since UNDO and !UNDO cause structure modification themselves, they also add an entry to UNDOLST. However, UNDO and !UNDO entries are skipped by UNDO. If you perform an INSERT and then an MBD, for example, the first UNDO will undo the MBD, and the second will undo the INSERT. However, you can also specify precisely which command you want undone. In this case, you can undo an UNDO command, (by typing UNDO UNDO), or undo a !UNDO command, or undo a command other than the most recent one.

22.11.4 UNDO-blocks: editing checkpoints

TEST

TEST adds a special entry called an UNDO-block at the front of the UNDOLST. The UNDO-block will terminate the operation of a !UNDO, thereby confining its effect to editing done since the block was added. Similarly, UNDO commands will not operate past the block. If you have reached a block either by !UNDO or a sequence or UNDO's, any further UNDO or !UNDO commands will print the message BLOCKED.

Note that TEST together with !UNDO provide a "tentative" mode for editing: you can perform a number of changes, and then undo all of them with a single !UNDO command.

When you leave the editor, the UNDOLST is saved (see 22.12). If you edit the same structure later, the UNDOLST is restored, and an UNDO-block is automatically added to the front of the UNDOLST as an added safety measure. Thus, if you re-edit a structure and immediately execute an UNDO or !UNDO, you will get the message BLOCKED instead of NOTHING SAVED.

UNBLOCK

This removes an UNDO-block. If there are no blocks on the UNDOLST, it will type NOT BLOCKED.

22.12 Leaving/recursing

22.12.1 Getting out

There are three ways of leaving the editor. The first two of them save the current state of the editor: the edit chain, the MARKLST, the UNDOLST, and UNFIND.

Whenever the editor is entered, it checks to see if it is editing the same structure as the last one edited. If so, it restores the state information.

OK

This is the usual command for leaving the editor. It goes back to the top of the expression (^) and saves the editor state information on the property list of the atom EDIT under the property name LASTVALUE. It also removes the property EDIT-SAVE from the property list of the function or variable being edited. (EDIT-SAVE is used by SAVE.)

SAVE

SAVE leaves the editor and saves the state information on the property list of the function/variable being edited under the property name EDIT-SAVE.

SAVE is useful when you are editing many different expressions since it saves the state information on separate property lists.

STOP

STOP leaves the editor via (ERR NIL). It does not save any state information. It is most useful when combined with the TTY: command.

22.12.2 Getting in deeper

TTY:

TTY: calls the editor recursively. You can then type in commands, and have them executed. The TTY: command is completed when you leave the inner level of the editor via one of the three exit commands.

The TTY: command is extremely useful. It enables you to set up a complex operation and perform interactive attention-changing commands part way through it. For example, the command (MOVE 3 TO AFTER COND 3 P TTY:) allows you to interact, in effect, with the lociation specification inside the MOVE command. Thus you can verify that the correct location has been found, or complete the specification "by hand." In effect, TTY: says "I'll tell you what you should do when you get there."

The TTY: command operates by printing TTY: and then calling the editor. The initial edit chain for the inner editor is the one that existed in the outer editor at the time the TTY: command was given. Until you leave the inner editor, any attention-changing commands you give affect only the inner editor's edit chain. (Of course, any structure-modification commands you give will modify the structure in both editors, since it is the same structure.) When the TTY: command finishes, the inner editor's edit chain becomes the edit chain of the outer editor.

All of the commands in the editor are executed under ERRSET. STOP provides a way of distinguishing between what you consider a successful or unsuccessful editing session. For example, if you type (MOVE 3 TO AFTER COND TTY:), and you leave the inner editor with an OK, the MOVE command will then complete its operation. If you want to abort the MOVE command in the outer editor, you should give the STOP command, which will bring you back to the outer editor without changing the outer-level edit chain.

22.12.3 Examples

```
#P
(NULL X)
#F COND P
(COND (& &) (T &))
#SAVE
FOO
  .
  .
  .
*(EDITF FOO)
EDIT
#P               ~ It remembers where we are (edit chain) ...
(COND (& &) (T &))
#< P             ~ ... and where we were (UNFIND).
(NULL X)
#


*(EDITF RL)      ~ recursive LENGTH function
EDIT:


#PP
(LAMBDA (X) (COND [(ATOM X) 1] [T (ADD1 (RL (CDR X)))]))


#~ We want to change the 1 to a 0. It's somewhere
#~ near the COND.
#REPLACE COND 1 TTY: WITH 0
TTY:


2#P      ~ Where are we?
COND


2#UP PP          ~ Too low. Look higher.
(COND [(ATOM X) 1] [T (ADD1 (RL (CDR X)))])


2#F 1 P          ~ Search for the 1.
... 1)


2#OK             ~ That's it. Now the REPLACE continues.


#PP
(LAMBDA (X) (COND [(ATOM X) 0] [T (ADD1 (RL (CDR X)))]))


#(DELETE T PP TTY:)      ~ We can delete the T if we like.
```

```
(T (ADD1 (RL (CDR X))))
TTY:

2#STOP                        ~ On second thought, let's leave it.
T  ?

#                             ~ The search for the T "failed."
#PP
(COND [(ATOM X) 0] [T (ADD1 (RL (CDR X)))])

#OK                           ~ All done.
RL
```

22.13 Programming in the editor

22.13.1 EVAL and EDITCOM: the interpreters

The top level of the LISP interpreter is:

```
(PROG NIL LOOP (PRINT (EVAL (READ))) (GO LOOP))
```

Likewise, the top level of the editor can be described (approximately) as:

```
(PROG NIL LOOP (EDITCOM (READ)) (GO LOOP))
```

That is, EVAL and EDITCOM (an internal function) are roughly counterparts. EDITCOM provides several ways to call EVAL, directly and indirectly, and there are several ways to call EDITCOM from EVAL. There is even one, happy fixed point: NIL.

<u>NIL</u>

As an editor command, NIL is a no-op.

22.13.2 Calling EVAL from EDITCOM

The simplest way to call EVAL is with the E command.

<u>E</u> x

The next input (x) is given to EVAL, and the result is printed.

Example:

```
#E (BREAK FIE FUM)
(FIE FUM)
#E (FOO)
(FIE BROKEN)
1:
```

Although most commands cannot be used in location specifications without a specific call to F, an exception is made for E. (INSERT X BEFORE E) is the same as (INSERT X BEFORE (F E)).

(E x)

This function performs (EVAL x) and prints the result on the teletype.

(E x T)

This is the same as (E x) but it does not print.

The (E x) and (E x T) commands are mainly intended for use by MACROS and subroutine calls to the editor; the user would probably type in a form for evaluation using the more convenient format of the (atomic) E command.

22.13.3 Calling EDITCOM from EVAL

(## "COM[1]" "COM[2]" ... "COM[N]")

is an FSUBR, not a editor command or editor function. It passes its parameters one at a time, unevaluated, to EDITCOM. Its value is what the current expression would be after executing the edit commands com[1] ... com[n] starting from the present edit chain. It generates an error if any of com[1] through com[n] cause errors. The current edit chain is never changed.

is intended to be used only inside the editor by some editor command, function, or program that calls EVAL. (That is, the backtrace includes EDITCOM - EVAL - EDITCOM - EVAL.)

The ## FSUBR is related to the special form (## com[1] ... com[n]) used by A, B, :, INSERT, REPLACE, and CHANGE. The effect of using the special form is the same as if the FSUBR were evaluated: the commands are passed to EDITCOM and resulting current expression is used for the insertion or replacement.

22.13.4 Editor program-forms

<u>(COMSQ com[1] ... com[n])</u>

COMSQ simply executes com[1] ... com[n]. (It corresponds to PROGN.)

<u>(COMS x[1] ... x[n])</u>

Each S-expression x[i] is <u>evaluated</u> and its value executed as a command.

For example, (COMS (COND (X (LIST 1 X)))) will replace the first element of the current expression with the value of X if non-NIL, otherwise do nothing (i.e., execute the editor command NIL).

COMSQ is mainly used in conjunction with the COMS command. For example, suppose you wish to compute an entire list of commands for evaluation, as opposed to computing each command one at a time as the COMS command does. You could then write (COMS (CONS 'COMSQ x)) where x computed the list of commands, e.g.,

```
(COMS (CONS 'COMSQ (GET FOO 'COMMANDS)))
```

<u>(I c x[1] ... x[n])</u>

This is the same as (c y[1] ... y[n]) where y[i] = (EVAL x[i]). If c is not an atom, it is evaluated as well.

Examples: (I 3 FOO) will replace the 3rd element of the current expression with the value of FOO.

(I N FOO (CAR FIE)) will attach the value of FOO and CAR of the value of FIE to the end of the current expression.

(I F= FOO T) will search for an expression EQ to the value of FOO.

(I (COND [(NULL FLG) -1] [T 1]) FOO), if FLG is NIL, inserts the value of FOO before the first element of the current expression, otherwise replaces the first element by the value of FOO.

(INSERT (## 3 2) AFTER 1) is equivalent to (I INSERT

(COPY (## 3 2)) 'AFTER 1).

(I R 'X (## (CONS :: Z))) replaces all X's in the current expression by the first CONS containing a Z.

(During the execution of an I-command, the structure-modification commands do <u>not</u> copy expressions when inserting, replacing, or attaching. See 22.15.1.)

22.13.5 Loops

<u>(LP . coms)</u>

LP repeatedly executes coms, a list of commands, until an error occurs.

When an error occurs, LP prints n OCCURRENCES, where n is the number of times COMS was successfully executed. The edit chain is left as of the last complete successful execution of COMS.

For example, (LP F PRINT (N T)) will attach a T at the end of every PRINT expression.

(LP F PRINT (IF (## 3) NIL ((N T)))) will attach a T at the end of each print expression which does not already have a second argument. The form (## 3) will cause an error if the edit command 3 causes an error, thereby selecting ((N T)) as the list of commands to be executed. The IF could also be written as (IF (CDDR (##)) NIL ((N T))).

<u>(LPQ . coms)</u>

LPQ is the same as LP but does not print n OCCURRENCES.

In order to prevent non-terminating loops, both LP and LPQ terminate when the number of iterations reaches MAXLOOP, initially set to 30.

22.13.6 Conditionals

<u>(IF x)</u>

("If") If (EVAL x) causes an error or (EVAL x) = NIL, generate an error.

<u>(IF x com)</u>

("If-then") If (EVAL x) is true, execute com; otherwise generate an error.

<u>(IF x com1 com2)</u>

("If-then-else") If (EVAL x) is true, execute com1; if (EVAL x) causes an error or is equal to NIL, execute com2.

For some editor commands, the occurrence of an error has a well-defined meaning; i.e., they use errors to branch on as COND uses NIL and non-NIL. For example, an error condition in a location specification may simply mean "not this one, try the next." Thus the location specification

```
(*PLUS (E (OR (NUMBERP (## 3)) (ERR NIL)) T))
```

specifies the first *PLUS whose second argument is a number. The IF command, by equating NIL to error, provides a more natural way of accomplishing the same result. Thus, an equivalent location specification is:

```
(*PLUS (IF (NUMBERP (## 3))))
```

The command (IF (NULL A) NIL (P)) will print the current expression, provided A = NIL.

<u>(ORR coms[1] ... coms[n])</u>

ORR begins by executing coms[1], a list of commands. If no error occurs, ORR is finished. Otherwise, ORR restores the edit chain to its original value, and continues by executing coms[2], etc. If each one causes some error, i.e., if ORR "drops off the end," then ORR generates an error. Otherwise, the edit chain is left as of the completion of the first command list which executes without error.

NIL as a command list is perfectly legal, and will always execute successfully. Thus, making the last argument to ORR be NIL will insure that the ORR never causes an error. Any other atom is treated as (atom). The example given below could be written as (ORR NX !NX NIL).

For example, (ORR (NX) (!NX) NIL) will perform a NX, if possible, otherwise a !NX, if possible, otherwise it will do nothing. Similarly, DELETE could be written as (ORR (UP (1)) (BK UP (2)) (UP (: NIL))).

22.13.7 Binding variables: S and BIND

(S var . $)

S sets var (using SETQ) to the current expression after performing (LC . $). The edit chain is not changed.

Thus (S FOO) will set FOO to the current expression. (S FOO -1 1) will set FOO to the first element in the last element of the current expression.

(BIND . coms)

This function binds three dummy variables #1, #2, #3 (all initialized to NIL), and then executes the edit commands coms. These bindings are in effect only while the commands are being executed. BIND can be used recursively; it will rebind #1, #2, and #3 each time it is invoked.

BIND is defined as:

```
(PROG (#1 #2 #3) (MAPC 'EDITCOM coms))
```

22.13.8 Defining functions: Editmacros

Many of the more sophisticated branching commands in the editor, such as ORR and IF, are most often used in conjunction with edit macros. The macro feature permits the user to define new commands and thereby expand the editor's repertoire. (However, built-in commands always take precedence over macros. The editor's repertoire can be expanded, but not modified.)

Macros are defined by using the M command. There are three forms for macro definitions: defining a new edit command (no parameters), defining a new editor function with a fixed number of parameters, and defining a new editor function with a variable number of parameters.

(M c . coms)

This defines c as an editor command. (If a macro is redefined, its new definition replaces its old.) Executing c is then the same as executing the list of commands coms.

For example, (M BP BK UP P) will define BP as an atomic command which does three things: BK, UP, and P. Macros may call other macros in their definitions. For example, suppose Z is defined by:

```
(M Z -1  (IF (NULL (##)) NIL (P)))
```

Z does a -1, and then if the current expression is not NIL, a P. Now we can define ZZ by (M ZZ -1 Z), and ZZZ by (M ZZZ -1 -1 Z) or (M ZZZ -1 ZZ).

(M (c) (arg[1] ... arg[n]) . coms)

This defines c as an editor functions with a fixed number of parameters (n). Executing (c e1 ... en) is then performed by substituting (not binding) the actual parameters e[1] ... e[n] for the formal parameters arg[1] ... arg[n] throughout coms, and then executing coms.

For example, we could define a more general BP by (M (BP) (N) (BK N) UP P). Thus, (BP 3) would perform (BK 3), followed by an UP, followed by a P.

(M (c) args . coms)

This defines c as an editor function of an arbitrary number of parameters; args is an atom. Executing (c e[1] ... e[n]) is performed by substituting the entire list of actual parameters (e[1] ... e]n]) for the single formal parameter, args, throughout coms (a la FEXPRs), and then executing coms.

For example, the command SECOND (see 22.3.2.3) is defined as:

```
(M (SECOND) X (ORR ((LC . X) (LC . X))))
```

Note that for all editor commands (built-in commands as well as commands defined by macros), atomic definitions and list definitions are completely independent. In other words, the existence of an atomic definition for c in no way affects the treatment of c when it appears as CAR of a list command, and the existence of a list definition for c in no way affects the treatment of c when it appears as an atom. In particular, c can be used as the name of either an atomic command, or a list command, or both. In the latter case, two entirely different definitions can be used.

Note also that once c is defined as an atomic command via a macro definition, it will not be searched for when used in a location specification, unless c is preceded by an F. Thus (INSERT -- BEFORE BP) would not search for BP, but instead perform a BK, an UP, and a P, and then do the insertion. The same also holds true for list commands.

22.13.8.1 Example: SW -

Occasionally, the user will want to employ the S command in a macro to save some temporary result. For example, the SW command could be defined as:

```
(M (SW) (N M) ~ Define SW as a function of 2 parameters.
        (NTH N)     ~ Find N and back up.
        (S FOO 1) ~ Set FOO to the CAR.
        MARK        ~ MARK this spot.
        0           ~ Back up one link.
        (NTH M)     ~ Find M and back up.
        (S FIE 1) ~ Set FIE to this CAR.
        (I 1 FOO) ~ Replace the CAR with FOO's value.
        __          ~ Go back to the marked spot,
                    ~ erasing the mark.
        (I 1 FIE))~ Replace the CAR with FIE's value.
```

A more elegant definition would be:

```
(M (SW) (N M)             ~ as before
              (NTH N)
              MARK        ~ Just MARK the spot.
              0
              (NTH M)
              (S FIE 1) ~ Set FIE as before.
              (I 1 (## _ 1)) ~ Replace the CAR with a the
                         _~ expression found after doing (_ 1),
                          ~ i.e., going back to the mark and
                          ~ getting the CAR, but restoring
                          ~ the edit chain.
                          ~ Now really go back to the mark,
              __          ~ erase it,
              (I 1 FIE))~ and replace the CAR with the value
                          ~ of FIE.
```

This would still use one free variable, which may have undesirable side effects, especially when the editor is called from deep inside a computation. To avoid having to make up unique names for dummy variables used in edit macros, which is bothersome, and to permit recursion, we use BIND. The algorithm is the same as our first one with FOO and FIE.

```
(M (SW) (N M) (BIND (NTH N)
                    (S #1 1)
                    MARK
                    0
                    (NTH M)
                    (S #2 1)

                    (I 1 #1)

                    (I 1 #2)))
```

22.13.8.2 Example: MAKEFN -

(MAKEFN form args n {m})

MAKEFN defines an EXPR. The name of the function is the CAR of form. The formals parameters are given by args, which should be a list (or NIL). The body of the function is composed of the *n*th through *m*th elements of the current expression, where each occurence of a variable in (CDR form) has been replaced by the corresponding formal parameter. (If *m* is omitted, it defaults to *n*.) Finally, the *n*th through *m*th elements are replaced by form.

For example:

```
#P
... (SETQ A NIL) (SETQ B T) (CONS C D))
#(MAKEFN (SETUP C D) (W X) 1 3) P
... (SETUP C D))
#E (PP SETUP)
(DEFPROP SETUP
 (LAMBDA (W X) (SETQ A NIL) (SETQ B T) (CONS W X))
EXPR)
#
```

MAKEFN is defined as:

```
(MAKEFN (EX ARGS N M)
        (IF 'M
            ((BI N M) (LC . N) (BELOW \))
            ((IF 'N ((BI N) (LC . N) (BELOW \)))))
        (E (MAPC '(LAMBDA (X Y) (EDITDSUBST X Y (##)))
                 'ARGS
                 (CDR 'EX))
           T)
        (E (APPLY# 'DE (CONS (CAR 'EX) (CONS 'ARGS (##)))))
        UP
        (1. EX))
```

22.13.9 USERMACROS

User macros are stored on the list USERMACROS (initially NIL). Thus if you want to save your macros, you should save the value of USERMACROS. (You should probably also save EDITCOMSL, the list of edit function names).

22.14 Miscellany

UNPACK
(UNPACK . $)

This command unpacks a packed string comment (see 9.2) into a list for ease of editing. The unpacking is permanent: the comment will remain in list form until written onto a file and read back in.

REPACK
(REPACK . $)

REPACK permits the "editing" of an atom or string.

For example:

```
#P
... "THIS IS A LOGN STRING")
#REPACK
EDIT:
2#P
(/" T H I S / I S / A / L O G N / S T R I N G /")
2#SW G N
2#OK
"THIS IS A LONG STRING"
#
```

REPACK operates by calling the editor recursively on UNPACK of the current expression, or if it is a list, on UNPACK of its first element. If the inner editor is exited successfully (via OK as opposed to STOP), the list of atoms is made into a single atom or string, which replaces the atom or string being "repacked." The new atom or string is always printed.

SORT
(SORT . $)

This command sorts the current expression or the expression at the specified location.

22.15 Implementation details

22.15.1 Structure changes use copies

For all replacement, insertion, and attaching at the end of a list, unless the command was typed in directly to the editor, *copies* of the corresponding structure are used, because of the possibility that the exact same command (the same list structure) might be used again.

Some editor commands take as arguments a list of edit commands, e.g., (LP F FOO (1 (CAR FOO))). In this case, the command (1 (CAR FOO)) is not considered to have been "typed in" even though the LP command itself may have been typed in. Similarly, commands originating from macros, or commands given to the editor as arguments to EDITF, EDITV, et. al., such as (EDITF FOO F COND (N --)) are not considered typed in.

Thus if the program constructs the command (1 (A B C)) via (LIST 1 FOO), and gives this command to the editor, the (A B C) used for the replacement will NOT be EQ to FOO. The u The u can circumvent this by using the I command, which computes the structure to be used. In the example above, the form of the command would be (I 1 FOO), which would replace the first element with the value of FOO itself. See 22.6.

22.15.2 How structures are modified

This section is included for applications where the editor is used to modify a data structure to which pointers are stored elsewhere. In these cases, the actual mechanics of structure modification must be known in order to predict the effect that various commands may have on these outside pointers. For example, if you did (SETQ FOO (CDR BAZ)) and then started editing BAZ, what will the commands (2), (3), (2 X Y Z), (-2 X Y Z), etc., do to FOO?

Deletion of the first element in the current expression is performed by replacing it with the second element and deleting the second element by patching around it. Deletion of any other element is done by patching around it; i.e., the previous tail is altered. Thus if FOO is EQ to the current expression which is (A B C D), and FIE is CDR of FOO, after executing the command (1), FOO will be (B C D) (which is EQUAL but not EQ to FIE). However, under the same initial conditions, after executing (2), FIE will be unchanged: FIE will still be (B C D) even though the current expression and FOO are now (A C D). (A general solution of the problem just isn't possible, as it would require being able to make two lists EQ to each other that were originally different. Thus if FIE is CDR of the current expression, and FUM is CDDR of the current expression, performing (2) would have to make FIE be EQ to FUM if all subsequent operations were to update both FIE and FUM correctly. Think about it.)

Both replacement and insertion are accomplished by smashing both CAR and CDR of the corresponding tail (that is, using RPLACA and RPLACD). Thus, if FOO were EQ to the current expression, (A B C D), after (1 X Y Z), FOO would be (X Y Z B C D). Similarly, if FOO were EQ to the current expression, (A B C D), then after (-1 X Y Z), FOO would be (X Y Z A B C D).

The N command is accomplished by smashing the last CDR of the current expression a la NCONC. Thus, if FOO were EQ to any tail of the current expression, after executing an N command, the corresponding expressions would also appear at the end of FOO.

In summary, the only situation in which an edit operation will _not_ change an external pointer occurs when the external pointer points to a _proper tail_ of the data structure, i.e., to CDR of some node in the structure, and the operation is deletion. If all external pointers are to _elements_ of the structure, i.e., to CAR of some node, or if only insertions, replacements, or attachments are performed, the edit operation will _always_ have the same effect on an external pointer as it does on the current expression.

22.15.3 LASTAIL and UP

The execution of UP is straightforward, except in those cases where the current expression appears more than once in the next higher expression. For example, if the current expression is (A NIL B NIL C NIL) and you type 4 UP, the current expression should then be ... NIL C NIL). UP can determine which tail is the correct one because the commands that descend save thave the last tail on an internal editor variable, LASTAIL. Thus after the 4 command is executed, LASTAIL is (NIL C NIL). When UP is called, it first determines if the current expression is a tail of the next higher expression. If it is, UP is finished. Otherwise, UP computes

```
(MEMQ current-expression next-higher-expression)
```

to obtain a tail beginning with the current expression. (The current expression should _always_ be either a tail or an element of the next higher expression. If it is neither, for example if you have directly (and incorrectly) manipulated the edit chain, UP generates an error.) If there are no other instances of the current expression in the next higher expression, this tail is the correct one. Otherwise UP uses LASTAIL to select the correct tail.

It is possible to get the edit chain into a state where LASTAIL cannot resolve the ambiguity; for example if there were two non-atomic structures in the same expression that were EQ, and you descended more than one level into one of them and then tried to come back out using UP. In this case, UP selects the first tail and prints LOCATION UNCERTAIN to warn you. Of course, we could have solved this problem completely in our implementation by saving both elements and tails at each descent. However, this would be a costly solution to a situation that arises infrequently and has no detrimental effects when it does. The LASTAIL solution is cheap and resolves 99% of the ambiguities.

22.16 Top-level editor functions

The basic editor function is EDITL, but there are several functions that save you the work of finding or constructing the proper parameters that EDITL requires. These tend to be the most commonly used editor functions.

22.16.1 Common user functions

(EDITF "FN" . "COMS")

EDITF is used for editing the function FN. COMS is an optional list of commands.

EDITF uses LASTWORD (see 21.2.2) as the name of the function to edit if no parameters are given, i.e., (EDITF).

EDITF returns FN.

In the most common case, FN is the name of a LISP function, and EDITF simply performs

```
(EDITE (CADR (GETL FN '(FEXPR EXPR MACRO))) COMS FN)
```

and sets LASTWORD to FN. If FN is not an editable function, but has a value, EDITF assumes the user meant to call EDITV, prints =EDITV, calls EDITV, and returns. Otherwise, EDITF generates the error: fn NOT EDITABLE.

(EDITE EXPR COMS ATM)

EDITE edits an expression. Its value is the last element of

```
(EDITL (LIST EXPR) COMS ATM NIL NIL)
```

EDITE generates an error if EXPR is not a list.

(EDITEXPR X)

If X is an atom, EDITEXPR simply returns X. Otherwise it calls the editor. Definition:

```
(DE EDITEXPR (X) (COND [(ATOM X) X]
                       [T (EDITE X NIL NIL)]))
```

(EDITV "VAL" . "COMS")

EDITV is used to edit values. VAL is the value. COMS is an optional list of commands.

If EDITV is called with no parameters, i.e., (EDITV), it uses the value of the global variable EDITV, which is analogous to LASTWORD but independent of it.

If VAL is a list, it is evaluated and its value given to EDITE; e.g. (EDITV (CDR (ASSOC 'FOO DICTIONARY))). In this case, the value of EDITV is T.

However, in most cases, VAR is a variable, e.g., (EDITV FOO), and EDITV calls EDITE on the value of the variable.

If the value of VAR is atomic, then EDITV prints a NOT EDITABLE error message.

When (if) EDITE returns, EDITV sets the variable to the value returned, and sets EDITV to the name of the variable.

The value of EDITV is the name of the variable whose value was edited.

(EDITP "ID" . "COMS")

EDITP is similar to EDITF and is used for editing property lists. Like EDITF, LASTWORD is used if there are no parameters. EDITP calls EDITE on the property list of ID. When (if) EDITE returns, EDITP RPLACD's ID with the value returned, and sets LASTWORD to ID.

The value of EDITP is the atom whose property list was edited.

(EDITFNS "L" . "COMS")

EDITFNS performs the same editing operations on several functions. L is evaluated to obtain a list of function names or a "prettyprint list" (see 17.5.3). (Both top-level atoms and any atoms appearing inside a prettyprint command in the list will be edited.) COMS is a list of edit commands. EDITFNS maps down the list of functions, prints the name of each function, and calls the editor (via EDITF) on that function.

For example, (EDITFNS FOOFNS (R FIE FUM)) will change every FIE to FUM in each of the functions on FOOFNS.

The call to the editor is ERRSET-protected, so that if the editing of one function causes an error, EDITFNS will proceed to the next function.

Thus in the example above, if one of the functions did not contain a FIE, the R command would cause an error, but editing would continue with the next function.

The value of EDITFNS is T. Definition:

```
(DF EDITFNS (X)
  (MAPC
   (FUNCTION
    (LAMBDA (I)
     (COND [(CONSP I)
            (COND [(AND [LITATOM I] [GET (CAR I) 'PPCOM])
                   (APPLY# 'EDITFNS
                           (CONS (LIST 'QUOTE (CDR I))
                                 (CDR X)))])]
           [T (ERRSET (APPLY# 'EDITF
                              (CONS (PRINT I) (CDR X)))
                      ERRORX)])))
   (EVAL (CAR X)))
  T)
```

22.16.2 EDITL

<u>(EDITL L COMS ATM MARKLST MESS)</u>

EDITL <u>is</u> the editor. Its first argument is the edit chain, and its value is an edit chain, namely the value of L at the time EDITL is exited. L is a SPECIAL variable, and so can be examined or set by edit commands. For example, ^ is equivalent to (E (SETQ L (LAST L)) T).

COMS is an optional list of commands. For interactive editing, COMS is NIL. In this case, EDITL types EDIT and then waits for input from the teletype.

If MESS is not NIL, then EDITL types it instead of EDIT. For example, the TTY: command is essentially (SETQ L (EDITL L NIL NIL NIL 'TTY:)).

Exit occurs only via an OK, STOP, or SAVE command.

If COMS is not NIL, no message is typed, and each member of COMS is treated as a command and executed. If an error occurs in the execution of one of the commands, no error message is printed, the rest of the commands are ignored, and EDITL exits with an error: the effect is the same as though a STOP command had been executed. If all commands execute successfully, EDITL returns the current value of L.

MARKLST is the list of marks.

On calls from EDITF, ATM is the name of the function being edited; on calls from EDITV, it is the name of the variable; on calls from EDITP, it is the atom of which some property of its property list is being edited. The property list of ATM is used by the SAVE command for saving the state of the edit. Thus SAVE will not save anything if ATM = NIL, i.e., when editing arbitrary expressions via EDITE or EDITL directly.

22.16.3 Stand-alone editor functions

<u>(EDIT4E PAT Y)</u>

EDIT4E is the pattern-matching routine. Its value is T if PAT matches Y. See 22.3.2.1 for the definition of "match."

Before each search operation in the editor begins, the entire pattern is scanned for atoms or strings that end in at-signs. These are replaced by patterns of the form

(CONS '/@ (EXPLODEC atom))

Thus from the standpoint of EDIT4E, pattern type 5 (atoms or strings ending in at-signs) is really "If car[pat] is the atom @ (at-sign), PAT will match with any literal atom or string whose initial character codes (up to the @) are the same as those in cdr[pat]."

If you want to call EDIT4E directly, you should use EDITFPAT to convert any patterns which contain atoms or strings ending in at-signs to the form recgnized by EDIT4E.

(EDITFPAT PAT FLG)

Makes a copy of PAT with all patterns of type 5 converted to the form expected by EDIT4E. FLG should be passed as NIL; FLG = T is for internal use by the editor.

(EDITFINDP X PAT FLG)

Allows a program to use the edit F command as a pure predicate from outside the editor. X is an expression, PAT a pattern. The value of EDITFINDP is T if the command F pat would succeed, NIL otherwise. EDITFINDP calls EDITFPAT to convert PAT to the form expected by EDIT4E, unless FLG = T. Thus, if the program is applying EDITFINDP to several different expressions using the same pattern, it will be more efficient to call EDITFPAT once, and then call EDITFINDP with the converted pattern and FLG = T.

22.16.4 Tracing the editor

EDITRACEFN

If the global variable EDITRACEFN is non-NIL, it is assumed to be the name of a function of one parameter; the editor will call the function before executing each command (at any level), giving it that command as the parameter. It is intended to help the user debug complex edit macros or subroutine calls to the editor.

For example, defining EDITRACEFN as

```
(LAMBDA (C) (PRINT C) (PRINT (CAR L)))
```

will print each command and the corresponding current expression. Defining EDITRACEFN as

```
(LAMBDA (C) (BREAK1 T T NIL NIL NIL))
```

will cause a break before executing each command. EDITRACEFN is initially equal to NIL.

22.17 Editor Command Summary

Table II
Editor Command Summary

The items in this table are presented in the same order as they are in the text, which you should consult for details.

The following abbreviations are used:

c-e	the current expression
p	pattern
m	integer or any parameter to NTH
n	integer
e	S-expression
c	editor command
fn	editor function
$	location specification
v	identifier

MOVING AROUND **

1	move to the first element
2	move to the second element
etc.	
-1	move to the last element
-2	move to the next-to-last element
etc.	
^	move to the top
0	move to the previous c-e
UP	move up a CAR-link
!0	move to a previous c-e that isn't a CDR
NX	move over to the next c-e on this level
BK	back up one c-e
!NX	move to the next c-e anywhere
<	go back to where we were before jumping
\	= <
<P	go back to where we were the last time we printed
\P	= <P
MARK	mark this spot
_	go back to the most recent mark
__	go back to the most recent mark and erase it

PRINTING COMMANDS **

P	print the c-e with (PRINLEV c-e EDITPLEV)
P;	= P with COMMENTFLG = T
PP	prettyprint the c-e

```
PP;      = P with COMMENTFLG = T
(P m)    print the mth element
(P 0)    = P
(P m n)  print the mth element to depth n
(P 0 n)  print the c-e to depth n
P1       = (P 0 1)
P2       = (P 0 2)
etc.
?        = (P 0 100)
```

SEARCH COMMANDS **

```
F p                look ahead for p
FP p               = F p P
(F p N)            = F p but without MEMQ-check
(F p T)            = (F p N) but without changing edit chain
(F p n)            = F p, repeated n times
(F p)              restrict search to top level of the c-e
(F p NIL)          = (F p)
(F p1 p2 ...)      = F p1 F p2 ...
(F= e p)           = F p, but p must be EQ to e
(ORF p1 p2 ...)    find first p that matches

BF                 look back for p
BFP p              = BF p P
(BF p T)           start at the end of the c-e
(BF p NIL)         = BF p
(BF p)             = BF p

&                  matches any single item
--                 matches any segment, including NIL
xxx@               matches any atom beginning with xxx
:::                allow matching on tails
```

LOCATION SPECIFICATIONS *********************************

```
(LC . $)           invoke location-specification procedure
(LCL . $)          restrict search to the c-e
(SECOND . $)       similar to (LC . $) (LC . $)
(THIRD . $)        similar to (LC . $) (LC . $) (LC . $)
(_ p)              match p with previous c-e's
(BELOW c x)        execute c [or (_ c) if c isn't a command],
                   then move back down (EVAL x)-many links
(NEX x)            = (BELOW x 1) NX
NEX                = (NEX _) = (BELOW _ 1) NX

(NTH $)            generalized NTH function
                   = (LCL . $) (BELOW <) UP

(p :: . $)         = (F p N) (LCL . $) (_ p)

($1 THRU $2)       construct segment from $1 to $2 (incl. both)
($1 TO $2)         construct segment from $1 to $2 (incl. $1)
($1 THRU)          = ($1 THRU -1)
```

```
($1 TO)            = ($1 TO -1)

INSERTION          ********************************************

(-1 e1 e2 ...)  insert e's before the 1st element
(-2 e1 e2 ...)  insert e'2 before the 2nd element
etc.

(N e1 e2 ...)   attach e's to the end of the c-e

(B e1 e2 ...)   insert e's before the c-e
                = UP (-1 e1 e2 ...)
(A e1 e2 ...)   insert e's after the c-e
                = UP (-2 e1 e2 ...) or UP (N e1 e2 ...)

INSERT e1 e2 ... BEFORE $       = (LC . $) (B e1 e2 ...)
INSERT e1 e2 ... AFTER  $       = (LC . $) (A e1 e2 ...)

DELETION           ********************************************

(1)             delete the 1st element
(2)             delete the 2nd element
etc.

DELETE          delete the c-e
(:)             = DELETE

(DELETE . $)    = (LC . $) DELETE

REPLACEMENT        ********************************************

(1 e1 e2 ...)   replace the 1st element with e1 e2 ...
(2 e1 e2 ...)   replace the 2nd element with e1 e2 ...
etc.

(: e1 e2 ...)   replace the c-e with e1 e2 ...

(REPLACE $ WITH e1 e2 ...)      = (LCL . $) (: e1 e2 ...)
(REPLACE $  BY  e1 e2 ...)      = same
(INSERT e1 e2 ... FOR $)        = same
(CHANGE $ TO e1 e2 ...)         = same

(R p e)         replace all p's with e
                = (DSUBST e (F p T) c-e)
(SW m1 m2)      switch elements m1 and m2

RESTRUCTURING      ********************************************

(MOVE $1 TO fn . $2)
                Locate $1, locate $2, use fn (e.g., AFTER,
                BEFORE, N) at $2, and delete $1

(MBD x)         embed c-e in x in spots marked with *
                = (SETQ c-e (SUBST c-2 '* x))
```

```
(EMBED $ IN . x)          = (LC . $) (MBD . x)
(EMBED $ WITH . x)        = same
(SURROUND $ WITH . x)     = same
(SURROUND $ IN . x)       = same

(XTR . $)                 replace c-e with (LCL . $)
(EXTRACT $1 FROM $2)      = (LC . $2) (XTR . $1)

(BI n m)        insert ( before nth element, ) after mth
(BO n)          remove both parens from nth element
(LI n)          insert ( before nth element, ) at end of c-e
(LO n)          remove ( from nth element, deleting n+1, ...
(RI n m)        move ) after nth element in, to just after
                its mth element
(RO n)          move ) after nth element to end of the c-e
```

UNDO MECHANISM **

```
UNDO    reverse effects of most recent structure change
!UNDO   UNDO everything up to the first UNDO-block
??      print list of UNDO-able commands
UNDO c  UNDO command c
TEST    add an UNDO-block
UNBLOCK remove an UNDO-block
```

LEAVING/RECURSING ***************************************

```
OK      ^ and exit normally
SAVE    exit and save state info on property list of
        edited structure
STOP    exit via (ERR NIL)
TTY:    call editor recursively
```

PROGRAMMING ***

```
NIL     do nothing
E x     (EVAL x)
(E x)   same
(E x T) same but don't print result

(COMSQ c1 c2 ...)         execute c1 c2 ...
(COMS x1 x2 ...)          execute (EVAL x1), execute (EVAL x2),
                          ...
(I c x1 x2 ...)           execute (c (EVAL x1) (EVAL x2) ...)
(LP c1 c2 ...)            repeat c1 c2 ... up to 30 times or
                          until an error occurs
(LPQ c1 c2 ...)           same but don't print how many times
                          it looped
(IF x)          if (EVAL x) causes an error or return NIL,
                generate an error
(IF x c)        if (EVAL x) neq NIL and doesn't cause an error,
                execute c
(IF x c1 c2)    if (EVAL x) neq NIL and doesn't cause an error,
                execute c; otherwise execute c2
```

```
(ORR c1 c2 ...) execute c1, then c2, ..., as long as
                there are errors
(S v . $)       locate $, set v to resulting c-e
(BIND c1 c2 ...)  = (PROG (#1 #2 #3) (COMSQ c1 c2 ...))

(M x c1 c2 ...) define new edit command v that executes
                c1 c2 ...
(M (x) (v1 ... vn) c1 c2 ...)
                define new edit function (x e1 ... en) that
                executes c1 c2 ... with e[i] substituted for
                corresponding v[i] in c1 c2 ...
(M (x) v.c1 c2 ...)
                define new edit function (x e1 e2 ...) that
                executes c1 c2 ... with list (e1 e2 ...)
                substituted for v in c1 c2 ...

MISCELLANY      *******************************************

UNPACK          unpack atom into list for editing
(UNPACK . $)    = (LC . $) UNPACK

REPACK          unpack, edit, and restore atom
(REPACK . $)    = (LC . $) REPACK

SORT            sort the c-e
(SORT . $)      = (LC . $) SORT
```

CHAPTER 23

COMPILED LISP

The first three sections of this chapter are intended to explain the structure of compiled functions, function calls, and accumulator usage. This discussion is relevant only if you intend to interface hand-coded functions or possibly functions generated by another system (such as FORTRAN) with LISP. In such a case, it is highly recommended that you examine the LAP code generated by the LISP compiler for some familiar functions.

Section 4 describes how to use LISPC, the LISP compiler. Section 5 discusses LAP, the function that loads the output from the compiler. Finally, section 6 discusses ways to increase the execution speed and decrease the storage requirements for compiled code.

23.1 Register usage

s means "sacred" to the interpreter
p means "protected" during garbage collection

```
NIL  = 0      s,p   Value cell for the atom NIL.
A    = 1        p   Results  from  functions,
                           1st arg to functions
B    = 2        p   2nd arg to functions
C    = 3        p   3rd arg to functions
AR1  = 4        p   4th arg to functions
AR2A = 5        p   5th arg to functions
T    = 6        p   used for LSUBR linkage
TT   = 7        p
T10  = 10       p   rarely used in the interpreter
S    = 11           used for atom relocation
D    = 12
R    = 13
```

```
P    = 14     s,p   Regular Pushdown List pointer
F    = 15     s,p   Free Storage List pointer
FF   = 16     s,p   Full-word List pointer
SP   = 17     s,p   Special Pushdown List pointer
```

23.1.1 Temporary storage

Whenever a LISP function is called from a compiled function, it is assumed that all accumulators from 1 through 10 are destroyed by the function (unless it is known otherwise). Therefore, the local variables and parameters in a compiled function should be saved in some protected cells such as the Regular Pushdown List.

23.1.2 Binding SPECIAL variables

SPECIAL variables in compiled functions are bound to special cells by:

```
PUSHJ   P, SPECBIND
XWD     n1, var1
XWD     n2, var2
      ...
start of function code
```

SPECBIND saves the previous values of var[i] on the Special Pushdown List and binds the contents of accumulator n[i] to each var[i]. The var[i] must be pointers to special cells of identifiers. Any n[i]=0 causes the var[i] to be bound to NIL.

Special variables are restored to their previous values by:

```
PUSHJ P,SPECSTR
```

which stores the values previously saved on the Special Pushdown List in the appropriate special cells.

23.2 Numbers: internal/external conversion

(NUMVAL X)

NUMVAL converts a number from its LISP representation to its machine representation.

At the assembly level, you can call NUMVAL directly by putting X in register A and calling

```
PUSHJ P,NUMVAL
```

which returns the machine-value of the number in A, and its type (either FIXNUM or FLONUM) in B.

(MAKNUM X TYPE)

MAKNUM converts a number X from its machine representation to its LISP representation. TYPE should be either FIXNUM or FLONUM; the default is FIXNUM. (Use FIXNUM for any integer, including INUMs.)

At the assembly level, you can call MAKNUM directly with

```
PUSHJ P,MAKNUM
```

after loading the machine number into A and the desired type into B. If the type is FIXNUM, you can also call

```
PUSHJ P,FIX1A
```

after loading the number into A. (MAKNUM calls FIX1A if type = FIXNUM). Both functions return the LISP number in A.

23.3 Function-calling UUOs

To allow ease in linking, debugging, and modifying of compiled functions, all compiled functions call other functions with special opcodes called UUOs. There are two kinds of function calls:

1. Calls of the form (RETURN (FOO X)) are called terminal calls and essentially "jump" to FOO.

2. Calls of the form (F X) where F is a computed function name or functional argument is called a functional call.

The function-calling UUOS are:

	non-terminal	terminal
non-functional	CALL n,f	JCALL n,f
functional	CALLF n,f	JCALLF n,f

where f is either the address of a compiled function or a pointer to the identifier for the function (the atom header), and n specifies the type of function being called as follows:

n = 0 to 5	specifies a SUBR call with n arguments
n = 16	specifies an LSUBR call
n = 17	specifies an FSUBR call.

The function calling UUOs are defined in MACRO by:

```
OPDEF CALL [34B8]
OPDEF JCALL [35B8]
OPDEF CALLF [36B8]
OPDEF JCALLF [37B8]
```

23.3.1 SUBR linkage

SUBRs are compiled EXPRs which are the most common type of function. Consequently, considerable effort has been made to make linkage to SUBRs efficient.

Arguments to SUBRs are supplied in accumulators 1 through n, the first argument in 1. There is a maximum of 5 arguments to SUBRs.

To call a SUBR named F from compiled code, use "<u>call</u> n,F", where n is the number of arguments, and <u>call</u> is the appropriate UUO.

The result from a SUBR is returned in A (register 1).

23.3.2 FSUBR linkage

FSUBRs receive one argument in A and return their result in A. FSUBRs which use the A-LIST feature (see 8.2) call:

```
PUSHJ P, *AMAKE
```

which generates in B a number encoding the state of the special pushdown pointer.

To call an FSUBR named F, use "call 17, F", where call is the appropriate UUO.

23.3.3 LSUBR linkage

LSUBRs are similar to SUBRs except that they allow an arbitrary number of arguments to be passed. To call an LSUBR, the following sequence is used:

```
        PUSH    P, [ret]   ;return address
        PUSH    P, arg1    ;1st argument
           ...
        PUSH    P, argn ;nth and last argument
        MOVNI   T, n    ;minus number of arguments
        call    16, F   ;the appropriate UUO
ret:                    ;the LSUBR returns here
```

When an LSUBR is entered, it executes:

```
JSP 3,*LCALL
```

which initializes the LSUBR. Register A will contain n. The ith argument can be referenced by:

```
MOVE    A,-1(P)
HRRZ    A,i(A)
```

Exit from an LSUBR with

```
POPJ P,
```

which returns to *LCALL to restore the stack.

23.4 The LISP compiler

The LISP compiler is a LISP program which transforms LISP functions defined by S-expressions into LAP assembly code. This can be loaded into Binary Program Space by LAP (LISP Assembly Program), a combined assembler and loader, which produces absolute machine code in core.

Compiled functions are approximately twenty times as fast as interpreted functions. Compiled functions also take up less memory space and relieve the garbage collector from marking function definitions. In a very large system of functions, this last point is particularly significant.

The LISP compiler exists as the system program LISPC, and is called by typing ".R LISPC" at the monitor level. Its top level is the same as LISP's.

<u>(COMPL "FILESPEC1" "FILESPEC2" ...)</u>

> The function COMPL takes as arguments an assortment of file names and device names in precisely the same way as the function DSKIN. The default device to be used for input in the event that none is supplied in the argument sequence is given by the value of the variable INDEV (initially DSK:).
>
> There is no provision for specification of an output device in the argument sequence. If you want the output on some device other than the your disk area, set the variable OUTDEV to that device. OUTDEV is initially set to DSK:. All error messages and comments are normally directed to the terminal. They can be sent to some other device by setting the variable LISTING (initially NIL). Files produced by the compiler have the filename extension LAP.

Examples:

1. (COMPL FOO SYS: TRACE)

will compile the file FOO from the your disk area and the file TRACE from the system area* to produce the files FOO.LAP and TRACE.LAP in your disk area.

----

* Since COMPL uses INPUT, the files FOO.LSP and TRACE.LSP will be read if FOO and TRACE are not found.

```
2.      (SETQ INDEV 'DTA2:)
        (SETQ OUTDEV '[2,123Q])
        (SETQ LISTING '(DSK: CMPMSG))
        (COMPL HAT SYS: SMILE)
```

b These commands will compile the file DTA2:HAT and the file SYS:SMILE to produce the files DSK:HAT.LAP[2,123] and DSK:SMILE.LAP[2,123]. All compiler messages will appear as the file DSK:CMPMSG.

23.4.1 Preparing files for compilation

<u>(DECLARE "D1" "D2" ...)</u>

Although the use of the compiler is quite straightforward, there are several declarations which can (and sometimes must) be made, so that the compiler has additional informaton about your code. In <u>LISP</u>, the function DECLARE is a no-op, equivalent to NILL; in <u>LISPC</u>, it is not.

There are several DECLARE-forms (parameters to DECLARE). The DECLARE call should normally occur at the beginning of your file.

1. If the compiler is generating a call to a function, it assumes that the function is an EXPR or SUBR unless it knows otherwise, either by having seen the definition of the function earlier in the compilation, by having the definition already on the function's property list, or by seeing a declaration of the form:

   ```
   (DECLARE (*FSUBR fun1 fun2 ...))
   or (DECLARE (*LSUBR fun1 fun2 ...))
   ```

   *FEXPR may be used in place of *FSUBR; *LEXPR may be used in place of *LSUBR.

2. Any variable which occurs free in any function must be declared SPECIAL prior to the definition of any function which binds it. This may be done with a statement of the form:

   ```
   (DECLARE (SPECIAL var1 var2 ...))
   ```

   Note that free variables that are used in (1) in-line LAMBDA expressions, (2) LAMBDA expressions that are arguments to the MAP functions, and (3) ERRSET expressions need <u>not</u>

be declared SPECIAL.

3. The UNSPECIAL declaration tells the compiler that certain variables are no longer to be considered SPECIAL and should be compiled as normal local variables in subsequent functions.

```
(DECLARE (UNSPECIAL var1 var2 ...))
```

This declaration is normally placed in the middle of a file.

4. Since macros are actually expanded at compile time, their definitions must occur earlier in the file than any function that uses them. Otherwise, the macro will be mistaken for an undefined EXPR.

Macro definitions are assumed to be used only by the functions in the file in which they appear, and hence are unnecessary after the file is compiled. Accordingly, they do not appear in the output (LAP) file. If you want to keep the macro definition and have it copied into the LAP file, you may do so with the GLOBALMACRO declaration:

```
(DECLARE (GLOBALMACRO fn1 fn2 ...))
```

5. Even though all undefined functions are assumed to be EXPRs and SUBRs, there are two cases where you must declare them as such.

A. If a function name is also used as a variable, it must be declared if it is referenced before it is compiled. Example:

```
(DECLARE (*SUBR BAZ))
```

B. Missing arguments to interpreted functions default to NIL. To compile references to such functions, the compiler must know how many formal parameters there are. To indicate that the function FOO takes three arguments, use the following form:

```
(DECLARE (*SUBR (FOO 3)))
```

*EXPR may be used in place of *SUBR.

6. Arrays may declared. *ARRAY is identical to *SUBR since arrays are actually implemented as SUBRs.

```
(DECLARE (*ARRAY BAZ))
```

7. The two remaining declarations, CALL and NOCALL will be discussed in 23.6.

23.4.2 Compiler messages

As the compiler goes about its business, it will make various comments and complaints about your code.

1. As the compilation of each function is begun, its name will be typed on the terminal by PRINA. Any other message will be set off by blank lines.

2. Whenever the compiler discovers a free variable which has not been declared SPECIAL, it declares it SPECIAL. At the end of any function (fn) in which it found such variables it will print out the message:

   ```
   * (var1 var2 ...) UNDECLARED FREE VARIABLES IN fn
   ```

3. If a PROG variable is unused in a function, the compiler will print the message:

   ```
   * var1 UNUSED PROG VARIABLE IN fn
   ```

   It will also declare the variable SPECIAL on the theory that if it was not used there, it must have been used somewhere else (e.g., in a function called from within the PROG) as a free variable.

4. Many minor errors in user code will unfortunately go undetected. Any serious error will produce the message *USER ERROR* followed by a description of what was wrong. This will halt the compiler.

5. The error message *COMPILER ERROR* indicates a bug in the compiler.

6. When the compiler has finished, it will type out the name of the file, the number of words of code produced, and the time taken. Following these will be lists of any functions called but not defined in the file and any auxiliary functions that the compiler generated.

23.4.3 Using compiled code

Since LAP code is self-loading, the loading of compiled files is the same as for interpreted functions. The allocations must be changed, however, since the code occupies Binary Program Space and not Free Storage. The compiler prints the amount of Binary Program Space required at the end of compilation.

The following example illustrates various aspects of the compiler's behavior. We show a collection of functions, the LAP code generated from it, and the comments made by the compiler in the process.

23.4.3.1 The input -

```
(DEFPROP FIRST (LAMBDA (L) (CONS 'CAR (CDR L))) MACRO)

(DEFPROP COUNTM
 (LAMBDA (SEXPR)
  (PROG (COUNT)
        {;; the variable COUNT has not been declared SPECIAL
            and will be treated as local}
        (SETQ COUNT 0.)
        (COUNT1 SEXPR)
        (RETURN COUNT)))
 EXPR)

(DEFPROP COUNT1
 (LAMBDA (SS)
  (COND [(ATOM SS) NIL]
        [T (INCR COUNT)
           {;; here it is discovered to be special but too
               late}
           (COUNT1 (FIRST SS))
           (COUNT1 (CDR SS))]))
 EXPR)

(DEFPROP SCALE
 (LAMBDA (NO)
  {;; SCALEF is found to be special}
  (TIMES NO SCALEF))
 EXPR)

(DEFPROP IT T SPECIAL)  {;; SPECIAL declaration}

(DEFPROP BAZ
 (LAMBDA (IT LIST)
  (FOO (FUNCTION (LAMBDA (X) (CONS IT X)))
       {;; The internal lambda becomes a separate function.
            Thus, the variable IT must be made SPECIAL.}
```

```
       LISP))
 EXPR)

(DEFPROP SETQQ (LAMBDA (L) (SET (CAR L) (CADR L))) FEXPR)
```

23.4.3.2 The LAP output -

```
(LAP COUNTM SUBR)
        (PUSH P 1Q)
        (PUSH P (C 0Q 0Q (QUOTE 0Q) 0Q))  <--- this is in
                error because COUNT wasn't declared SPECIAL
        (CALL 1Q (E COUNT1) S)
        (MOVE 1Q 0Q P)
        (SUB P (C 2Q 0Q 2Q 0Q))
        (POPJ P)
        NIL

(LAP COUNT1 SUBR)
        (PUSH P 1Q)
        (CALL 1Q (E ATOM) S)
        (JUMPE 1Q TAG2)
        (MOVEI 1Q (QUOTE NIL))
        (JRST 0Q TAG1)
 TAG2   (MOVE 1Q (SPECIAL COUNT) S)  <-- reference to the
                SPECIAL variable COUNT, which has not been
                bound properly
        (CALL 1Q (E ADD1) S)
        (MOVEM 1Q (SPECIAL COUNT) S)
        (HLRZ@ 1Q 0Q P)
        (CALL 1Q (E COUNT1) S)
        (HRRZ@ 1Q 0Q P)
        (CALL 1Q (E COUNT1) S)
 TAG1   (SUB P (C 1Q 0Q 1Q 0Q))
        (POPJ P)
        NIL

(LAP SCALE SUBR)
        (MOVE 2Q (SPECIAL SCALEF) S) <-- detected in time
        (JCALL 2Q (E *TIMES) S)
        NIL

(LAP SUBFUN1BAZ SUBR)  <-- generated by the internal LAMBDA
        (MOVE 2Q (SPECIAL IT) S)
        (JCALL 2Q (E XCONS) S)
        NIL

(LAP BAZ SUBR)
        (JSP 6Q SPECBIND)
        (0Q 1Q (SPECIAL IT) S)
        (MOVE 3Q 2Q)
        (MOVEI 2Q (QUOTE NIL))
        (MOVEI 1Q (QUOTE SUBFUN1BAZ) S)
```

```
        (CALL 3Q (E FOO) S)
        (JRST 0Q SPECSTR)
        NIL

(LAP SETQQ FSUBR)
        (HRRZ@ 2Q 1Q)
        (HLRZ@ 2Q 2Q)
        (HLRZ@ 1Q 1Q)
        (JCALL 2Q (E SET) S)
        NIL
```

Note that the macro definition and the special declaration do not appear in the output.

23.4.3.3 Comments to the TTY -

```
FIRST COUNTM COUNT1

* COUNT LOCAL AND SPECIAL
* (COUNT) UNDECLARED FREE VARIABLES IN COUNT1

SCALE

* (SCALEF) UNDECLARED FREE VARIABLES IN SCALE

BAZ

* (IT) UNDECLARED FREE VARIABLES IN SUBFUN1BAZ

SETQQ

TEST COMPILED 43Q WORDS 3Q CONSTANTS 3Q SECONDS

UNDEFINED FUNCTIONS
FOO

GENERATED FUNCTIONS
SUBFUN1BAZ
```

23.4.4 Ignoring input

The compiler normally works by compiling all function definitions in the file (putting the compiled code in the LAP file), and copying all other expressions into the LAP file unchanged (except for comments, macros, and DECLARE expressions). It is sometimes desirable to change this standard convention. For example, the GLOBALMACRO declaration causes macros to be used by the compiler and also copied to the LAP file. Certain functions may have their compilation suppressed (with the symbolic definition copied to the LAP file) by placing their definitions inside a PROGN (the MBD: prettyprint command is useful for this).

If you want certain expressions to be evaluated when the LSP file is loaded, but to not be copied to the LAP file, place the expressions inside a NOCOMPILE (which acts like a PROGN when evaluated). For example, the prettyprint package causes PPL prettyprint lists to disappear at compile time by placing the variable binding inside a NOCOMPILE expression.

23.5 LAP, the LISP assembler

LAP is a primitive assembler designed to load the output of the compiler. Normally, it is not necessary to use LAP for any other purpose. LAP is self-loading. It returns a list consisting of the name of the function loaded followed by the number of words of Binary Program Space required for the compiled code.

The format of a compiled function in LAP is:

```
(LAP name type)

<sequence of LAP instructions>

NIL
```

where name is the name of the function, and type is either SUBR, LSUBR, or FSUBR.

A LAP instruction is either:

1. A label which is a non-NIL identifier.

2. A list of the form:

   (OPCODE AC ADDR INDEX)

   a. The opcode is either a PDP-10 instruction which is defined to LAP and optionally suffixed by @ which designates indirect addressing, or an 18-bit number which specifies a numerical opcode. Opcodes are defined by putting an 18-bit (not 9-bit) number on the opcode's property list under the name SYM. Examples:

   ```
   (DEFPROP SOJGE 365000Q SYM)

   (DEFPROP ILDB@ 134020Q SYM)
   ```

   b. The AC and INDEX fields should contain a number from 0 to 17, the atom P which designates register 14, or the atom S which designates register 11.

   c. The ADDR field may be a number, a label, or a list of one of the following forms:

   (QUOTE S-expression) to reference list structure.

   (SPECIAL x) to reference the value of identifier x.

   (E f) to reference the function f.

(C OPCODE AC ADDR INDEX) to reference a literal constant.

If the ADDR field refers to atoms or lists (e.g., QUOTE, SPECIAL, or E), then the INDEX field must be S (register 11) to indicate that the atom is relocatable. Exception: (QUOTE NIL) needs no relocation.

For example, the function ABS could be defined:

```
(LAP ABS SUBR)
(CALL 1 (E NUMVAL) S)
(MOVMS 0 1)
(JCALL 2 (E MAKNUM) S)
NIL
```

Warning

(1) The order of arguments is the same for all instructions. An unconditional jump to label TAG1 is written (JRST 0 TAG1), not (JRST TAG1).

(2) If an opcode has no SYM property, LAP will use an opcode of zero, which is, of course, an illegal instruction.

23.6 Further optimization: NOUUO and NOCALL

The function-calling mechanism described earlier, also known as the UUO handler, is used whenever a function is called from compiled code. This requires some overhead, such as checking the property list of the called function, before the function actually begins. The benefit of this extra work is that the function can be redefined, traced, and broken, and the number of arguments can be checked.

For completely debugged code, however, this may be unnecessarily expensive. It is possible to have the CALL UUO replaced by a PUSHJ instruction, and the JCALL UUO by a JRST instruction, either at runtime (NOUUO), at compile-time (NOCALL), or at load-time (NOCALL). CALLF and JCALLF cannot be eliminated since their addresses may change every time they are called.

23.6.1 NOUUO

If the NOUUO flag is NIL, then the UUO handler actually replaces the CALL (or JCALL) instruction with a PUSHJ (JRST) instruction when the CALL (JCALL) is first executed.

<u>(NOUUO X)</u>

> NOUUO sets the special flag to the value of X and returns the previous setting of the flag. The flag is initially T.
>
> Warning
>
> Once the CALL (or JCALL) has been removed, it cannot be put back. The function call cannot be traced or broken. Even if the function is redefined, the old definition will be used.

23.6.2 NOCALL property

If a function FN has a non-NIL NOCALL property at compile time (when running LISPC), the compiler will translate all calls to FN as PUSHJ's and JRST's to the entry point of FN, with no reference to the atom FN itself. When LAP sees such an instruction, it adds the name of the function to the list on the variable REMOB, so that functions that are not major entry points can be REMOB'ed later to save storage (e.g., via the function DUMPATOMS, described below).

The NOCALL property can be added to a list of functions by:

```
(DECLARE (NOCALL fn1 fn2 ...))
```

23.6.3 NOCALL = T

If the global variable NOCALL is T when LAP is loading compiled code, then <u>all</u> function calls will be changed to direct jumps. NOCALL is initially NIL and should be set back to NIL after loading.

Specific exceptions can be made. If a function has a non-NIL CALL property at load time, LAP will keep the CALL UUO. If the statement

```
(DECLARE (CALL fn1 fn2 ...))
```

appears in the LISP file being read by LISPC, LISPC will write that out to the LAP file as

```
(DEFLIST (fn1 fn2 ...) T CALL)
```

which will give fn1, etc., a non-NIL CALL property.

This is optional is some cases (e.g., you may wish to trace a particular function) and necessary in others.

LAP keeps a list of NOCALL functions on the list NOCALL. If a NOCALL function is defined when LAP sees a reference to it, it will put the address of the function in the instruction. If you subsequently <u>redefine</u> a NOCALL function, it will not be able to put the new address back in -- the old address will remain -- and it will print the message:

```
*WARNING - NOCALL Function <name> Redefined
```

If you want to redefine a NOCALL function, put the new definition <u>ahead</u> of any references to it, so that the new, correct address will be put in the instruction, or remove that function's SUBR, FSUBR, or LSUBR property, so that LAP will think that the function is <u>undefined</u>.

If a NOCALL function is undefined when LAP sees a reference to it (either because no definition has ever been seen or because you REMPROP'ed the definition away), it puts the property UNDEF on the function's property list.* When loading is finished, any atom with a non-NIL UNDEF property will cause the following error message:

```
*WARNING - NOCALL Function <name> Not Yet Defined
```

23.6.4 SPECIALs and compiled code

SPECIAL variables that are referenced only from compiled code do not need to keep their property lists around after the code has been loaded, because only the special cell (see 13.2) is referenced by the compiled code. Accordingly, the NOCALL procedure extends to them as well: CALL and NOCALL apply to SPECIAL variables just as they do to functions.

There is a difficulty, however, with backtraces of SPECIAL variables access from compiled code. In order to print variable bindings in backtraces (e.g., BKV), the CAR of the special cell points to the atom header. When the variables are bound by LAMBDA or PROG, a CONS-cell is pushed on the Special Pushdown List. As described in Chapter 19, the CAR of that cell is the address of the variable's special cell, and the CDR points to the previous value, so the CAAR of that cell is the atom header, which is passed to PRINT to get the variable's name. However, the CAR of special cells of SPECIAL variables that are referenced from compiled code must be NIL, since indirect addressing is used, and that involves bits in the left half of the word. So when LAP sees a reference to a SPECIAL variable in compiled code, it sets the left half (CAR) of the special cell to NIL, but adds a new CONS-cell to the front end of the list LAPLST. Its CAR is the address of the value cell and its CDR is the address of the atom header. When TRACE is printing variable names and finds a NIL in the CAR of SPDLFT, it looks in LAPLST (with ASSOC) for the special cell. If found, the CDR of that will point to the atom header. The code that prints variable names (from the Break Package):

```
(PRINC (COND [(CAR (SETQ SPEC (SPDLFT %SPD)))]
             [(SETQ NAM (ASSOC SPEC LAPLST)) (CDR NAM)]
             [T '?]))
```

where %SPD is the stack pointer.

Since this means a 2-word overhead for each SPECIAL

----

* The UNDEF property is a list of locations where the undefined function was called. If the definition is later loaded by LAP, each location is patched with the new address, and the property is removed.

variable, there is a flag which controls the adding of items to LAPLST. SPECIAL variables are added to LAPLST iff the variable SPECIAL is non-NIL. SPECIAL is initially T.

23.6.5 Other LAP-lists

In addition to LAPLST, LAP maintains three other lists, which, like LAPLST, the naive user should leave alone.

1. LAPKLST points to constants within compiled code.
2. LAPQLST points to quoted expressions referenced from compiled code and to make them known to the garbage collector.
3. LAPSLST is a list of special cells of NOCALL variables for use by the garbage collector.

23.6.6 Clearing the storage

The NOCALL declarations are intended to flag identifiers that are not necessary after a LAP file has been loaded. To REMOB the variables, but without permanent damage, two functions are provided:

<u>(DUMPATOMS "FILESPEC")</u>

DUMPATOMS may be called to REMOB all NOCALL atoms after first creating a file (if omitted, it uses DSK:REMOB.LSP), writing out all the SUBR, FSUBR, LSUBR, VALUE, and SYM properties of each NOCALL atom. The file can be read back in later, either by UNDUMPATOMS or DSKIN, restoring all those properties. The file contains PUTPROP calls for all the atoms, and a DEFV for REMOB.

<u>(UNDUMPATOMS "FILESPEC")</u>

UNDUMPATOMS reads the file back in. (If the file name is omitted, it also uses DSK:REMOB.LSP.) If the variable SPECIAL is NIL, UNDUMPATOMS simply calls DSKIN. Otherwise, it reads and evaluates each expression in the file. If it reads an expression of the form:

```
(PUTPROP X Y 'VALUE)
```

it adds (CONS Y X) to the front end of LAPLST so that backtraces will include variable names once again.

CHAPTER 24

THE LOADER

24.1 LOAD

A modified version of LOADER* is available for use in LISP. You can call the loader into a LISP core image at any time by executing:

(LOAD X)

When a * is typed, you are in the (LOAD X) loader, and the loader commands are expected. As soon as an altmode (or /G) is typed, the loader finishes and returns to the top level of LISP.

The loader is read from LSP:LISP.LOD and placed in expanded core. (LSP: is where the LISP system resides. It may be SYS: at some installations.) If X = NIL (or missing) then loaded programs are placed in Expanded Core; otherwise they are placed in Binary Program Space. The loader removes itself and contracts core when it is finished.

In the following discussion a "RELOC" program will refer to any program which is suitable for loading with the loader. FORTRAN, MACRO, and FAIL, for example, produce RELOC programs (.REL files).

While LISP uses the OBLIST and the property lists as its "symbol table," the .REL-file loader uses the more standard symbol table produced by most assemblers and compilers, sometimes called the DDT symbol table. If the address of a LISP function or atom is declared EXTERNAL in the RELOC

----

* LOADER is no longer used as the standard linking loader on SYS:. It has been replace by LINK-10. LISP uses LOADER version 57(151)-1. Consult old manuals for detailed documentation, switches, etc.

program, then the loader will look for it in the symbol table. If it's not there already, then you must put it there with PUTSYM. Often these addresses will be taken from the property lists (via GET), and they may have to be converted from their LISP representation to the machine representation (via NUMVAL). Consequently, _before loading, you may have to call PUTSYM, GET, and NUMVAL_.

After loading, the opposite situation holds. Addresses in the RELOC program that you want to access from LISP are declared INTERNAL (or ENTRY) so that the loader will add them to the symbol table. In order to use them from LISP, you must retrieve them from the symbol table with GETSYM. Often these addresses are added to the property lists (PUT), and they may have to be converted from the machine representation to the LISP representation (via MAKNUM). Consequently, _after loading, you may have to call GETSYM, PUT, and MAKNUM_.

24.2 Accessing the symbol table

(*GETSYM S)
(*RGETSYM S)

*GETSYM searches the DDT symbol table (which LOAD automatically loads) for the symbol S and returns its value. It returns NIL if the symbol was not found.

*RGETSYM is like *GETSYM except that it adds the atom relocation amount to the result. (If Binary Program Space is expanded, all the memory areas above it are moved up. This includes Free Storage, where all the atoms are stored.) If the result of adding the relocation to the symbol-table entry is a location outside Free Storage, *RGETSYM causes an error: NOT A CONS CELL. *RGETSYM is provided only as an "inverse" to *RPUTSYM. Normally, the only way to put an _unrelocated_ value into the symbol table is with *RPUTSYM. If (LOAD T) is used, the loader puts, in the symbol table, addresses that are located in Binary Program Space and therefore not subject to relocation. If (LOAD NIL) is used, the addresses will be in Expanded Core, not Binary Program Space, but those aren't really subject to relocation either, since all Expanded Core is removed ("dislocated"?) whenever any storage area, such as Binary Program Space, is expanded.

(GETSYM "P" "S1" "S2" ...)
(RGETSYM "P" "S1" "S2" ...)

GETSYM uses *GETSYM to search the DDT symbol table for each of the symbols S[i], and it places the value on the property list of S[i] under property P.

RGETSYM is the same, except that it uses *RGETSYM.

NOTE

In order to load the symbol table, either /S or /D must be typed to the loader. Symbols which are declared INTERNAL and ENTRY are always in the symbol table without the /S or /D. In the case of multiply defined symbols (a symbol used in more than one RELOC program), a symbol declared INTERNAL or ENTRY takes precedence, the last symbol otherwise.

```
(DF GETSYM (L)
  (MAPCAR
   (FUNCTION
    (LAMBDA (X)
     (PROG (V)
           (SETQ V (*GETSYM X))
           (COND [V (PUTPROP X (NUMVAL V) (CAR L))]
                 [T (TTYMSG -1 X
                            " not in Symbol Table."
                            T)])
           (RETURN V))))
   (CDR L)))
```

(*PUTSYM S V)
(*RPUTSYM S V)

*PUTSYM puts the symbol S into the DDT symbol table with value V. (If V is a FIXNUM or FLONUM, *PUTSYM and *RPUTSYM convert it via NUMVAL first.) *RPUTSYM also checks that V is a CONS-cell (a location in Free Storage), and if so, subtracts the atom relocation amount before storing the value in the symbol table. If not, it causes an error: NOT A CONS CELL.

(PUTSYM "X1" "X2" ...)
(RPUTSYM "X1" "X2" ...)

PUTSYM uses *PUTSYM to place symbols in the DDT symbol table. If X[i] is an atom, then the symbol X[i] is placed in the symbol table with its value pointing to the atom X[i]. If X[i] is a list, the symbol in (CAR X[i]) is placed in the symbol table with its value (EVAL (CADR X[i])). PUTSYM is useful for making LISP atoms, functions, and variables available to RELOC programs. Symbols must be defined with PUTSYM before the LOADER is used. PUTSYM returns NIL.

RPUTSYM is like PUTSYM except that it uses *RPUTSYM.

```
(DF PUTSYM (L)
  (MAPC
   (FUNCTION
    (LAMBDA (X)
     (COND [(ATOM X) (*PUTSYM X X)]
           [T (*PUTSYM (CAR X) (EVAL (CADR X)))])))
   L))
```

24.2.1 Example: SYS:DDT

DDT is assembly-level debugger for the PDP-10. If you're familiar with the 10's assembly code, and you know how to use DDT, it can be an invaluable aid in debugging code loaded either by LAP or the loader, when it's beneath the level that the Break Package can access. A typical case is troubleshooting a function that works fine in LISP and doesn't after it's compiled into LAP, or checking a hand-coded LAP function. To load DDT into LISP, use:

```
  *(LOAD)                ~ Load into Expanded core.
  *SYS:DDT/G             ~ SYS:DDT.REL
LOADER 5K core           ~ message from the loader
  *(GETSYM SUBR DDT)     ~ Make DDT known to LISP.
  *(DDT)
```

At this point, you're in DDT. You can return to LISP with the DDT command

```
POPJ 14, $X
```

If you want to look at a particular LAP function FOO, find it location before calling DDT. For example, suppose we had hand-coded a function to call the monitor SLEEP UUO. LAP, the assembler, knows the opcodes for some of the instructions, but not all. In this example, what we <u>didn't</u> have in the LAP file was the declaration

```
(DEFPROP CALLI 047000Q SYM)
```

We use DDT to patch the bug:

```
*(TYPE (S.LAP))
(LAP SLEEP SUBR)
        (CALL   1,(E NUMVAL),S) ~ Convert sleep time from
                         ~ LISP number to machine number.
        (CALLI  1,31Q)  ~ SLEEP UUO
        (MOVEI  1,'NIL) ~ return NIL.
        (POPJ   P)
NIL

*(DSKIN (S.LAP))
(SLEEP 4)

*WARNING - NOCALL Function CALLI Not Yet Defined.
Files-Loaded

*(SLEEP 1)       ~ Try it.
?
?Illegal UUO at user PC 001244
Interrupt (Help=?): ^D  ~ Go back to top level.

*(LOAD)          ~ Call the loader.
****SYS:DDT/G

LOADER 5K CORE
```

```
*(GETSYM SUBR DDT)
(19091)

*(CDR 'SLEEP)    ~ We need SLEEP's starting address.
(SUBR #1243 PNAME (#41707))

*(DDT)
DDT

1243/   34051,,UNBOUN+170       = 34051,,3517
[We display the first instruction. The opcode 034 is CALL.
 The "=" re-displays the instruction in numerical form.]

1244/   .JBUUO,,31      = 40,,31     047040,,31
[We go to the next instruction. The opcode is zero: we
 forgot to define CALLI as opcode 047. We use "=" to
 re-display, and then directly type in the correct
 instruction.]

;CALLI 1,31
[The ";" re-displays the instruction. OK now.]


POPJ 14,$X
[We return to LISP.]

NIL

*(SLEEP 1)      ~ One second elapses, then...
NIL
```

24.3 Accessing LISP from MACRO-10

Although the examples here are in MACRO-10, the comments apply to any compiler or assembler that produces a .REL file.

Assume the file is named EXAMP.MAC and contains ENTRY points (or INTERNAL symbols) MFN1, MFN2, and MFN3. After doing the required PUTSYM's, if any, the user would type:

```
     *(LOAD)           ~ or (LOAD T)
     *EXAMP$           ~ $ means altmode. Same as EXAMP/G
 LOADER nK CORE        ~ message from LOADER
     *(GETSYM SUBR MFN1 MFN2 MFN3)  ~back at top level
```

All symbols in the MACRO that refer to LISP must be declared external, either explicitly (EXTERNAL CONS) or implicitly (CONS##).

There are three cases to consider:

1. If the symbol is already in LISP's symbol table, no PUTSYMs are needed. The initial symbol table is listed in Table 24-1 at the end of this chapter. Example: to use CONS from MACRO, use:

   ```
   MOVE    1,<first arg>
   MOVE    2,<second arg>
   PUSHJ   14,CONS##          ;cannot be TRACE'd
   ```

   There is no advantage in using CALL 2,CONS##. It merely requires more overhead by going through the UUO handler. It does not permit tracing, since CONS## is not the atom header but the location of the actual code.

2. If the symbol refers to something in Free Storage, you must use RPUTSYM before you load. To access the LISP atom VAR100, type:

   ```
   *(RPUTSYM VAR100)
   ```

   to LISP before LOADing. The MACRO program accesses it thus:

   ```
           MOVE    1,VAR100##(11)
   ```

If the LISP variable is more than 6 letters long or uses characters not in the RADIX-50 character set (0-9, A-Z, period, dollar, percent, and null), put a synonym in the table:

```
*(RPUTSYM (DMPATM 'DUMPATOMS))
```

The MACRO program accesses it thus:

```
        MOVE    1,DMPATM##(11)
```

The MOVE instructions above put the <u>atom header</u> in register 1. You can do anything you normally do with an atom: PUSHJ to EVAL or GET, for example. If the atom is the name of a function, you can call it by going through the UUO handler. E.g.,

```
        CALL    0,DMPATM##(11)  ;CALL = 034Q.
                                ;0 means no args.
```

That function call can be traced because it goes through the property list of the atom. If DUMPATOMS were redefined, this call would use the new definition.

3. If the symbol refers to some point <u>outside</u> Free Storage, such as a location in Binary Program Space or the high segment, use PUTSYM before LOADing. For example:

```
*(PUTSYM (MEMBER (GET 'MEMBER 'SUBR)))
```

The MACRO program would refer to it thus:

```
                PUSHJ   14,MEMBER##   ;no relocation
```

Again, there's no advantage to going through the UUO handler by using CALL 1,MEMBER##. Likewise, if the identifier is more than 6 characters long or uses characters not defined in RADIX-50, use a synonym. E.g.,

```
*(PUTSYM ($NCONC (GET '*NCONC 'SUBR)))
```

It is referred to in the MACRO program as:

```
                PUSHJ   14,$NCONC##
```

If you want to access the value of a LISP variable efficiently (without going through EVAL every time), put the value cell in the symbol table by using *RPUTSYMV:

<u>(*RPUTSYMV S A)</u>

*RPUTSYMV puts the value cell of the atom A in the symbol table under the name S. The PNAME of S must have 6 or fewer RADIX-50 characters. *RPUTSYMV uses a LAP function (LAPEVAL) to do the same bookkeeping as LAP does when it sees a reference to a SPECIAL variable from compiled code (replacing the CAR of the value cell with NIL, etc., as described in 23.6.4).

If A is missing, S will be used. Definition:

```
(DE *RPUTSYMV (S A)
  (*RPUTSYM S (NUMVAL (LAPEVAL (LIST 'SPECIAL (OR A S))))))
```

For example, to access the values of MYVAR, LONGATOM, IBASE, and #MARK#, type in LISP:

```
*(*RPUTSYMV 'MYVAR)
*(*RPUTSYMV 'LNGATM 'LONGATOM)
*(*RPUTSYMV 'VIBASE 'IBASE)
*(*RPUTSYMV 'HSHMRK '#MARK#)
```

They could be referred to in the MACRO program thus:

```
MOVE    1,MYVAR##(11)
...
HLRZ    3,@LNGATM##(11) ;gets CAR of LONGATOM
...
MOVEI   1,^D10
MOVEM   1,VIBASE##(11)  ;set IBASE to 10.
...
SETZM   HSHMRK##(11)    ;sets #MARK# to NIL
```

24.4 Accessing MACRO-10 from LISP

We've already seen that GETSYM can be used after LOAD to put SUBRs on the property lists of atoms: *GETSYM reads the symbol that LOAD put in the table. LOAD will always put global symbols (INTERN and ENTRY) from the MACRO program into the symbol table; it will also put local symbols in the table if the /S switch is used in the command to the loader:

```
*(LOAD T)
*A.REL/S
```

If you wish to use a MACRO function named %THIS% and refer to it in LISP by a synonym such as, *THIS*, use *GETSYM directly:

```
*(PUTPROP '*THIS* (*GETSYM '%THIS%) 'SUBR)
```

If you wish to define a location (VFOO) in the MACRO program as the value cell of a LISP atom (FOO), use:

```
*(PUTPROP 'FOO (CONS 'FOO (*GETSYM 'VFOO)) 'VALUE)
```

If the atom FOO is to be accessed from LAP, use:

```
*(PUTPROP 'FOO (CONS NIL (*GETSYM 'VFOO)) 'VALUE)
```

24.5 FORTRAN Functions in LISP

It is possible to use the FORTRAN Math Functions in LISP. This allows the user to perform computations that are difficult to do in LISP. All functions return FLONUMs for values but may have either a FLONUM or a FIXNUM for an argument.

To load the Arithmetic Package execute the following at the top level of LISP:

```
*(DSKIN LSP: (ARITH.LSP))
*(LOAD NIL)
*LSP:ARITH$
LOADER nK CORE
*(ARITH)
```

In this example, LSP: is the name of the disk area where the LISP system resides. It may be SYS: at some installations. If it is a particular disk area with no ersatz device name, use the PPN in list form for DSKIN (e.g., (4777Q 2Q)) and in standard PDP-10 form for the loader (e.g., ARITH[4777,2]).

This will load the Arithmetic Package into expanded core. To load the package into Binary Program Space, type (LOAD T) instead of (LOAD NIL). In this case BPS should first be expanded by 1300 (octal) words (e.g., via (EXPBPS 1300Q)).

After the loader loads ARITH.REL, it will look for SYS:JOBDAT.REL and SYS:FORLIB.REL (where the actual function definitions are).

Available Functions

Function Name	Meaning
SIN	Sine with argument in radians
SIND	Sine with argument in degrees
COS	Cosine with argument in radians
COSD	Cosine with argument in degrees
TAN	Tangent
ASIN	Arc Sine
ACOS	Arc Cosine
ATAN	Arc Tangent
SINH	Hyperbolic Sine
COSH	Hyperbolic Cosine
TANH	Hyperbolic Tangent
LOG	Log base e
EXP	Take e to a power
SQRT	Square Root
FLOAT	Convert to a FLONUM
RANDOM	Generates a random number between 0.0 and 1.0

24.6 Predefined symbols in LISP

The LISP symbol table will be loaded into Expanded Core from LSP:LISP.SYM by LOAD. These are the initial symbols in the table, accessible via GETSYM after using LOAD.

Table 24-1

ACONS	AIN.2	AIN.4	AIOP	AOUT.2	APPEND
ARRAY	ATMOV	ATOM	BNINIT	BSTRGC	CADAR
CHANNE	CHCT	CHNSUB	CHRCT	CHRTAB	CHTAB
CONS	CORUSE	CTY	DEV	DEVDAT	ENTR
EQUAL	ERR	ERRSET	EVAL	EXPLOD	EXT
FALSE	FIX	FIX1A	FIXNUM	FLATSI	FLONUM
FLOOV	FLTYIA	FP7A1	FSCNT	FWOCNS	FWCNT
FWCONS	GC	GENSYM	GET	GETL	HGHDAT
IDFLD	IGSTRT	INC	INCH	ININBF	INPUT
INTERN	INUMO	INUMIN	IOPPN	IOSUB	ITYO
LAST	LENGTH	LINL	LIST	LISTAT	LOOKIN
MAKNAM	MAKNUM	MAPCAR	MAPLIS	MEMQ	MORCOR
MOVDWN	MYPPN	NCONC	NCONS	NOINFG	NUMVAL
NXTIO	OEVAL	OLDCH	OLDCU	OPR	OUTC
OUTCH	OUTERR	OUTPUT	PATOM	POPAJ	PPN
PRIN1	PRINC	PRINT	PROMPT	PUTPRO	RATFLD
RATOM	RDFILE	READ	READCH	READLI	REALLO
REMOB	REMPRO	REVERS	RUN	RUNCCL	SASSOC
SET	SETIN	SETQ	SIXATM	SIXMAK	SMAC
SPECBI	SPECST	STNIL	STRFLD	STRT	SYSINO
SYSIN1	SYSINI	SYSINP	TABSR1	TABSRC	TERPRI
TRUE	TYI	TYI2	TYI2E	TYI2Z	TYI3B
TYIA	TYO	TYO2X	TYO5	TYOD	UFDINP
UNBOUN	XCONS	.APPEN			

CHAPTER 25

MISCELLANY

25.1 Other functions

(RUN "DEV:" "PPN" "FILE")

RUN uses a RUN UUO to simulate the monitor command ".RUN ...". If DEV: and PPN are both missing, it uses SYS:FILE. If DEV: is missing, it uses DSK:FILE[PPN]. If PPN is missing, it uses DSK:FILE.

This function never returns to LISP. The monitor handles all errors.

(RUNCCL "DEV:" "PPN" "FILE")

This is like RUN, except that the named file is run at its CCL entry point (1 + the starting location). This is typically used after a command file has been written for the program to be run.

(TIME)

TIME returns the number of milliseconds your job has computed since you logged into the system.

(DTIME)

DTIME returns the time of day in milliseconds past midnight.

(DATE)

DATE returns the current date as a numerical list of the form:

(month day year-1900)

(TIMER "EXPR1" "EXPR2" ...)

TIMER serves as either an evaluation timer or an incremental timer. If any arguments are present they are evaluated, the execution time, the portion of that time spent garbage collecting, elapsed clock time, and number of conses are printed, and the value of the last expression is returned. For example, (TIMER (GC) (GC)) times two garbage collections.

If TIMER is called with no arguments (i.e., (TIMER)), the execution time, etc., since the last evaluation of (TIMER) is printed and a value of NIL is returned. The intent here is that TIMER will be called once to initialize it, a number of expressions will be evaluated, and then TIMER will be called again to check the incremental execution time, etc.

(EXAMINE N)

EXAMINE returns as an integer the contents of memory location N.

(DEPOSIT N V)

DEPOSIT stores the integer V in memory location N and returns V.

(INITFL "FILESPEC1" "FILESPEC2" ...)

INITFL sets up the files that get read in at startup, or after (ERR 'ERRORX) after a SYSCLR (see below). If FILESPEC1 is not found, no error will occur, but any file past that, if any, must be found or an error will be generated. The initial INITFL-list is ((LISP.INI)). INITFL returns the previous INITFL-list.

Example:

```
*(INITFL (INIT1.LSP) (MYFILE.LSP) FOO)
((LISP.INI))
```

(SYSCLR)

SYSCLR re-initializes LISP to read the INITFL-list when it returns to the top level, e.g., after an (ERR 'ERRORX) or START. SYSCLR also resets the GC time indicator to 0, resets the CONSCOUNT to 0, and calls EXCISE.

25.2 Functions for the system builder

The UCI LISP system has a sharable high segment which contains the interpreter, the Editor, the Break Package, and all of the utility functions ("built-in" or "system" functions). If you wish to create your own system, you must be able to load code into the high segment. To do this, you must both own the file and have write privileges. To be write-privileged, you must either create the system from LISP.REL or use SETSYS (see below). The following four functions are for loading code into the high segment; they require write privileges.

<u>(HGHCOR X)</u>

If X = NIL, then the hiseg write-protect flag is turned on (via SETUWP UUO). (The hiseg is initially write-protected.)

Otherwise, X should be a number specifying the amount of space needed for compiled code. The space is then allocated, expanding core if necessary, the write-protect flag is turned off.

In either case, HGHCOR returns T.

<u>(HGHORG X)</u>

If X = NIL, then HGHORG returns the address of the first free location in the hiseg (cf. BPORG).

Otherwise, the first free location in the hiseg is set to X and the old value of the first free location is returned.

<u>(HGHEND)</u>

HGHEND returns the address of the last unused location in the hiseg (cf. BPEND).

<u>(HGHIN "FILESPEC1" "FILESPEC2" ...)</u>

HGHIN is DSKIN for the high segment; i.e., compiled code will be loaded into the high segment. Definition:

```
(DEFPROP HGHIN
 (LAMBDA (L)
  (PROG (BPORG BPEND)
        (SETQ BPORG (HGHORG NIL))
        (SETQ BPEND (HGHEND))
        (SETQ L (ERRSET (APPLY# 'DSKIN L) ERRORX))
        (HGHORG BPORG)
        (HGHCOR NIL)
        (COND [(ATOM L) (ERR L)] [T (RETURN (CAR L))])))
 FEXPR)
```

(SETSYS "DEVICE" "FILE")

SETSYS enables you to create your own sharable system. DEVICE is either a project-programmer number (e.g., (4777Q 2Q)) or a device name (e.g., DSK:). FILE is the name of the sysem to be created. To create the system, type (EXIT NIL), type (at the monitor level) ".SSAVE FILE", then ".RUN FILE". After this procedure, you will have write privileges and may load code into the sharable high segment. You do *not* need to do this to save only a low segment.

Most users who create their own LISP-based system will want to save only the low segment of their core image, with LISP's sharable high segment loaded at run time. This may be accomplished by exiting from LISP via (EXIT NIL) (or (EXIT) or ^C ^X), which removes the high segment so that SAVE will create only a low segment file instead of low and high segment files. When such a save file is later RUN, LISP's standard sharable high segment will automatically be loaded. Note that an EXCISE or a SYSCLR should always be done before exiting and saving LISP. If this is not done the I/O buffers will be allocated as available space, causing the ALLOC? message to appear each time the saved program is run.

Although it is suggested that most LISP-based systems share the standard LISP high segment as outlined above, it may be desirable that a heavily-used system with large amounts of compiled code have its own sharable high segment. In order to do this you must have write privileges for the system, and you must execute a HGHCOR to allocate space for compiled code in the high segment. The compiled code may then be loaded with HGHIN.

The following summarizes the procedure necessary to create a sharable system:

```
.R LISP
*(SETSYS (<proj>,<prog>) <name of system>)
*(EXIT T)
.SSA <name of system>
.RU <name of system>
*(HGHCOR <# of words of compiled code>)
*(REALLOC <other space allocations> . . .)
*(SETQ NOCALL T)
*(HGHIN <your files>)
*(SETQ NOCALL NIL)
*(SYSCLR)
*(INITFN '<fn to print header>)
*(EXIT T)
.SSA <name of system>
```

CHAPTER 26

ERROR MESSAGES

Section 26.1 contains an alphabetical list of LISP error messages, their types in brackets (see Chapter 18), their cause, and in some cases, their remedy.

Section 26.2 lists the error messages that appear on two lines, such as:

```
FOO
UNBOUND VARIABLE - EVAL
```

These messages are listed here as:

X MESSAGE

Finally, section 26.3 lists the error messages having to do with input and output.

26.1 Interpreter messages

ARRAY SUBSCRIPT OUT OF BOUNDS
[2] All array references are checked in advance.

ASCII VALUE OUT OF BOUNDS
[2] You specified an illegal argument to one of the scanner functions (e.g., MODCHR) described in Chapter 16, or to TYILIST (Chapter 15).

BINARY PROGRAM SPACE EXCEEDED
[3] ARRAY, EXARRAY, LOAD, or LAP has exceeded Binary Program Space. Allocate more Binary Program Space next time.

CAN'T CHANGE HIGH SEG. WRITE PROTECT
[2] You called HGHCOR to get write-privileges to the high segment, and it failed. (SETUWP UUO failure)

CAN'T EXPAND CORE
[2] INPUT, OUTPUT, LOAD, or REALLOC failed to expand core. Your job is too large.

CAN'T EXPAND HIGH SEGMENT
[2] HGHCOR failed to expand core. Your job is too large.

CAN'T REMOB NIL
[2] You used REMOB on NIL. Don't.

DOT CONTEXT ERROR
[2] READ does not like dots adjacent to parentheses or other dots, or more than one per list; e.g., (A . B . C).

FLOATING OVERFLOW
[2] An arithmetic operation exceeded the range of PDP-10 floating-point numbers, or READ tried to construct such a number.

GARBAGED OBLIST
Some member of the OBLIST has been garbaged, or the variable named OBLIST has a strange value. You are in trouble. (Try ^C ^R.)

GO WITH NO PROG
[2] You used the function GO outside a PROG.

ILLEGAL OBJECT - READ
[2] READ objects to syntactically incorrect S-expressions.

INTEGER OVERFLOW
[2] An arithmetic operation has exceeded the range of PDP-10 integers, or READ tried to construct such a number.

MORE THAN ONE S-EXPRESSION - MAKNAM
[2] MAKNAM and READLIST object to a list which constitutes the characters for more than one S-expression.

NO FREE STG LEFT
[3] All of Free Storage is bound to the OBLIST, protected cells, arrays, and bound variables on either the Regular Pushdown List or the Special Pushdown List. Unbinding to the top level will usually release the storage. You might also try REALLOC (see Chapter 20).

NO FULL WORDS LEFT

[3] All of Full-Word Space is being used for print names and numbers. The problem and its solution are similar to NO FREE STG.

NO LIST - MAKNAM

[2] MAKNAM and READLIST object to an empty list.

NON-INTEGRAL OPERAND

[2] REMAINDER, DIVIDE, and GCD require integers.

NON-NULL TAIL - MAP

[2] The MAP functions operate only on lists: the CDR of the LAST element must be NIL.

NON-NULL TAIL - NCONC OR APPEND

[2] NCONC and APPEND operate only on lists: the CDR of the LAST element must be NIL.

OVERFLOW

[2] Some arithmetic function caused overflow - either fixed or floating.

PDL OVERFLOW FROM GC - CAN'T CONTINUE

[3] There is not enough room in the Regular Pushdown List to finish garbage collection. You lose. Try REALLOC (see Chapter 20).

READ UNHAPPY - MAKNAM

[2] MAKNAM and READLIST object to a list which is not an entire S-expression.

REG PUSHDOWN CAPACITY EXCEEDED
SPEC PUSHDOWN CAPACITY EXCEEDED

[3] A pushdown list has overflowed. This is usually caused by non-termination of recursion. Sometimes you need to ALLOCATE or REALLOC more space for the pushdown list.

TOO MANY ARGUMENTS SUPPLIED - APPLY

[1] APPLY checks all calls on interpreted functions for the proper number of arguments.

ZERO DIVISOR

[2] The second argument to *QUO, QUOTIENT, REMAINDER, or DIVIDE was zero.

26.2 2-line error messages

X CAN'T BE RPLACD'D (NIL OR INUM)
[2] Don't use RPLACD on NIL or numbers.

X CAN'T BE USED AS A VARIABLE
[2] You attempted to assign a value to NIL, T, or a something that isn't a LITATOM, such as a number or a list. Don't.

X HAS NO PRINT NAME
[2] You've either REMPROP'ed the PNAME from an identifier, or you asked for (via GET) the PNAME of a number. (X is the address of the atom header.)

X IS AN ATOM, CAN'T BE RPLACA'D
[2] You used RPLACA on an atom. Use RPLACA only on CONS-cells.

X MADE ILLEGAL MEMORY REFERENCE
[4] The function X referred to an illegal address. This is usually caused by taking the CAR or CDR of an atom or number.

X NOT AN ATOMIC SYMBOL - PUTPROP
[2] The first argument to PUTPROP must be a LITATOM.

X NON-NUMERIC ARGUMENT
[1] Arithmetic functions require that their arguments be numbers.

X PROGRAM TRAPPED FROM
An illegal instruction was executed in function X.

X UNBOUND VARIABLE - EVAL
[1] EVAL tried to evaluate an identifier and found that it had no value. You probably forgot to QUOTE some atom or to initialize it.

X UNDEFINED COMPUTED GO TAG IN
[2] A GO in some compiled function had an undefined label.

X UNDEFINED FUNCTION - APPLY
[1] The function X is not defined.

X UNDEFINED PROG TAG - GO
[1] A GO in some interpreted function had an undefined label.

X UNDEFINED READ MACRO
[2] The character X had a Read-Macro type in CHRTAB (RATAB = 12, see Chapter 16), but there was no

READMACRO property on X's property list.

26.3 Input/output errors

26.3.1 Device errors

CAN'T GET PATH
[2] A call to (PATH ...) failed. You may have called (PATH CHAN) where CHAN points to a non-disk device, or perhaps the PATH UUO is not implemented in your system.

CAN'T READ DIRECTORY
[2] The PPN you specified to DIR or DIRF either does not exist or is protected.

DEVICE NOT AVAILABLE
[2] INPUT or OUTPUT found the specified device unavailable. Some other job is probably using it.

ILLEGAL DEVICE
[2] INPUT or OUTPUT was attempted to either a non-existent device or to a device of the wrong type, such as INPUT from the lineprinter.

INPUT ERROR
[2] Bad data was read from the selected device.

NO I/O CHANNELS LEFT
[2] INPUT or OUTPUT failed to find a free I/O channel. There is a maximum of 14 active I/O channels.

NO INPUT - INC
[1] An attempt was made to select a channel for input with INC which was not initialized with INPUT.

NO OUTPUT - OUTC
[1] An attempt was made to select a channel for output with OUTC which was not initialized with OUTPUT.

OUTPUT ERROR
[2] Data was improperly written on the selected output device, possibly a write-locked DECTAPE.

26.3.2 File errors

These errors are all of type 2. They occur after a device has been INIT'ed. Internal LISP errors should be reported to your local LISP maintenance person. Monitor errors and hardware errors should be reported to your system manager.

FILE NOT FOUND - you specified a non-existent file.

INCORRECT PPN - no such directory exists. E.g., [0,4].

PROTECTION FAILURE - you may not read/write the file.

FILE BEING MODIFIED - someone else is updating the file.

ALREADY EXISTING FILE NAME - a RENAME error.

ILLEGAL SEQUENCE OF UUOS - internal LISP error.

TRANSMISSION ERROR - hardware problem. Not your fault.

DEVICE NOT AVAILABLE - not assigned to you.

NO SUCH DEVICE - possibly you forgot to use a DEVPPN property.

NO ROOM OR QUOTA EXCEEDED - output error.

WRITE-LOCKED - output error to DECtape or magtape.

NOT ENOUGH MONITOR TABLE SPACE - Monitor error.

CANNOT SUPERSEDE A DIRECTORY - don't write directly on UFDs or SFDs.

CANNOT DELETE NON-EMPTY DIRECTORY - the UFD or SFD still has files.

SUB-FILE-DIRECTORY NOT FOUND - incorrect SFD.

SEARCH LIST EMPTY - use ".R SETSRC" to reinstate your search list.

SUB-FILE-DIRECTORY NEST LEVEL TOO DEEP - each system has a maximum.

NO-CREATE FOR ALL SEARCH LISTS - use ".R SETSRC" to fix it.

FILE CANNOT BE UPDATED - internal LISP error.

INDEX